Changing your child's Heart

STEVE SHERBONDY

Tyndale House Publishers, Inc.
WHEATON, ILLINOIS

OTHER AACC-TYNDALE BOOKS

Family Shock: Keeping Families Strong in the Midst of Earthshaking Change by Gary R. Collins, Ph.D.

Intimate Allies: Rediscovering God's Design for Marriage and Becoming Soul Mates for Life by Dan B. Allender, Ph.D., and Tremper Longman III, Ph.D.

"Why Did You Do That?" Understand Why Your Family Members Act As They Do by Wm. Lee Carter, Ed.D.

Questions Couples Ask behind Closed Doors: A Christian Counselor Explores the Most Common Conflicts of Marriage by James Osterhaus, Ph.D.

High-Maintenance Relationships: How to Handle Impossible People by Les Parrott III, Ph.D.

Fresh Start: 8 Principles for Starting Over When a Relationship Doesn't Work by Thomas Whiteman, Ph.D., and Randy Petersen

Simplify Your Life and Get More out of It! by H. Norman Wright, M.A.

Into Abba's Arms: Finding the Acceptance You've Always Wanted by Sandra D. Wilson, Ph.D.

Soon to Be Released

On the Threshold of Hope: Opening the Door to Healing for Survivors of Sexual Abuse by Diane Mandt Langberg, Ph.D.

BOOKS IN THE AACC COUNSELING LIBRARY

Psychology, Theology, and Spirituality in Christian Counseling by Mark R. McMinn, Ph.D.

Counseling Children through the World of Play by Daniel S. Sweeney, Ph.D.

Promoting Change through Brief Therapy in Christian Counseling by Gary J. Oliver, Ph.D., Monte Hasz, Psy.D., and Matthew Richburg, M.A.

Counseling Survivors of Sexual Abuse by Diane Mandt Langberg, Ph.D.

The American Association of Christian Counselors is an organization of professional, pastoral, and lay counselors committed to the promotion of excellence and unity in Christian counseling. The AACC provides conferences, software, video and audio resources, two professional journals, a resource review, as well as other publications and resources. Membership is open to anyone who writes for information: AACC, P.O. Box 739, Forest, VA 24551.

Visit Tyndale's exciting Web site at www.tyndale.com

The author takes full responsibility for the content of this book and welcomes all comments and questions. Write to him in care of Tyndale House Publishers, Box 80, Wheaton, IL 60189.

Designed by Melinda Schumacher
Edited by Lynn Vanderzalm

Library of Congress Cataloging-in-Publication Data

Sherbondy, Steve, date
    Changing your child's heart : parenting tools to change your child's attitude, not just
  behavior / Steve Sherbondy.
       p.   cm.
    Includes bibliographical references.
    ISBN 0-8423-0429-0 (sc : alk. paper)
    1. Parenting—Religious aspects—Christianity.   2. Attitude change in children.   I. Title.
  BV4529.S432   1998   98-19890
  248.8′45—dc21

Printed in the United States of America

03   02
8   7   6   5   4

To the legacy of Gordon and Marion Blossom.
Pastor, your fatherly vision set my life on course.

contents

a c k n o w l e d g m e n t s

Let me say a few words of thanks to

Vince and MaryAnn Barlow: I never would have started this without your encouragement. We are all proof that God can do amazing things through ordinary people.

Dana Sherbondy: Your numerous late nights at the computer saved me many hours of frustration. It's a privilege to call you my brother in life and in Christ.

Mark Mittelberg: For whatever gave you the inspiration to refer me to Gary, I thank you for your simple act of encouragement. Little things really do mean so much.

Dave Veerman: Thank you for presenting my rough thoughts to Tyndale and for your behind-the-scenes work.

Gary Collins: Your vision of seeking out new authors was a godsend for me. Thank you for taking the risk of believing in me and the material in this book.

Lynn Vanderzalm: Your discernment and gentle guidance brought my rough drafts to life. The extent to which my words make sense and communicate is due to your wise counsel.

Jeff and Barb Valerio: Your leadership gave Sharon and me the experience to implement these child-rearing tools not only in the Dominican Republic but also with our own children. We will always remember your friendship. Those late-night visits gave us the strength to survive the demands of working with teenagers.

Dugan and Breeze: You both got the best of what your mother

and I could offer you. I thank God for letting me be your dad. You have taught me so much about growing up and being a father.

Sharon: Speaking of growing up, I couldn't have teamed up with anyone better. God really knew what he was doing when he brought us together. You should really be listed as a coauthor for this book; your suggestions and insights were always direct and helpful. But since you already have six published books of your own, thanks for letting me take credit for this one. Your patience with my writing perfectionism was extraordinary for anyone else but typical for you. Your firm but gentle love is exactly what I need. While many people enjoy your contagious humor, I get the pleasure of laughing with you as often as I want. Thank you for sharing your life with me. I hope you will "always be like this"!

part one

Engaging in the Battle of the Wills

My child, don't ignore it when the Lord disciplines you, and don't be discouraged when he corrects you. For the Lord corrects those he loves, just as a father corrects a child in whom he delights.

— P r o v e r b s   3 : 1 1 - 1 2

1

A Loving Plan for Discipline

"Scott, what about the garbage cans?" Scott's dad asks as he comes into the house after work.

Scott yells over his shoulder, hoping to get out the door quickly, "Dad, I gotta go. I'll do it tomorrow."

"Scott, I told you last night you had to take out the garbage cans."

Giving his dad an impatient glare, Scott shoots back, "I forgot." He hopes his honesty will mollify his dad so that he can get out to his friends.

"So, you'll do it now before you go."

"But, Dad, they're waiting for me," Scott persists, with a slight whine to his voice.

"They can wait five more minutes."

Scott realizes his dad isn't going to let up. He doesn't want to risk being any later to the game, so he decides to let his dad win this battle. But Scott has to let his dad know that he hasn't won the war. As Scott leaves, he mumbles a parting shot: "Fine, I'll do it. I'll take out your stupid gar- . bage."

Scott's dad is angry with his son's attitude. He wonders, *What should I do? Should I just let that rude comment go? After all, Scott is finally doing what I asked him to. But his attitude sure is lousy. Should I call him back and yell at him? Come to think of it, he has been pretty mouthy lately. He's been lazy. He's been rude to his sister. And he hardly even talks to us anymore. Maybe I should make him stay home from playing with his friends. Boy, would that set off the fireworks!*

What would you do?

■ ▒ ▒

What about this scene? Does it sound familiar?

"Melissa, I don't want to have to tell you again. Stay in this seat! If you don't sit still this time, you'll have to sit here for ten minutes!"

As Melissa's mom walks away, Melissa stays in her seat. However, she stomps her feet and screams loudly at her mom.

"And if you keep screaming, there will be no TV for the rest of the day!"

Melissa stomps her feet more loudly.

"And if you keep stomping your feet, there will be no TV for the rest of the week."

Melissa's mom walks into the next room, falls into a chair, and lets out an exhausted sigh. *Well, at least she's finally quiet. When they are good, they are very good. But when they are bad, they are horrid.* She wonders, *What has happened to kids today? What makes them think they can act this way? I never got away with acting like this in front of my mom and dad. All my kids seem to want to do is fight me. Even when one is cooperating, the other one isn't. Why is raising kids such a battle?*

■ ■ ■

Sound familiar? Do you have to repeat yourself to get your children to do their chores? Have you ever felt like pulling out your hair in desperation because your kids won't listen to you? Have you ever had to grit your teeth, hoping you wouldn't explode into a torrent of hurtful words? Do you feel at a loss for knowing how to handle your children's tests of authority? Are you dreading the day your children become teenagers? Or are you in the midst of it right now and at a loss for how to handle the challenges they throw at you?

Or maybe you worry that you are too hard on your kids. Do you worry that your spouse is too harsh when he or she disciplines the kids? Do you ever wonder if you may be damaging your kids' tender hearts by expecting too much from them?

This book is for you if you have ever felt or said any of the following statements:

1. I want to have a close, open, respectful relationship with my children—not a battleground.
2. My children grumble about every little thing I ask them to do.
3. Time-outs, threats, and groundings aren't working anymore. What can I do?
4. My children obey me on the outside, but I can tell that they are rebelling on the inside.
5. I am at my wits' end with my children's bad attitudes.
6. I want some real answers about *what* to do, *how* to do it, and *when* to do it.
7. I would like to have some practical, proven tools that will guide me in disciplining my children.

8. I want to have confidence in my ability to handle whatever challenges my children throw at me.
9. My children sometimes are out of control. What can I do to handle them?
10. What does God think about disciplining children? How would he want me to do it? Does he understand how hard this is?

I Wasn't Always Ready for the Battle of the Wills

How do we *lovingly* handle our children's tests of authority? Some of you are in the grip of a "Battle of the Wills." You may be thinking, *I've tried everything! Sometimes it works for a while, but then I'm right back to where I was before. No, I take that back; it is worse than before because now I feel even more defeated and a little more helpless and hopeless. I can feel myself losing my children's respect. I just don't have the influence that I used to have with them. And what really scares me is that the stakes are so much higher for my teenager than when I was a kid. I don't want to lose my children to their friends or to something horrible like drugs, jail, pregnancy, or some deadly disease.*

I must confess to a certain irony in writing this book. Before I had kids of my own, I would brag to my older brother-in-law that Sharon and I would not need to spank our kids. We would just talk to them and explain the merits of cooperation. Our family would fulfill the fantasy of an egalitarian democracy.

Boy, did I have a lot to learn! Thankfully, I did learn. I have seen the value of lovingly yet authoritatively rearing children. In parenting my own two children (thirteen-year-old Dugan and ten-year-old Breeze) and in my work (as a professional counselor, a houseparent in a private Christian school, and the disciplinarian in a public school setting), I have experienced the fact that when we lovingly administer discipline to children, *everyone* is happier.

I want to challenge you to take seriously the importance of lovingly disciplining children. It is critical in passing on the kind of character and values we pray our children will have.

We *can* generate warmth in our family, even when our kids seem intent on simply generating friction. We don't have to let our family become hostage to uncooperative, selfish, pouting, or demanding children bent on getting their own way. We can rekindle the dream of making our family one of kindness, peace, and safety.

I am a softhearted person. I would rather make peace than waves. Upsetting children is not my idea of a good time. My chosen profession is counseling. I'm one of those how-does-that-make-you-feel types. I'm in my forties. By doing the math, you can figure out that I'm a child of the sixties—in every sense of the word.

My early values and beliefs were greatly influenced by the thinking of the day. The philosophy was reflected in phrases such as "Do your own thing" and "If it feels good, do it" and "Make love, not war" and "Don't trust anyone over thirty." I now see the subliminal messages these slogans were sending: "Don't let *anyone* tell you what to do!" and "Pain is bad" and "Don't interfere in anyone else's life" and "Feeling good is most important" and *"Work* is a four-letter word."

All of these cultural messages shaped how I thought I wanted to parent. I was going to be a "cool" dad and let my kids have lots of freedom. We would just be great friends and do lots of fun things together. It all sounds so silly now, but it sounded great back then in the idealistic sixties.

When I graduated from college, I got a job as a child-care worker. I was going to help kids who weren't loved and cared for by their parents. I naïvely thought that all I had to do to repair these damaged lives was to listen to their problems and play games with them. We played games all right, but I was played for the fool. They would take all I had to give them, but that is all they wanted to do. The kids weren't interested in changing, and I didn't get the feeling that my supervisors were that concerned. Eventually I became as resigned to their fate as everyone else seemed to be.

Don't get me wrong. I really liked some of those kids. I would even bring some of them to family events on my day off. But I was not making much of an impact on them. Their bruised and damaged hearts were still about the same when I left. I didn't have the knowledge, wisdom, or experience that I needed to be an effective child-care worker. At the time I wondered if their damaged hearts and lives were too much for me to help them change. I don't think so. I just needed better tools.

After that first job, I worked for two years in a Christian school that specialized in teenagers who had pretty severe attitude and behavior problems. There I learned some better tools to use with children. After spending two years at that school, I returned to the first school to work in a different capacity. I was the disciplinarian. When the kids would act up enough in class to warrant kicking them out of class, I was the guy the teachers would call. Keep in mind that this was a special-education school with one teacher and an aide for each group of six students, so they weren't kicked out for chewing gum or talking out of turn. I would be called on to manage students who were unwilling to listen to the teacher, who were fighting with another student, or who were simply "out of control."

I had an opportunity to use the new tools I had learned— tools that I will offer to you in this book—and I would often have dramatic results. My goal was much higher than to play prison guard until the unruly kids were calm enough to rejoin their classmates. I would work with them until they understood the seriousness of their offense and were ready to apologize to the offended party, student or teacher. Some of the teachers were baffled with what I was doing, but they all knew that the problem would be handled when I was called. The teachers loved me, and I had a reputation with the students as being firm yet fair. Teachers would tell me that even when they would merely mention to the student that they were going to call me in, the problem would immediately be resolved.

At that point I had a better understanding of what real love is. I was helping these kids in a much more significant way than just entertaining or baby-sitting them for a while. I was affecting their character. I was able to improve their relationships with their classmates and teachers. I was teaching them self-control, integrity, and kindness—qualities that may influence them for life.

Before I learned about these effective tools, I had a very immature view of love. I equated love with feeling good. That's what I saw portrayed in the media and in the relationships around me. But I have learned that love is much broader than simply feeling good.

PARENTING WITH A MATURE LOVE

When it comes to loving our children with a mature love, I visualize a spectrum. On one end of the spectrum is *soft love.* Soft love is nurturing, like a mother with her nursing infant. It attends, listens, and comforts. Soft love expresses itself when you read your children's favorite book to them for the hundredth time. It is cuddling them. It is sharing their delight in finding a butterfly in the driveway. It is telling them how sorry you are when their friend ignores them at a ball game.

In the middle of the spectrum, we find *everyday love*. It is practical. Everyday love is driving your children to their baseball practice or music lessons. It is getting off the couch to kick a soccer ball with them, even though they tell you that you don't kick it right. It is allowing them the chance to sleep over at a friend's house. Everyday love tells them clearly what you expect them to do and teaches them how to do it. Everyday love answers their never-ending questions about life. The majority of the love we express to our children is this kind of love. It isn't very dramatic, intense, or flashy. We usually express this love without much emotion at all. Everyday love is a pleasant habit. It is something we usually do without a second thought.

At the other end of the spectrum is *firm love*. Firm love warns your children not to touch the electrical outlet. Firm love scolds your daughter when she doesn't tell you where she went after school. Firm love takes away your son's driving privileges when your neighbor tells you he saw him racing. Firm love enforces the household rules.

The Spectrum of Parental Love chart illustrates the full range of parental love.

Spectrum of Parental Love

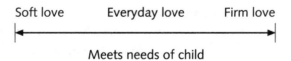

The focus of the entire spectrum of love is on the children. Mature love, which uses the full spectrum, takes care of all your children's needs.

Many parents think the best strategy is to find the balance between the two extremes of love and stay there. Balance is *not* the goal. *Your children need you to express the full spectrum of love in your relationship with them.* At times they need you to be soft. Other times they need you to be firm.

Much of this book focuses on the firm kind of love. That is not because it's more important than soft love. It's just that many other books already describe how to do the soft-love things with our children. Very few books are willing to tackle the tough side of the spectrum. If your children don't have any attitude or behavior problems, then you may want to give this book to someone who you think may need it.

I do want to give you a little warning about this book. You may not agree with some of the ideas here. You may have the same reaction I did when I first heard about some of these tools. I felt very uncomfortable at first. You may too. Some of the ideas may even seem unbiblical or unloving. But I'm confident that if you stick with reading the entire book, you will find that it will address most of your doubts or questions.

My goal in writing this book is to help you have a deeply loving relationship with your children while you take an active role in shaping their attitudes and behavior. I have a passion for families challenged with willful children. I pray that this book gives you hope as well as some practical, proven tools to foster optimally loving relationships.

GOD IS OUR FATHER AND ROLE MODEL

God calls himself our "father" (Ps. 68:5; Jer. 3:19; John 14:6). God could have referred to himself as our grandfather or uncle or cousin if he wanted to be thought of like that. But he doesn't. He wants to be thought of as a dad. God invites us to call him Father. Jesus told us we could even call him Abba, which in English is the equivalent of "Daddy" (Matt. 6:9).

But that wasn't always true. Early in history, God referred

to himself as "the God of Abraham," or "the God of Abraham, Isaac, and Jacob," or simply, "the Lord." Beginning with Moses, God associated himself with the people of Israel more intimately. God first called Israel his "son" when he called Moses to lead Israel out of Egypt (Exod. 4:22-23). God attached a new identity to himself. He is "God, the Father of Israel." He is proud to be identified with his children.

Ponder the awesome truth of God wanting to be our father. He invites us to be his children. Now consider this following deduction: Since God is our heavenly father, we can look to him as an example of how to parent our children. As we read Scripture and learn about how God parented his children, we can learn how to parent our children more effectively. What better role model could we ask for? God the Father is the perfect parent.

God's children were less than perfect. Truth is, they were quite rebellious. Israel had periods of obedience, but that was usually after God had disciplined them.

God tried to teach his children about who he was and how much he loved them. They were not always responsive. God laments, "'I would love to treat you as my own children! I wanted nothing more than to give you this beautiful land—the finest inheritance in the world. I looked forward to your calling me "Father," and I thought you would never turn away from me again'" (Jer. 3:19).

There is some comfort in knowing that even though God is the perfect father, his children still chose to rebel. I may work at being a godly parent, but even that doesn't guarantee godly children. However, we can't use that as an excuse for our children's rebelliousness. God never stops trying to make his children appreciate the importance of obeying him. We should be just as diligent and committed to our children.

Let us not forsake our God-given responsibility. Thank God we have a record of his example to teach us. Throughout this book, as we discuss the importance of discipline, we will also glean insights from how God the Father disciplined his children.

Summary

This book will give you a step-by-step outline of what to do when your children have attitude problems. It will also describe some powerfully effective, practical tools that you can use to develop your children's character. Because it is important to make sure that our discipline is in line with God's ideas, we will compare the tools with some that God used when he disciplined his children, the people of Israel.

It's important to keep in mind what the goal of effective discipline is. It is more than getting our kids to do what we say, although that sounds good. It is more than having our kids do what we say and do it with a good attitude, although that sounds even better. The goal of discipline is a warm, harmonious relationship with our children.

When you think about it, having a "warm, harmonious relationship with our children" is why many parents do *not* discipline their children; they are afraid that if they confront their children's disobedience and bad attitudes, they will harm the relationship. But nothing can be further from the truth. And that's what this book will try to demonstrate.

In the rest of part 1, we will look at three important truths that form the foundation stones of loving discipline: (1) attitude is more important than behavior; (2) submissiveness is the key to attitude; (3) conflict enhances our relationships. We then will evaluate several common discipline methods that I believe are ineffective.

Part 2 details some effective tools that will not only change your children's attitudes but also knit your hearts together in harmony. Those tools are setting expectations, enforcing logical consequences, assigning work, and assigning exercises. The first two tools are fairly ordinary. You may already be using them, and these chapters will help you use them even more effectively. The last two tools are what I call power tools, and they are to be used to give your children an "attitude adjustment." These tools may be new to you, but they may be the very tools you've been groping for. Chapter 9 will help you discern when your children's attitudes have softened. Chapter 10 will explain how to reconnect with your children and restore intimacy after an attitude-adjustment session.

Part 3 explores some issues in making sure you use the tools well. It discusses some cautions, some questions you may have about the tools, and the importance of working together as a parental team. It also looks at the whole issue of spanking.

Part 4 offers insight on how these tools can be used effectively in single-parent families and in blended families, where parents face some unique challenges. Chapter 19 discusses specific ways that the tools can be used effectively with teenagers.

As you read this book, I pray that God will speak to you and give you hope and direction as you work on one of the most important responsibilities he has given you: to train your children and shape their character.

▧ ▧ ▧ Reflection Questions

Take a few minutes to think about these questions. If possible, discuss them with your spouse, another parent, or a group of parents. If you want to chart your growth and your children's growth as you read this book and try the strategies, start a journal. Write down your observations, feelings, and goals.

1. What would you have done with Scott? with Melissa?
2. Where are you most often on the spectrum of love?
3. In what ways do you express soft love? everyday love? firm love?
4. Do you agree that love needs to be expressed in various ways?
5. Do you think of love and discipline as connected?
6. What is the easiest way for you to express love to your child? What is the hardest?
7. What are some of the tools God used when he disciplined his children?
8. What are the areas that you most want to see change in your children?
9. What are the areas that you most want to see change in yourself?

People judge by outward appearance, but the Lord
looks at a person's thoughts and intentions.

— 1 Samuel 16:7

2
Attitude Is More Important Than Behavior

"OK, *now* can I go over to Bethany's house? She's been waiting for me all day while *you* made me do all this work."
Samantha's voice drips with contempt.

"All right, all right. Go ahead," Samantha's mother, Jean,
concedes with a sigh. "And thank you for putting away your
things." Jean is trying to sound positive. After all, the experts
say that parents should praise their children when they do a
good job.

So why does Jean feel so hurt and angry? And why does
Samantha treat her as if she is being so mean? Is Jean expecting too much?

"Well, when are you going to take me to Bethany's?"
Samantha demands, impatient that her mother hasn't already
grabbed her car keys.

"Sam, honey, I can't take you now. I have to get to the store
so I can start getting ready for our company tonight."

"What do you mean you can't take me? Bethany can't come

to pick me up." Samantha starts pouting and throws her jacket on the floor.

"Why can't Bethany come?"

"You know her mom takes the car to work at ten o'clock."

"Well, honey, I'm sorry."

"Why do I always have to work, and you never do anything?"

"Samantha, that's ridiculous. You knew last night that you had to put your stuff away before you could go to Bethany's house. But you watched TV until you got too tired. Now it's too late."

Samantha doesn't even hear her mom. "This is what always happens. It's because of *you* that I don't have any friends." She storms up to her room and slams the door.

Samantha's mother wonders, *Is making Sam pick up her own stuff worth all this grief? Am I too hard on her? Maybe I should just take her to Bethany's. But it's over an hour there and back, and I just don't have that much time to spare. But Samantha is so upset.*

◼ ◼ ◼

What would you say to Jean? Would you tell her to relax? After all, Samantha did put away her stuff. Isn't that enough? Aren't parents supposed to be satisfied with obedience? Does Jean simply need to understand that Samantha is disappointed?

Samantha is more than disappointed; she is acting selfishly and talking rudely. Samantha's feeling upset is *not* the problem. She is blaming her mother, even though she was told to pick up her things the night before. That is plenty of fair warning.

What is most harmful is that Samantha probably will not be held responsible for her obstinate attitude. She is barely being held responsible for the items she left around the house, let alone the attack she is throwing at Jean. Samantha has successfully shifted the issue from her not doing her simple chore to her mother's making her too late to go to her friend's house.

The other tragedy is that Jean is buying into it. Jean feels guilty. She hopes that if she just ignores Samantha's rudeness, it will eventually stop. But Jean has been waiting for that to happen for fifteen years! When will this strategy kick in and get some results? It has gotten to the point that Jean just expects that kind of treatment from Samantha. Rudeness has become part of Samantha's standard operating procedure. Samantha has no appreciation for her mother's schedule; the daughter acts as if the world revolves around her life. Yes, she did put her things away. But her attitude is that she did her mother a favor. Her *attitude* is the problem. Her minimally obedient behavior is overshadowed by her rude attitude.

Jean focused more on the "obey" part and tried to ignore the "rude" part. Big mistake. The rude part is the bigger problem. Samantha needs to change her attitude. Samantha needs to honor her mother and treat her with respect. Unfortunately, Samantha has no interest in doing so. And Jean has no clue how to motivate her, except to give in to Sam's demands.

■ ■ ■

Stu closes the garage door, goes into the house, and puts down his briefcase. "Derek, how many times have I told you not to leave your bike by the street? Now go put it away."

"But, Dad, let me finish watching this."

"No. That's how your last bike got stolen. Go get it now."

"But, Dad, the program is almost over," Derek persists, with a whine.

Stu knows Derek will forget. His requests just go in one ear and out the other. Besides, how many reminders are enough? Stu decides to take some action this time. He walks over to the television set and turns it off.

Derek starts yelling, "What are you doing? I was watching that! Mom says you can't touch the TV if somebody else is watching something."

"We've already had this conversation. When we got your new bike, you agreed to keep it in the backyard. Go get it *now*, young man!"

"But, Da-a-d, the show is almost over."

"And the bike is sitting out front where it doesn't belong."

"But, Da-a-d, I'll get it afterward."

"No, Derek. Now!"

Derek just sits there staring at his dad.

"OK, no TV for the rest of the week," Stu spits out in desperation.

"Whatever."

"OK, now it's for the rest of the month."

"Why don't you just make it for the rest of my life and get it over with?" Derek retorts, rolling his eyes.

"OK, if that's what you want."

"Whatever."

"Don't make me get my belt."

"Do whatever you have to do." But Derek finally starts moving, even though a slug would pass him up.

Derek and his dad glare at each other as Derek heads off to get his bike.

Stu's blood is boiling, but he doesn't know what to say. He is also afraid that if he does say something, he might lose control. He just swallows hard and goes upstairs to change out of his work clothes. At least his son is moving in the right direction. But he can't help wondering, *Why does a simple expectation have to be such an ordeal?*

■ ■ ■

Is Stu being too strict with Derek? Did he really have to turn off the television and threaten him with the belt? Couldn't he have waited to see if Derek would follow through? Of course, he could have given Derek another chance. But Stu has already tried waiting for Derek to get around to it, and nothing changes.

This little scene is about something far bigger than a bike left out at the street. Derek has another agenda in mind. He wants to see how far he can push his get-off-my-back attitude. This little episode isn't just about the television program or the bike. Derek is testing his dad's strength and resolve.

Stu almost lost control. He doesn't want to beat his son with a belt, but he doesn't know what else to do. He's not even sure he would use the belt. He is relieved when Derek finally obeys. But Stu is also still angry. He no longer has confidence in his ability to handle Derek's challenges. He feels he's at the end of his options for dealing with Derek.

So who do you think won this encounter? I would say Derek won, hands down. He knows he pushed his dad to the brink without any serious consequences. Sure, he had to go get the bike and he missed the ending of his show, but his dad is steaming. He knows that his dad will think twice before he asks Derek to do anything again in order to avoid the aggravation.

Is Derek's compliance enough? Not unless Stu is willing to endure the same scenario each time he asks Derek to do something.

What is the message behind Derek's snail's pace? The message is, "I'm only going to do what I absolutely have to do, and I'm going to try to make you pay for making me do what I already agreed to do."

Does Stu have options in handling a situation like this? Yes, most definitely. It is *not* with the belt, or a spanking, or restricting TV. Arguing and threatening just bring Stu down to Derek's level. They may get Derek to comply minimally, but the relationship will probably be severely damaged. There are other tools that would be more effective.

Derek has an attitude problem. He needs an attitude adjustment.

■ ■ ■

Little Michael is fascinated with the Christmas tree. Every morning he and his mom spend some time "oohing and ahhing" about the lights and ornaments. Every morning he wants to touch the tree. His mother, Maryann, realizes he is just curious. She allows him to touch the tree occasionally to feel its prickly needles. Michael understands "hot" and doesn't touch the lights. No matter how much time Maryann spends supervising Michael's exploration of the tree, she can't trust him to be alone with it.

But Michael doesn't seem satisfied with his mother's supervised touching. Whenever his mom is preoccupied with something, he heads right for the tree. Unfortunately, the living room doesn't have doors to shut out Michael and his curious fingers. Several times Maryann has found him just before he would have pulled the tree down on top of himself.

One morning, after Michael has been reminded several times not to touch the tree, he decides he has had enough of this rule. He starts hitting Maryann and yelling *no* as loudly as he can. Maryann is flabbergasted. Her older son never acted this way. She tells Michael to stop hitting, but he doesn't stop. She doesn't want to spank him or slap his hands while telling him to stop hitting her, but she doesn't know what else to do.

Michael gets more out of control. He throws himself on the floor, wildly kicking his feet and flailing his arms. Maryann has read books that advise parents just to ignore these tantrums. What can she do? She had tried being patient. She had let him satisfy his curiosity to touch the tree as long as she was right next to him. So why is he doing all this? What should she do? He looks so out of control and angry. Is this normal?

Michael has reached the limits of his ability to control himself. At this point, his compliance is contingent on his mother's presence in the room. He just can't stand to obey his mommy anymore, and his tantrum reveals that he can no longer contain his frustration. He wants what he wants, when he wants it! And right now he wants to touch that tree.

Does Michael have a bad attitude? Yes. He is taking a position of defiance. Fortunately, Michael is too young to know how to bury his attitude very deeply. He lays it all out for the world to see, and it's not a pretty sight. He tried to keep it inside for a while, but he couldn't keep up the charade. Without any effort whatsoever, Maryann brought Michael's ugly attitude to the surface. But is ignoring it the best way to handle it? Sure, it may blow over this time, but what about when he is older? It may not be quite as harmless then.

WHAT IS ATTITUDE?

What exactly is attitude? The word comes from the Latin word *aptus*, which originally described physical "fitness." Several other definitions help reveal the flavor of this word. An attitude is

- an internal posture with regard to a fact or state
- the arrangement of the parts of a body or figure
- sometimes refers to a feeling or emotion toward a state or fact

The definition that best suits our discussions in this book is the first one: *An attitude is an "internal posture."* In biblical language, our internal posture is what is referred to as the "heart."

The embodiment of the word *attitude* is illustrated by the first grader who repeatedly ignores the teacher's requests to stay seated. Eventually the teacher has to walk back to his desk and make him sit down. As the teacher returns to the front of the class, the child screams out, "I may be sitting on the outside, but I'm standing on the inside!" That youngster has described perfectly his internal posture. That child has a bad attitude.

How Is Attitude Related to Feelings and Behavior?

You may notice that one of the definitions says that the word *attitude* is "sometimes used as a feeling or emotion toward a state or fact." This reflects a common usage of the word. Let me make an important distinction between attitude and feelings. A feeling is a subjective response to a person, thing, or situation. It is a reaction. Feelings are very important. I like to think of them as little messengers that are trying to give us information about who we are inside. Sometimes we welcome that information, and sometimes we are ashamed of how we feel. However, feelings are neither good nor bad. What we do with our feelings is the moral issue. Feelings make great servants but poor masters. If we allow them free rein, feelings can lead us down a deadly path.

Behavior consists of a person's actions or words. Behavior is external. It is observed or heard. Feelings usually find their expression in our behavior.

The *internal position* we take is our attitude. This internal position applies to anything. If I like what I'm feeling, my behavior will probably be free and spontaneous. My attitude would be, "Life is awesome, and I want to share it with you."

However, if I'm feeling hurt and my attitude is, "I'm gonna get even with you for hurting me," then my attitude reveals my selfishness and immaturity. My behavior will be destructive. If I feel hurt and my attitude is, "I respect you and I also respect me, and I expect you to respect me," then my behavior will be quite different. I've recognized my feelings, and I have several choices on how to express them. My behavior will reveal not only my feelings but my attitude toward others and myself.

One way to think of the relationship between these three terms is to imagine the old-fashioned cart and horse. The horse represents our behavior, and the cart represents our feelings. Emotions follow the motion of the horse. The attitude is represented by the driver. The driver is in close touch with the feelings. He decides where the horse (behavior) will go. The feelings will eventually follow.

If the driver's attitude is halfhearted, he will not make much progress. If his attitude is careless, they will all end up in a ditch. If his attitude is bitter, he will abuse the horse and risk damage to the cart and himself. And if the driver tries to put the cart before the horse, then he is in big trouble.

Let's go back to the three scenarios at the beginning of this chapter and look at the feelings, attitudes, and behavior in each one. Samantha's feelings are persecution. Her attitude is rude. Her behavior is to argue with her mom, to be sarcastic, and to complain.

Derek's feelings are annoyance that he has to move his bike. His attitude is irritatingly arrogant. His behavior is to take verbal jabs at his dad and move very slowly to make his dad mad.

Michael's feelings are frustration because he is not allowed to touch the Christmas tree as much as he wants to. His attitude is combative and rebellious. His behavior is to hit, kick, and scream.

Our behavior (including the words we speak) reveals to everyone what is happening inside of us. If we let our feelings have free rein, we soon earn the reputation of being "hot-headed" or "selfish" or "lazy" or "undependable." Why? Because we do what we feel like doing. The Bible calls that "living in our sinful nature."

However, if we maintain an attitude of caring and humility, we do not surrender to the slavery of unbridled feelings. Since we are created in the image and likeness of God, we have the ability to choose how to react to situations.

When I tell my daughter she cannot have her friend Briana come over to play because she has to go to softball practice, she feels disappointed. What she *does* (words or behavior) with those feelings of disappointment reveals her attitude. If she says, "I hate softball. I wish I had never signed up for that stupid game!" then she reveals a bitter attitude. If she had a better attitude, she might say, "Oh-h Dad. I don't want to play softball. I'd rather see Briana." This would express those same feelings without letting them grow into a bad attitude.

The real test of her attitude comes when I make her stick to her commitment to go to practice. A person's ability to handle a disappointment—like a dad's saying no to a request—is the quickest way to uncover a child's true attitude.

Should children be encouraged to express their feelings,

wants, and opinions? Yes, children should be heard as well as seen. Parents should welcome their children's developing personalities and emotions. We should do everything in our power to foster their strength, talents, and individuality. At the same time, we also need to be guiding them in how to express themselves in appropriate, polite, respectful ways.

ATTITUDE ADJUSTMENT

Samantha, Derek, and Michael all have a bad attitude. They have it for different reasons, and they express it differently. Samantha's attitude is a little more controlled, but it is obviously snotty. Derek's attitude is sneakier and subtler, but he is certainly disrespectful. Michael's attitude is raw, unadulterated, out-of-control rebellion.

All three of them need an attitude adjustment. They don't need another chance. They don't need someone just to understand them and give them a hug. They don't need a lecture or a bribe or a good spanking. They need parents who are committed to them enough to stop them from heading down the path they are on. They need parents who can save their children from themselves. If parents don't correct negative, critical, rebellious, rude attitudes, then they are condoning their children's disrespect and condemning them to a life of misery.

Samantha needs someone to say to her, "You are the one who decided to watch TV rather than clean up last night. And I didn't know you needed a ride over there. Stop trying to make me feel guilty for your not being able to see Bethany today. But beyond all that, you are not allowed to talk to me in that rude tone of voice. If you don't change your attitude quickly, then I will have to help you."

Derek needs his father to say, "Listen, Son, not only have

you had plenty of warnings about leaving your bike outside, you haven't been keeping your promise to be more cooperative when we ask you to do things around here. Let me sum it up for you: Your attitude is unacceptable, and it's going to change starting right now. You have a choice as to whether you do it with my help or without my help. What's it going to be?"

Michael needs his mom to tell him, "Michael, that's enough of that. Now stand up and pull yourself together. I won't stand for that. If you need my help, then just keep screaming like you are and I'll help you, but you may not like it."

Children's attitudes are more significant than their behavior. Behavior reveals the inner attitude. In order to have truly well-behaved children, parents must focus their discipline on their children's attitudes.[1]

I've been using the phrase "attitude adjustment" without defining what that means. An attitude adjustment is the process of turning a bad attitude into a good attitude. This adjustment is a collaborative effort by both the parents and the children. Obviously, if the children have bad attitudes, they are not going to be very enthusiastic about this attitude adjustment. In fact, they will be quite vehemently opposed to this entire procedure. You can count on it. The children's cooperation will be minimal if not negligible. That means most of this attitudinal turnaround will be left up to the energy and motivation of the parents. That is the bad news.

The good news is that once you are skilled at using some attitude-adjusting tools and your children know you will use them whenever necessary, they quickly learn it is better to maintain a good attitude or at least change their attitude on their own, rather than depend on your help. Adjusting attitudes is never easy, but nothing of real value ever is.

When the core issue of attitude is resolved, spontaneous,

eager-to-learn, friendly children will flourish. Show me a child who complains about every rule, and I'll show you a miserable child. Show me a child who listens to the coach and referee, and I'll show you a child who loves to play the game. We aren't talking simply about soccer; this is about life.

When a child's attitude is positive, it helps make the family a nice place to be. A family is a place to learn how to develop and maintain good relationships. If one person's attitude is rotten, it can spoil it for everyone.

This book cannot guarantee that your children will always want to do the right thing, but it will help you ensure that they know what the right thing is and how good it feels when they do it. Once your children have experienced how sweet cooperation can taste, they will be less likely to return to the bitterness of rebellion. Families are meant to enjoy the fruits of love, peace, and joy. As we tutor our children in the critical importance of attitude, we will be giving them the tools to build a strong family of their own.

GOD IS CONCERNED WITH OUR ATTITUDES

Our attitudes affect our relationships. God is concerned about our relationships—to him and to other people. Derek, Samantha, and Michael are all examples of how a negative attitude damages relationships.

God is very interested in our internal posture. He sees right through our behavior to our attitudes. He says of some people who worship him, "These people come near to me with their mouth and honor me with their lips, but their hearts are far from me. Their worship of me is made up only of rules taught by men" (Isa. 29:13, NIV). God knows when his children try to fool him with their external behavior. God is warning them that he sees beyond the facade of external obedience. He knows when we close our hearts to him.

> This is what the Lord Almighty, the God of Israel, says: . . . For when I brought your forefathers out of Egypt and spoke to them, I did not just give them commands about burnt offerings and sacrifices, but I gave them this command: Obey me, and I will be your God and you will be my people. Walk in all the ways I command you, that it may go well with you. But they did not listen or pay attention; instead, they followed the stubborn inclinations of their evil hearts. They went backward and not forward. From the time your forefathers left Egypt until now, day after day, again and again I sent you my servants the prophets. But they did not listen to me or pay attention. They were stiff-necked and did more evil than their forefathers. (Jer. 7:21-26, NIV)

From the very beginning of Jesus' ministry, he let people know that God's standard is more than mere obedient behavior. God doesn't just want us not to murder; he wants us not even to harbor anger or bitterness toward anyone (Matt. 5:21-22). God doesn't just want us not to commit adultery; he wants us not even to contemplate violating our wedding vows (Matt. 5:27-28). At the end of Matthew 5, Jesus delivers the punch line to his entire challenge. He tells the crowd of people to "love your enemies" and "turn the other cheek" when mistreated by others. Jesus challenges us to obey a law even tougher than the Old Testament ones. It is the "law of love." Our hearts, our internal posture, our attitudes are what God is most concerned with.

Jesus' harshest words were for people who pretended to

have God-honoring attitudes. Those people were the religious leaders or Pharisees. Jesus calls the Pharisees hypocrites (Matt. 23:13). The Jews knew exactly what that meant. The word *hypocrite* is the Greek word for an actor, someone who performs on a stage. It was definitely not a compliment. Jesus was accusing the Pharisees of just pretending to love God by their behavior. Jesus constantly exposed their hypocrisy, saying their hearts were full of wickedness.

Jesus' own disciples found this standard hard to understand. I'm paraphrasing here, but at one point Jesus got so frustrated that he asked his disciples, "How stupid can you guys be? It doesn't matter what food you eat! What counts is the condition of your hearts! When are you guys gonna get it?" He even lists the sins that make people impure so there is no misunderstanding. Jesus concludes his lesson: "All these evils come from inside and make a man 'unclean'" (Mark 7:18-23, NIV).

Summary

Our children's attitudes are more important than their behavior. Therefore, our goals for training and discipline should not stop at behavior. Since God is so interested in our hearts, we should be sure we focus on our children's hearts as well. We desire a good relationship with them, not just their obedience. In the next chapter we'll look at submissiveness, which is the key to a healthy attitude.

Reflection Questions

Take a few minutes to think about these questions. If possible, discuss them with your spouse, another parent, or a group of parents. Write down your observations, feelings, and goals in a journal.

1. How do your children express bad attitudes?
2. What body language do they use to express their resistance to you?
3. What are the phrases they use to try to get you to back down?
4. What do you do when your children have negative or rude attitudes?
5. What kind of results do you get?
6. How do you feel when you face their attitude problem?
7. Observe your children during the next few days. Note attitudes that may need adjustment.
8. Meditate on Proverbs 22: 6. In what "path" do your children need to go? What methods have you tried to get them to go that direction?
9. In what ways did your parents use their authority well? Did they ever abuse their authority? If so, how?
10. How do you feel about your parental authority/ responsibility?
11. In what ways do your children need you to exercise your authority?
12. In what ways did you see your children's attitudes expressed in their behavior in the last week?
13. Name three specific instances in which you over looked bad attitudes you probably should have dealt with in your children.
14. How did your dad prepare you for seeing God as your "heavenly Father"?
15. Study the Sermon on the Mount in Matthew 5, allowing God to show you how important your children's attitudes are to him.

For I have come down from heaven to do the will of
God who sent me, not to do what I want.

— J o h n   6 : 3 8

3

Submissiveness Is the Key to Attitude

The word *no* means different things to different people. When parents say no to their children, the children often hear it as a negative response to anything that smacks of a good time, happiness, a future, or a reason to live. However, the parents are saying no because they love and want to protect their children. Parents live in hope that someday when the kids are older, they will thank them for saying no as often as they did. In their dreams.

Columnist and humorist Erma Bombeck said it well:

> I actually sat down once with one of my kids and tried to explain the meaning of no. "It means I love you enough to want you to have as smooth a journey through life as is possible. I don't pretend to know where all the chuckholes are, but I've fallen in a few, and I want to save you from doing the same thing. When I see you going in the wrong direction, I have to say no to get you back on track.

"I don't want you to be hurt or hurt someone else. A lot of noes can make this possible. I want your trust that I will say yes as often as I can, but no when I must.

"I'll be honest with you. When I say, 'We'll talk about it later,' or 'I'll ask your father,' there isn't a chance of a snowball in Phoenix in the summer that the answer will be yes. I'm stalling because I don't enjoy the look of disappointment on your face and I want to be loved."

My son sat there for a long time without speaking. Then he said, "So, why don't you ever want me to have a good time?"[1]

Kids just can't understand why we have to say no. They don't *want* to understand. They want their own way.

"But, Da-a-ad. Why do I have to?" We've all heard that familiar whine. In a stronger tone of voice it sounds like, "Ah c'mon, Dad, no one else has to do that." The next level sounds like, "There's no way I'm gonna do that. That's stupid!" And if it gets stronger, you may hear, "Forget it. I'm outta here!" If we try to make children obey at that point, it could get physical or even ugly if we aren't careful.

What is the problem here? Why do our kids behave that way? Well, I may be the bearer of bad news here, but we are all sinners, even our children (Rom. 3:23). I hope that doesn't come as a surprise. Our children may look like perfect angels while they sleep, but unfortunately they have inherited the same sinful nature we have. Sin is woven into the very fabric of our nature. It is a deadly condition that can kill our bodies and our souls (Rom. 6:23). Part of our job as parents is to teach our children how to overcome the effects of their sin, and that starts with their hearts.

IT'S A MATTER OF THE HEART

Attitudes begin in the heart. The heart is the place of our internal posture. Solomon knew that our hearts are important: "Above all else, guard your heart, for it affects everything you do" (Prov. 4:23).

So, what do we aim for in our children's hearts? We work toward the same thing God wants in our hearts: submissiveness. Submissiveness is the cornerstone of our relationship with God. In the Garden of Eden, God expected Adam and Eve to submit to his instructions about what not to eat. Their lack of submissiveness (i.e. rebellion) was catastrophic. If Adam and Eve had maintained their attitude of submission, we wouldn't be in this mess.

God is very concerned about our submissiveness. It is the *first* rule God gives to Moses. In Exodus 20 God says (in the "Sherbondy paraphrase"), "Listen up, people! You know who I am, right? Just in case you forgot, I'm the one who got you out of Egypt. You'd still be slaving away making bricks in the hot sun if it weren't for me. Now I have some serious instructions to tell you. The first one is 'Don't let anyone or anything become more important than I am! Don't even think about it! When I talk, you listen.'"

If that tone sounds harsh to you, I invite you to read the original. God tells Moses to warn the Israelites not even to touch Mt. Sinai or they would die (Exod. 19:21). Moses explains that the reason God is revealing his awesome power is to make them afraid in hopes they would not sin.

If you didn't know any better, you would think God is pretty stuck on himself. It sounds as if he thinks he's better than the rest of us. He is, in every way. But he isn't telling his children that because he needs their applause. He wants his children to recognize who he is and to listen to him. He knows if they don't trust him, they will get into serious trouble. He wants his children to obey his life-enhancing expectations.

It sounds pretty clear what sort of posture, internal and external, God wants his children to have in relation to him. He is the Creator, and we are the creatures. We are to submit to him.

SUBMISSIVENESS

What exactly does it mean to be submissive? It is "a yielding to the will or power of another; obedience; humility; an acknowledgment of one's inferiority." Submissiveness is not humiliation or shame. It is respectfully honoring someone of greater knowledge, wisdom, discernment, and authority—all attributes parents should possess.

Submissiveness is not the same as obedience. Submissiveness is the internal posture; obedience is the outward manifestation of the internal posture. Submissiveness is the heart condition; obedience is the behavior.

Submissiveness gets a lot of bad press. It is equated with weakness, victimization, lack of confidence, and all sorts of other negative qualities. That is a foolish way of looking at it. It takes more strength and character to submit than it takes to fight back. Consider Roberto Alomar. Mr. Alomar is the professional baseball player who spit in the face of the umpire who called him out on strikes. It would have taken more strength and maturity to yield to the authority of the umpire than to lash out in anger.

Don't you hope that your children will never do something as shameful as spitting at an umpire? But how about arguing with an umpire? How about gossiping about an umpire? How about just giving an umpire a dirty look? Don't all these gestures expose a shameful attitude?

A story illustrates the point.

Donald Jensen of Terre Haute, Ind., was umpiring a Little League game when he was struck on the head by a thrown bat. He continued to work the game, but later that evening he was placed in a hospital for observation. While being kept overnight for observation, Jensen composed a letter for the parents of Little Leaguers.

"I'm an umpire. I don't do it for a living but only on Saturdays and Sundays for fun. . . . I feel deep down I'm providing a fair chance for all the kids to play the game without disagreements and arguments. With all the fun I've had, there is still something that bothers me about my job.

"Some of you folks don't understand why I'm here. Some of you feel I'm there to exert authority over your son. For that reason, you often yell at me when I make a mistake or encourage your son to say things that hurt my feelings.

"Let me tell you more about my game today. There was one close call that ended the game. A runner for the home team was trying to steal the plate on a passed ball. The catcher chased the ball down and threw to the pitcher covering the plate. The pitcher made the tag, and I called the runner out.

"As I was getting my equipment to leave, I overheard one of the parents comment, 'It's too bad the kids have to lose games because of rotten umpires.' Later at the concession stand a couple of kids were telling their friends, 'Boy, the umpires were lousy today. They lost the game for us.' I felt terrible when I got home. Here was a group of kids who had made a lot of mistakes. . . .

"A parent or adult leader who permits the younger player to blame his failures on an umpire is doing the worst kind of injustice to that youngster. Rather than learning responsibility, such an attitude is fostering an improper outlook toward the ideas of the game itself. This irresponsibility is bound to carry over to future years. . . .

"I was umpiring behind the plate for a pitcher who pantomimed his displeasure at any call on a borderline pitch. He wanted the crowd to realize he was a fine, talented player who was doing his best, but that I was a black-hearted villain who was working against him. The kid continued acting like this for two innings, while at the same time yelling at his own players who dared to make a mistake.

"For two innings the manager watched this. Finally the manager called him aside. In a voice loud enough that I was able to overhear, the lecture went like this: 'Listen, Son, it is time you make a decision. You can be an umpire, an actor, or a pitcher. Right now it is your job to pitch. And you are basically doing a lousy job. Leave the acting to actors, the umpiring to umpires, or you won't do any pitching here. Now what's it going to be?'

"The kid chose to pitch. After the game the kid followed me to my car. Fighting to keep back the tears, he apologized and thanked me. He said he had learned a lesson. I can't help but wonder how many more fine young men are missing their chance to develop into outstanding ball players because their parents encourage them to spend time umpiring, rather than working harder to play the game as it should be played."

The following morning, Donald Jensen died of a brain concussion.

That arrogant, young pitcher had been more concerned with finding someone else to blame than with looking in the mirror. When kids don't learn the value of submitting to authority, they are severely handicapped. As they get older, the consequences will get more serious. Childhood is the perfect time to teach children valuable lessons like that wise, strong coach. "Teach your children to choose the right path, and when they are older, they will remain upon it" (Prov. 22:6).

God is not only concerned with telling his children how much he loves them. He also wants us to see the big picture. God wants his children to "fear" him. That's right—fear God! "Fear of the Lord is the beginning of knowledge. Only fools despise wisdom and discipline" (Prov. 1:7).

Fearing God does not mean that we live in terror of him. It means that we so thoroughly respect and submit to him that the closest way to describe that kind of posture is fear. Respect always contains at least a dash of fear.

Obviously we don't want our children to tremble when they are around us. Parents should be the epitome of safety and security. But sometimes safety and security mean we have to protect them from their own selfish desires, foolish choices, and negative attitudes. When our children decide to flex their willful muscles in a dangerous or negative manner, we need to answer their challenge with commensurate strength of our own. Teaching children the importance of having a submissive posture sometimes boils down to saying something like this: "The reason you have to do this is because I'm older and wiser and I know what is best for you. The risks of letting you learn the hard way are just too great." Or to put it another way: "Because I said so."

If the only reason children will respect and obey us is

because we are stronger or more powerful, then that's *their* choice. Our first choice is that they would respect and obey us because we love them. We hope that they love us in return and that out of that love grow obedience and then trust.

JESUS MODELED SUBMISSIVENESS

As always, Jesus is our role model. He demonstrated how children should submit to their parents. "During the days of Jesus' life on earth, he offered up prayers and petitions with loud cries and tears to the one who could save him from death, and he was heard because of his reverent submission. Although he was a son, he learned obedience from what he suffered" (Heb. 5:7-8, NIV).

Jesus was submissive, and he had to *learn* obedience. What an amazing thought. The Creator of the universe, in human form, had to learn how to be obedient.

Do you think his earthly parents had anything to do with his submissive attitude? God, the Father, was pretty particular about the parents he chose to foster parent his Son. As loving and wise as Joseph and Mary may have been, Scripture does not say that they were perfect parents. They were blessed, as all parents are, by having children. I imagine Jesus had plenty of practice honoring and obeying his imperfect, earthly parents. He may have even had to suffer because of their imperfect parenting. But Jesus and the entire human race benefited from his submissiveness to his earthly parents.

If Jesus hadn't been submissive to his heavenly Father, things might have turned out differently in the Garden of Gethsemane. Jesus respectfully begged his heavenly Father for some other way to redeem our souls. But God's will was to stick to their original plan, and, thankfully, Jesus submitted his Father's will.

SUBMISSIVENESS BRINGS REWARD

God expects his children to respect him, not because he needs an ego boost, but because he wants his children to live fulfilling lives. When God gave the Ten Commandments, he instructed children to honor their fathers and mothers. This is the only one of the commandments with a promise: "Honor your father and mother. Then you will live a long, full life in the land the Lord your God will give you" (Exod. 20:12). God offers an incentive for obeying this commandment. Children should honor their parents because it is for their own benefit. As the saying goes, "This is for your own good."

The same principle applies to rearing our children. We set a curfew to protect our kids from numerous temptations and dangers. We don't allow rude back talk so our children will learn the importance of respecting people. We set a bedtime because children need sleep in order to function well. Our children don't always see the rewards of submissiveness, but that's all right. We need to remember that because of our discipline and training, they will reap rewards in their lives.

Knowing children as we do, *submissive* is not always the first word that comes to mind when we think of them. You may not want to make it number one on your list, but let's at least put it in the top five or six. After all, God made submitting to parents number five on his top-ten list. He even put it ahead of murder, adultery, stealing, and lying. He must think it is pretty important. And for us adult children, he made submitting to him the number one issue. God said as clearly and simply as possible, "I come first! *Nothing* should come before me" (paraphrase of Exod. 20:3).

Just in case that isn't clear enough, commandment number two further clarifies God's concern with respect, honor, and submission. "Do not make idols of any kind, whether in the shape of birds or animals or fish. You must never worship or bow down to them, for I, the Lord your God, am a jealous God who will not share your affection with any other god! I do not leave unpunished the sins of those who hate me, but I punish the children for the sins of their parents to the third and fourth generations. But I lavish my love on those who love me and obey my commands, even for a thousand generations" (Exod. 20:4-6).

Summary

As parents, the core attitude we need to look for in our children is submissiveness—their ability and willingness to yield their will to ours. If we are going to make any serious changes in our children's rebellious attitudes, it will be much easier on everyone if we begin this process when our children are young. But remember that it's never too late to start.

The next chapter will help build our courage as we begin to help our children develop attitudes that foster healthy relationships.

Reflection Questions

Take a few minutes to think about these questions. If possible, discuss them with your spouse, another parent, or a group of parents. Write down your observations, feelings, and goals in a journal.

1. How does your children's lack of submission surface? When they are doing chores? In their appearance? In their choice of friends? In their choice of entertainment?
2. How do your children show their respect to you? to your spouse? to siblings? to teachers? to coaches?

3. How do your children express their frustration or anger with others?
4. How would you describe your ability to submit to your authorities? employer? civil authorities? God?
5. How can you model a submissive attitude to your children?
6. How good were you at submitting to your parents?
7. Do you want your children to do better than you did? Why?

Happy are those whom you discipline, Lord, and
those whom you teach from your law.

— P s a l m   9 4 : 1 2

4

Conflict Enhances Our Relationships

As Christy heads out the door after dinner, her dad calls out in a rather cheery voice, "Christy, where are you going?"

"Out."

"Who are you going out with?" asks Christy's mom.

"Some friends," says Christy through clenched teeth.

Feeling as if he is forced to drag information out of his daughter, Christy's dad continues, "When are you coming back?"

"I don't know. Sometime."

Christy's dad is frustrated. Not wanting to get into an argument but wanting to make his expectations clear, he announces, "No later than one o'clock."

"Why?"

"Because one o'clock is late enough."

Pouting, Christy shoots back another question: "Why do you have to put a time limit on me?"

"Because you're only sixteen."

"So are the rest of my friends, but they don't have to be home at a certain time."

"We're not the rest of your friends' parents."

"What do you think I'm going to do?" Christy starts to whine.

"I don't know. You won't tell us."

"I'm going over to Jill's house. Are you satisfied? We're not going to get drunk and watch porno movies. We're just meeting some friends over there. What is the problem?"

"I repeat, Christy. Staying at Jill's house until one o'clock is long enough to be with friends."

Uncomfortable at the rising pitch in her daughter's voice, Christy's mom comments, "Bill, since it's just at Jill's, that should be all right."

"*Mom* trusts me," Christy responds. She knows she's winning now.

Feeling that he is losing ground, Christy's dad asserts, "Now wait a minute. I want you home by one o'clock and no later. If you aren't home by then, you will be grounded."

"Mom." Christy looks imploringly at her mom. "That's not fair."

Turning to her husband, Christy's mom says in a soft voice, "Honey, I think she will be all right."

"No. One o'clock is late enough. Christy, if you don't want to come home by then, you can just stay home all night."

Exasperated at how the conversation is moving, Christy shouts, "Fine. I may as well just stay home forever." She storms off to her room.

"That's fine with me," her dad says cryptically.

"Oh, honey . . ." is all Christy's mom can say.

■　■　■

This scene didn't go too well. The conflict did not end well. All three people lost, and their relationships were torn. Christy is pouting. Her mom is scared. Her dad is irritated at both Christy and his wife.

What if he had let the conversation finish something like this?

"I'm going over to Jill's house. Are you satisfied? We're not going to get drunk and watch porno movies. We're just meeting some friends over there. What is the problem?"

"I repeat, Christy. Staying at Jill's house until one o'clock is long enough to be with friends."

Uncomfortable at the rising pitch in her daughter's voice, Christy's mom comments, "Bill, since it's just at Jill's, that should be all right."

"*Mom* trusts me," Christy responds. She knows she's winning now.

"Well, Carolyn, what time do *you* want Christy to be home?"

"I don't know. Christy, how late were you thinking?"

"I don't think about time. I just think about being with my friends. When we're done being together, I come home."

"Bill, that seems harmless enough to me."

Christy's dad is exasperated. "Fine, stay out as long as you want. I don't care."

"Well, Christy, don't stay out too late," her mother calls after her.

■ ■ ■

Is this much better? No harsh words were spoken. Was the conflict successfully handled, or was it only avoided? Are the relationships still strong, or are they strained? Christy got what she wanted only because her mom joined her side and her dad gave up. Christy's mom feels relieved that she temporarily dodged a bullet. Her dad feels betrayed, frustrated, and confused.

Actually, neither scenario is healthy for the family. Everyone lost, even Christy. She may have some feeling of "winning," but she probably has some sense of loss, even though she may not be aware of it, let alone admit it. Christy lost some of her parents' protection and guidance. She may even feel a tinge of fear at having so much power, similar to that feeling when you start down a giant roller coaster. It's exhilarating but scary.

Christy's mom feels stuck in the middle. She's frustrated that her husband and daughter don't get along better. In response, the mother surrendered some of her parental authority. The next time she wants to use it, she will have a hard time asserting it. Christy's dad feels frustrated with both women. He feels "out of the loop" with the family unit. He lost his wife's support and loyalty. He also lost some of his daughter's respect since she was able to recruit her mom to gang up against him.

What is important to note is that in both situations the parents temporarily avoided conflict. The first conflict ended prematurely; it died before it could bear any fruit. The second conflict was aborted by the parents; they lost an opportunity to strengthen their family. But all they have really done is postponed the conflict until things build up so much that one of the three explodes in anger. That's when things get ugly.

Christy and her parents avoided conflict because they fear conflict would harm their relationship. I contend that exactly the opposite happened. Because they avoided conflict, the relationships were all weakened. If the parents had been willing to embrace conflict as a necessary part of shaping their daughter's attitude, all three people would end up winners. The upcoming chapters will explain in detail how to make this happen.

AVOIDING CONFLICT HURTS OTHERS

Christy's parents aren't the only ones who want to avoid conflict. And they aren't the only ones to reap the consequences of avoiding conflict. Listen in on this conversation:

"Hi, Laurie. How did it go with Tommy?" Marian Hoyt asked Laurie Parker, the baby-sitter.

"Hi, Mom," greeted Tommy.

"Hey, pal. What are you doing up?" Marian's husband asked their six-year-old son.

"Mr. Hoyt, Tommy wouldn't go to bed when I told him to," said Laurie.

"You wouldn't go to bed, Tommy? Aren't you tired?" his mother asked.

"Nope."

Feeling frustrated, Laurie continued, "He really wouldn't listen to anything I said."

Smiling down at Tommy, Mr. Hoyt responded, "He does have a mind of his own. Tommy, were you being ornery?"

"She was being bossy." Tommy pointed to Laurie.

Embarrassed that the six-year-old was making her look bad, Laurie added, "I tried to get him to pick up his stuff, but, well, he wouldn't do it."

"Well, that's OK," said Tommy's dad as he moved to his son's side. He tousled the boy's hair playfully.

"Tommy has never been one to sleep, Laurie. Even when he was a baby, he took only fifteen-minute naps," added Marian.

"He also tore my jacket," Laurie persisted, hoping she could get these parents to support her.

"I was only trying to get it off the hook for her," Tommy blurted out with a whine.

"Tommy, I asked you not to pull at it."

"Laurie, I'm sure Tommy was just trying to be helpful. Can we pay you for the repair to your jacket?"

"No, that's OK. I'll just go home now."

"So, Laurie, are you available next week to baby-sit for Tommy?"

"Uh, no, sorry. I'm busy."

"Ah, that's too bad."

■ ■ ■

Tommy's parents either don't know how to make Tommy behave, or they don't want to. Maybe they just don't see his growing defiance. Laurie sure does. She was trying to supervise him well, but Tommy isn't used to obeying. But the boy really isn't to blame. He is only doing what comes naturally for kids. Children just want to do whatever they feel like at the moment; they don't like limits. Unfortunately, Laurie was the recipient of Tommy's insolence. And she won't be the last.

If Tommy's parents don't get the message soon and do some things differently, they will be giving their son the wrong message. They will be teaching him that he should always get what he wants. Those messages lead to arrogant, spoiled attitudes. Pretty soon, it won't be just Laurie who doesn't want to be with Tommy. The only ones who will tolerate Tommy are other insolent kids. Then Tommy's only friends will be ones he can dominate or ones who will control him. Tommy needs to be taught how to treat others with respect.

Since Tommy's parents are avoiding the little conflicts when he is young, he will undoubtedly have bigger conflicts when he is older. Not everyone will tolerate his demands the way his parents do now. Someone will put Tommy in his place, and it may not be done very nicely. That's why it's important for Tommy's parents to work with him at a young age. If they are willing to take responsibility, they can shape Tommy's attitude in loving and effective ways.

Dealing with the conflict would enhance everyone's relationship with Tommy by making him a much more pleasant person to be with. Tommy may not want to learn those lessons, but who does?

CHILDREN INVITE CONFLICT

Parents should not be surprised when their children place them in conflict situations. By nature, children will oppose our moves toward making them do anything they don't want to do. We should expect conflict in our relationship to our children. Ashley's mom should not be taken off guard by her daughter's stubbornness.

"Ashley, it's time to pick up your toys."

"No, I don't want to."

"Yep, we've got to clean up."

"I want to keep playing."

"I know. Come on. You help me."

"No."

"Look, see how I'm putting them all away. You help me."

"No."

"Ashley, here, you put your doll in its bed."

"No." Ashley throws her doll.

"Ashley, that's not very nice. That hurts your dolly."

Ashley responds by throwing another toy.

"Ashley, go sit in your chair. Right now. You're going to sit there until I get this picked up, and then you're going to take a nap."

"No."

"Yes."

■ ■ ■

What lesson is Ashley learning from this encounter? This scene taught her that if she doesn't want to do something, she can have a tantrum and then sit down while her mom does the work. Ashley is learning that her mother is afraid to make her do what she tells her to do. Ashley is learning that her mom doesn't like conflict and is very hesitant to use her authority to correct and teach her daughter. Ashley is most likely also learning that conflict is bad.

Poor Ashley will not have much opportunity to learn how to navigate the rough waters of conflict. She will grow up thinking that the only response to conflict is separating herself from it when it begins.

PREPARE TO ENGAGE IN THE BATTLE OF THE WILLS

Scientists are currently discussing the feasibility of a manned space trip to Mars. One of the problems facing the astronauts is the damage to their muscles and bones caused by weightlessness. Bones lose calcium and get brittle while muscles lose their strength. Ironically, this is all caused by the lack of a stressful environment. Gravity places a certain amount of stress on our bones and muscles to keep them strong. They were made to function better with some stress.

Relationships are similar. Some people falsely believe that a relationship without conflict is the ideal. The truth is that a relationship without conflict is dead. Show me a marriage without periodic conflict, and I'll show you two people living as distant roommates. They are both dying a slow, lonely death. As the old joke says, "If two people agree on everything, then one of them isn't necessary."

Healthy relationships have conflict. "As iron sharpens iron, a friend sharpens a friend" (Prov. 27:17). Sure, there will be sparks, but that makes it exciting. Unless we push, pull, challenge, and test the strength of our commitments to our spouse and children, those commitments will grow weak and flabby. If we want our relationships to be strong, they have to

be tested. That is why kids push so hard against their boundaries. They want to see how secure they are. They want to feel
safe. Don't abandon your kids to the weightlessness of float-
ing through life with no limits, no expectations, or no challenges.

This book will offer you some practical, effective tools with
which to help you adjust your children's bad attitudes. But
like any tool, they won't work unless you are willing to use
them.

If someone is trained as an airplane pilot but is afraid to
fly, of what value is the training? If someone passes all the
tests to be certified as a firefighter but is terrified of getting
burned, then that person is of little use to the fire depart-
ment.

Our willingness to change our children's bad attitudes is
vital. We parents have to be willing to engage our children in
the battle of the wills. We should not provoke our children
unnecessarily, but we also should not retreat from their challenges. We must establish our authority. Everyone needs to
know who is in charge.

A bad attitude is like a fire; it continues to grow in intensity
and destructiveness if it is left unattended. If we see a fire
starting, we would be foolish to think that because it is only a
small fire, it will soon burn itself out. An untended fire will
only strengthen in intensity. If we run from it, it will spread.
If we try to cover it up, it will smolder. If we fight it with a
water pistol, it will create some steam. The best way to handle
a growing fire is to fight it with the proper equipment.

The most effective way to handle a bad attitude is to engage
in the battle. You are welcome to use whatever tools you
think will work, but if the results are not satisfactory, then
keep reading.

The truth about well-handled conflict is this: *Conflict with kids connects them with parents.* Many parents are afraid that conflict will drive their kids away. That is true only if the conflict is handled poorly. If conflict is handled well, it serves to knit people's hearts together. If a fire is contained in the hearth, everyone gathers around it. A campfire provides intimacy, warmth, and comfort. Just as fire handled carelessly will destroy, conflict without boundaries will harm relationships.

Conflict offers parents one of the most valuable teaching opportunities. The richest teachable moments you could ever ask for are right in the midst of conflict. When your children challenge you and your authority, recognize the challenge as a valuable opportunity to teach them the importance of respect and submission in a God-honoring way. You won't ever have to lecture them on the ways to resolve conflict; they will be learning it by how you treat them.

LOVE PURSUES CHILDREN

God was often faced with the fact that his children repeatedly rejected him. The Israelites ignored his commands and rudely went their own way. But God continued to pursue them. God continually embraced conflict to bring them back to his heart.

When the people of Israel rebelled, God would raise up a prophet. The prophets would warn the people that God loved them very much, and because he loved them so much, he was *very* angry.

God expressed his frustration through prophets like Isaiah and Jeremiah: "The children I raised and cared for have turned against me. Even the animals . . . know their owner and appreciate his care, but not my people Israel. No matter what I do for them, they still do not understand" (Isa. 1:2-3). "The anger of the Lord will not diminish until it has finished all his plans. In the days to come, you will understand all this very clearly" (Jer. 23:20).

God's purpose in exposing sin is to cleanse the sinner. God pursues us until our rebellion is revealed in all its ugliness. Through his perfect Son, Jesus, God the Father offers his rebellious children a new relationship based on their brokenness, repentance, forgiveness, and restoration. God's pursuit is ultimately an expression of his love for us.

Similarly, our purpose in disciplining our children is to pursue them so that we can expose their bad attitudes and help them change. Our goal should be to seek our children's hardened hearts with the intent to soften them, not break them. Our pursuit should be an expression of our love.

In the New Testament, Jesus expresses this principle of pursuing rebellious children. Luke 15 tells the familiar parable of the shepherd leaving the ninety-nine sheep in the fold to search for the one lost sheep. Jesus underscores this principle by immediately giving another illustration of a woman who lights a lamp and sweeps every nook and cranny of her house until she finds the one lost coin.

In the same way we must pursue our children's bad attitudes. We can't be deceived into thinking that our children will eventually learn the value of submission and honoring parents on their own. Pursuing what is important is a vital principle of parenting. Our children need to be pursued the most when they are disobedient.

The reason pursuit is so necessary is that bad attitudes distance kids from parents. Bad attitudes tend to isolate people from each other and harden hearts. If parents don't pursue their children when they have a bad attitude, parents run the risk of losing their children's hearts for good. Loving parents do not risk losing their children's hearts due to lack of effort.

WHY ARE WE AFRAID OF CONFLICT?

When I was young, I went to a youth camp where we would ride horses every afternoon. I loved it. The only part I didn't care for was when it was time to return to the stables. The horses knew we were heading back and would try to break into a full gallop. It took all my strength to restrain those powerful beasts.

Can you imagine trying to ride an animal with the power of over a hundred horses? If you could handle the terror, the thrill would be awesome. If you lived on a farm, you could use an animal like that to accomplish an enormous amount of work.

Do you realize you handle over a hundred horses every day without even giving it a second thought? It's your car. When you drive your car, you are guiding the power of over a hundred horses. Sometimes that power gives us a rush. Other times we are sobered by that power when we see the damage it can do in an accident.

Anger is like horsepower. Anger gives us a tremendous rush of power. Whether or not that power is under our control is up to us. Just as we need lessons to learn how to drive, we could all use some practice learning how to harness our anger.

Some people think anger is harmless. They drop angry words like *stupid* or *good-for-nothing* on their children and think nothing of it. But careless words or cruel glares can leave lifelong damage. A harsh tone of voice can echo inside our heads for years. Speaking as a counselor, I hear examples of these things every day. You may have your own to tell.

Other people are afraid of anger and don't want anything to do with it. They work very hard to keep calm at all times. We could live without our cars and not have anything to do with them. But for most of us, that just isn't realistic. Instead we opt to learn how to drive a car well. Likewise, we should learn how to harness our anger and use it for good.

Many of us parents are afraid of conflict with our children. I can think of three reasons why we often feel this way.

First, we are afraid conflict will damage our children either internally or externally. This is the fear of losing control. Perhaps you have been the object of poorly handled conflict or anger. As a result, you may be afraid of your own anger. You don't want to be anything like the people whose anger is out of control. Or maybe you never saw your parents angry, and you feel guilty for your own anger at your children. You never saw your parents model how to be angry yet not sin. Fear of conflict is based on not knowing whether you can handle the energy, strength, and power that anger generates inside you.

I hope that by reading this book you will learn some reasonable, practical tools to use in handling conflict with children. I will suggest an outline to follow in your head so you can feel as if you know where you are heading with your anger. As you gain experience, your confidence will mature and you will be free to benefit from the positive side of anger.

Second, we are afraid to engage in conflict because it may cause our children not to like us. If this is the case, then you need to do some thinking. God does not give us children to meet our own social or emotional needs. If that is how we see our children, then we can cause damage. If we do not express our anger at our children because we want them to like us, we are using our children to get what we should be getting elsewhere. Let children be children. Let them grow up gradually.

Parents should get their social and emotional needs met from the other spouse, from family members, or from friends. That is how the body of Christ is supposed to function.

Third, we may be afraid of conflict because we fear our children's anger. If this applies to you, then you need some support to face your children. Spouses need to support each other. A husband can use his wife's encouragement. A wife can use her husband's strength in her role as chief disciplinarian. Talk to other parents who have challenging children to rear. Encourage each other. Ask a respected church leader if you should let your children do some of the things you aren't sure about. If necessary, talk to a professional who can help you evaluate whether you are doing the right thing by not giving in to your children's demands.

Children do not want to win the battle of the wills. They will fight like cats and dogs sometimes, but they are trying to reassure themselves that you love them enough to set limits for them.

Children feel things deeply. When they have a feeling, they feel it 110 percent and they let you know about it. That can be very scary for kids sometimes. The roller coaster of their feelings, especially strong ones like anger, can overwhelm children. Your children want to know if you are big and strong enough to handle the uncontrollable urges they feel. Are you?

You may not feel as trained, knowledgeable, and experienced with handling anger as you are with your car, but you can be.

How Can We Handle Conflict with Children Well?

The first thing we need to do when handling conflict with our children is to handle our own anger well. This is a key factor in successfully disciplining children. Part 2 will unpack some tools you can use with your children.

God expressed anger. "It's [God's] anger that wakes us up and reveals the intensity of His love."[1] The opposite of anger is not love; it's apathy. Unless we care about someone or something deeply, we wouldn't bother to get angry about it. We should "notice how God is both kind and severe" (Rom. 11:22). When we discipline our children, it is evidence of our love for them. "The Lord disciplines those he loves, as a father the son he delights in" (Prov. 3:12, NIV).

If someone hurts my children, intentionally or not, I get angry at that person. If my children are rude to each other, I'm annoyed that they don't treat each other with respect and that they are acting so selfishly. If they persist in their rude behavior, I get angry that they ignore my expectation to treat each other better.

Should I get angry when my children are disrespectful to someone else or to me? Let me put it this way: If I *don't* get angry, then I don't care enough about my children, others, or myself. My anger at them for their misbehavior or bad attitude is one of the ways to gauge how much I care about them and/or myself. We should not let our children treat others disrespectfully.

GOD'S ANGER

If we are to emulate God, how do we do that with our anger? Let's start by looking at how God handles his anger. In his book *The Surprising Side of Grace* Stephen Bly cites seven important facts to remember about God's anger. All of them can apply directly to how parents handle anger with their children.

1. God's anger is always justified.
2. God's anger is always initiated by disobedience.

3. God is slow to anger.

4. God often restrains his anger.

5. God's anger remains until it accomplishes its purposes.

6. God's anger is neutralized by our repentance.

7. God's anger does not last long.[2]

Let's look more closely at each of these statements.

1. God's anger is always justified. Psalm 7:11 reminds us that "God is a judge who is perfectly fair. He is angry with the wicked every day." It is comforting to know that God's anger is fair. He doesn't fly off the handle for no good reason. No one can reasonably complain that God has no right to be upset.

Parents should always know why they get angry. Are you angry for some legitimate reason? What specific thing did your children do or say to warrant this anger? Take some time to identify the problem. This will help to make it clear to your children. They need to know what to do or what not to do next time. Identifying the source of your anger will help you teach your children what you expect from them. Your anger will serve a good purpose rather than just explode.

Remember that these are your children and you are trying to teach them how to make themselves do what they don't feel like doing. When you manage your anger well, you will be demonstrating for them that we can make ourselves do what we don't feel like doing, even if it is difficult.

2. God's anger is always initiated by disobedience. Jeremiah 44:3 says, "Because of all their wickedness, my anger rose high against them." God's anger is fueled by rebellion. Throughout Scripture, God was always very clear to tell his children exactly what he expected from them, and when they disobeyed him, he became angry.

When we set expectations for our children, we should have a rationale for why we are setting the expectations. If our children do not meet the expectations, then we are justified in getting angry for their disobedience. If we have a legitimate reason for our anger, then we can be fairly sure it is a righteous anger, not destructive anger.

In evaluating your anger, ask yourself these questions: Do I demand obedience because it somehow benefits my children or because I need to feel big and strong? Will my children learn a valuable lesson or just think that I need to feel powerful? Do I get angry over petty offenses or only those things that are truly disobedience? Those are tough questions to answer at times.

3. God is slow to anger. The psalmist tells us, "But you, O Lord, are a merciful and gracious God, slow to get angry, full of unfailing love and truth" (Ps. 86:15). God had prophets warn his children of his impending anger. Healthy anger gives plenty of warnings. It is predictable. It doesn't catch people off guard, causing them to live in constant fear.

We should give plenty of chances for our children to change their attitudes. That is why when I warn my children about the consequences of their disobedience, I tell them it doesn't have to be that way if they will only change their attitudes. I try to give them plenty of opportunities to turn their attitudes around and head in a positive direction.

4. God often restrains his anger. "Many a time he held back his anger and did not unleash his fury! For he remembered that they were merely mortal" (Ps. 78:38-39). God does not let us feel the full strength of his anger. He tempers it because he knows we would be blown away if we had to endure what we deserve.

We parents should be careful about revealing the intensity

of our anger with our children. I speak from much experience with this one. Sometimes I really struggle with keeping my anger corked. I don't have a problem with bad language or name-calling. But I forget how intimidating my deep male voice can sound to someone half my size, how sensitive little kids' ears are to sounds and how my critical tone of voice can cut deep into my children's hearts.

Anger is like a knife. What is important is whether the knife is in the hands of a mugger set out to harm or destroy or a surgeon ready to heal. If you think your anger is too quick or unrestrained, try some of these methods of controlling your anger:

- Count to fifty before you say anything else.
- Tell your children not to say anything until you tell them they can talk again. (This gives you time to develop a game plan.)
- Ask more questions of your children to be sure you have all the facts straight.
- Have your spouse relieve you for a few minutes and go clear your head before you return to finish the confrontation.
- Call a time-out for yourself and go get a cup of hot tea or chocolate before you resume resolving the conflict. You can keep your child with you, but don't say anything until you are under control.
- Take five deep breaths and repeat in your head, "This child may deserve annihilation, but then so do I sometimes. I will teach him, not destroy him."
- Take a quick walk around the block (alone or with your child) or do ten quick push-ups to release some of your own anger and tension.

We must look for balance. We don't want to shy away from necessary anger either. Harnessed anger can give us the much needed energy to build a harmonious relationship. Sometimes it feels as if the relationship is starting from scratch, and it can get discouraging. Anger can give us the necessary jump start as long as we are headed in the right direction.

5. God's anger remains until it accomplishes its purposes. "The anger of the Lord will not diminish until it has finished all his plans. In the days to come, you will understand all this very clearly" (Jer. 23:20). Ineffective anger stops short of its purpose. It is like a surgeon who does exploratory surgery and discovers the infected appendix but doesn't take it out.

Some parents stop short when they confront their children and then storm off in frustration when the children look disinterested or start to talk back. Once you have started this process, you have to finish it. If you haven't known what to do before, then this book could help you develop a game plan of what to do and in what order. Don't expect your children to enjoy this intense process of confrontation and attitude adjustment. If you stop the process in midstream, your children will be even more confused, angry, and scared.

Anger is like strong medicine: Use only when necessary; use only what is necessary; but use all that is necessary.

6. God's anger is neutralized by our repentance. The goal of God's anger is our repentance. "Return, O Israel, to the Lord your God, for your sins have brought you down. Bring your petitions, and return to the Lord. Say to him, 'Forgive all our sins and graciously receive us, so that we may offer you the sacrifice of praise. Assyria cannot save us, nor can our strength in battle. Never again will we call the idols we have made "our gods." No, in you alone do the orphans find mercy.' The Lord says, 'Then I will heal you of your idolatry and faithlessness, and my love will know no bounds, for my anger will be gone forever!'" (Hosea 14:1-4).

Repentance should be what we are looking for in our children. Repentance is what will allow us to rebuild the broken relationship. Anger has accomplished its purpose when our children repent. Once your children repent, your anger is no longer necessary; it will only demoralize them (Col. 3:21).

If you are anything like me, it takes some time for all that adrenaline to work its way out of my system. I have a hard time shutting off my anger. What works for me is keeping my mouth shut for several long minutes. I still look intently at my children. Their genuine repentance helps me calm myself. I am able to see their brokenness, and it becomes hard to stay mad at them.

Sometimes that doesn't work. I have gotten on my little soapbox and pulled out a favorite sermonette to deliver to my children. Fortunately, my wife gives me the "cut" sign by pretending to slash her throat with her finger. This friendly reminder helps me stop before I do any more damage. If I have gone on too long, I apologize to my children for beating them up with my words. I should model to them how to let go of anger when it is no longer necessary.

7. *God's anger does not last long.* God's anger "lasts for a moment, but his favor lasts a lifetime! Weeping may go on all night, but joy comes with the morning" (Ps. 30:5). The psalmist is saying that relatively speaking, God's anger doesn't last long, when we have truly repented. During the time of his anger, it may seem never-ending, but rejoicing will come soon enough.

Practice letting go of your anger after it has achieved the purpose of bringing your children to repentance. Once they have repented, then all this is ancient history. "[Love] keeps no record of when it has been wronged" (1 Cor. 13:5). Children need to see that you are no longer angry. Hug them or play with them to show that the relationship has returned to normal. *How* we express our anger is vitally important. I've spent considerable time talking about *what* God's anger is like. Now let me say a couple of things about *how* to express anger in healthy ways.

Healthy anger is expressed

- with strength, yet restraint
- with confidence, yet humility
- with determination, yet composure
- with resolve, yet temperance
- with force, yet gentleness
- with conviction, yet kindness

Probably the best word to describe how to express anger is with *meekness*. Even though this word rhymes with *weakness*, that is not at all what it means. Moses was described as the meekest, most humble man on the face of the earth (Num. 12:3). He successfully challenged the most powerful man (Pharaoh) in the world at that time. Moses faithfully governed an unhappy, unruly, dissatisfied nation of more than 10 million people for over forty years.

The original definition of the word *meek* came from the world of training animals and racing chariots. It described the power of the animals under the control of the trainer or chariot driver. Anger should be expressed with the power of a wild animal but under the control of the trainer. Healthy anger is expressed with meekness.

Practically speaking, what does this look like? Watch the reaction you get from your children when you are angry with them. If they are backing away or if their eyes get real big or if they start to cry, then you may be coming on too strong and scaring them. Show them that you are in control of yourself by

- not talking for a minute
- lowering the volume of your voice
- whispering what you have to say
- bending down to talk to them face-to-face
- having them stand up, face you, and look you in the eyes so they can see the love behind your anger

You don't have to stop challenging them on their misbehavior. Just change the approach so they can hear you and not be terrified of you.

On the other hand, your children may not be affected at all by your attempts to express godly anger. They may try to put you off or ignore you by

- looking away
- rolling their eyes
- scratching their forehead
- fidgeting
- crossing their arms
- putting their hands on their hips
- pulling their cap down low
- standing on one leg
- sighing as if they are bored
- tapping their fingers or toes

This is their attempt to reject your influence over them. They are trying to say to you, "Leave me alone! Who do you think you are? I don't have to listen to you. No, I don't want to!" They may not be saying the words aloud, but their body language is communicating loudly and clearly.

Don't pretend you don't hear them. This is when you may

need to raise the intensity to break down their attempted defense against your influence. You may need to

- stand up
- talk louder
- silence them from arguing
- refuse to tolerate their excuses or back talk

Tell your children to stop whatever they are doing with their bodies to try to put you off. Don't tell them why you are doing it because they will only deny their intent and it will lead to more arguing. If they ask you why they can't do that anymore, say, "Because you need some practice obeying me." If you need to say it in a stronger way, say, "Because I said so, and I am your parent."

Sometimes you may even have to deal with your children when they try to intimidate or threaten you. Occasionally it is almost cute or funny, but don't be fooled by their lack of power. This would sound something like

- "I'm never coming out of my room."
- "I'll never talk to you again."
- "I'm going to tell Mommy [or Daddy or my teacher] on you."
- "My friend is right. You're nothing but a jerk!" (or something much worse)

Friends, if your children say these kinds of things, this is a wake-up call for you to do something serious and drastic. This would be the time to use some of the power tools I will describe in part 2 of this book.

Conflict is not my idea of a good time. It is scary. Resolving conflict is never easy. Pastor Bill Hybels refers to conflict as a "tunnel of chaos." The main reason to struggle through conflict is to break through to the other side into the peace and tranquillity of a harmonious relationship. Parents are in a fight for their children's hearts. Parents who have the courage, strength, determination, and skill to navigate through the tunnel will enjoy that sweet communion with their children.

MANAGE YOUR OWN ANGER

Managing anger is one of the keys to resolving conflict. Anger is one of those very powerful feelings. It is like gasoline, which can be used constructively or destructively. When gasoline is put into an engine and ignited by a spark plug, its power is harnessed to drive the pistons in a useful way. Its power can be throttled down or turned off very quickly. But if gasoline is thrown into a building and lit with a match, it becomes destructive. Once the fire is blazing, it usually destroys or severely damages the structure. It takes a long time to rebuild after that kind of destruction.

This book is something like a firefighter's training manual. It gives you a plan to use when you are in the midst of those intense feelings between you and your children. Before you use the tools outlined in part 2, be sure you are ready. People must have a certain level of physical strength and health before they are accepted into firefighter training. The same principle applies to using these parenting tools. Using parenting tools requires a certain level of emotional strength to ensure that these tools are not used carelessly. The following guidelines will help you prepare to manage your anger.

Keep your goal in mind. Continually remind yourself *why* you are disciplining your children. You want to return to a harmonious relationship. You do this by expecting a considerate, cooperative, submissive attitude from your children. At times it may appear all you are trying to do is dominate or control your children. What you are doing is teaching your children the importance of being teachable. It may appear self-serving on the surface, but the real motivation is for the good of the children.

Try to mentally screen everything you say or do through the filter of this question: "How will my words or actions help to get my message through to my children?" Part of your message is to convince them that their attitudes are damaging the relationship. This may have to be communicated in a direct, confrontive manner. A firm, tough tone of voice with carefully chosen words is much different from a harsh, abusive tone of voice with rude or insulting words. Don't shy away from the challenge of taking your children on this journey even though they may be dragging their feet. But don't use more force than necessary to accomplish this task.

Go slowly. Confronting children with bad attitudes can appear so easy, until your children don't do what you expect them to do. It's easy for our anger to pick up so much momentum that it gets out of control. Then we are in danger of running them over unless we find some way to stop quickly.

Managing anger takes a lot of practice. Practice expressing your opinion strongly yet respectfully. If you find yourself gaining too much speed, sit down, stop talking, and breathe deeply for a minute until the adrenaline rush has passed. Then try it again. Develop the discipline to shut your mouth long enough to regain control over your emotions. Go slowly.

If you are having trouble going slowly, stop completely. Sit there in silence until you can go on. "Don't sin by letting anger gain control over you. Think about it overnight and remain silent" (Ps. 4:4). If it takes all night to compose yourself, then take it. But maybe a few long, deep breaths would suffice. Do whatever it takes to regain your self-control.

Stick to the subject. We've all been involved in arguments that have started out with one issue and ended up with our hauling out everything that ever bothered us about the other person. We need to be careful to focus on whatever started the problem. Remind your children that the reason they are being disciplined is because of what they did or said. Tell them specifically what they did wrong so they know. But don't use this occasion to drag out anything else they have done. One issue at a time is sufficient to handle. This will help you stay focused and will help them feel that your discipline is fair.

Say as little as possible, but as much as necessary. No one likes to be lectured. Make your point. Have them repeat it if necessary. Move on. Don't get yourself worked up. You want them to feel chastised, not bludgeoned, for their misbehavior. Make sure they know exactly what they did or said wrong. Explain to them why it was wrong in terms they can understand.

Keep it private. Disciplining children is not a spectator sport. Some siblings seem to derive much pleasure from watching this event. Not only do you want to protect the dignity of your children, but you also don't want to give them the opportunity to show you up. If you and your child are alone, you are both less likely to play to the crowd. The only one you should try to impress is your child. You are trying to impress on him or her the seriousness of the bad attitude.

If your children act up in public, take them to a private place, even if they scream that you are hurting them as you take them there. Keep in mind that their screaming is usually an attempt to embarrass you, so if you don't let that dissuade you from disciplining them, they will soon learn that they have to obey in public places also.

Check your own attitude. If your attitude is harsh or overly critical, either ask your spouse to take over for you or sit still for as long as it takes to regain your composure. There is nothing wrong with thinking through exactly what you want to say before you say it. It helps to remember the goal of reconciliation.

Summary

I hope these guidelines help. What this book cannot provide for you is the experience. But as with any skill, the more you use it, the more confidence you will gain. You may lose some sleep and maybe even suffer a broken heart at times. But when you persevere, you will experience the rewards of intimacy with your children.

As the saying goes, "It is much easier to put out a brush fire than a forest fire." We need to prepare ourselves for the challenge. Let's learn how to win the battle of the wills without losing our children's hearts. We want to do much more than just put out the fire of rebellion in our children's hearts. We want to save their hearts from becoming disconnected from ours.

In the next chapter, before we look at the discipline tools in part 2, we will review why some of our common methods of discipline are ineffective or damaging.

Reflection Questions

Take a few minutes to think about these questions. If possible, discuss them with your spouse, another parent, or a group of parents. Write down your observations, feelings, and goals in a journal.

1. How do you react to conflict?
2. How did your parents handle conflict when you were growing up?
3. How do your spouse and children know when you are angry?
4. What are your strengths and weaknesses in harnessing your anger?
5. In what recent situation did you ignore conflict with your children? What were the results?
6. In what recent situation did you embrace conflict with your children? What were the results?
7. What frightens you the most about handling conflict?
8. In what ways would facing conflict help your children?
9. What are some possible positive results of your willingness to manage conflict with your children?

*And now, dear brothers and sisters, let me say one
more thing as I close this letter. Fix your thoughts
on what is true and honorable and right. Think
about things that are pure and lovely and
admirable. Think about things that are excellent
and worthy of praise.*

— P h i l i p p i a n s   4 : 8

5

Evaluating Ineffective
Methods of Discipline

Since the overall goal of discipline is to improve our relationship with our children, our disciplinary tools should help us
attain that goal. Before I suggest some effective tools that will
help you reach that goal, let's look at the benefits and draw-
backs of the most common methods of discipline.

The National Committee to Prevent Child Abuse commis-
sioned a telephone survey in 1994. More than 1250 parents
responded to this question: "How did you discipline your
children last year?" These are the results:

- Taking away privileges   79%
- Confining children to their rooms   59%
- Spanking or hitting   49%
- Insulting or swearing   45%[1]

At one time or another, we have all used some of these
techniques to discipline our children. Sometimes they work
quite well, and other times they don't seem to be enough. As
we evaluate these methods, ask yourself these four questions:

1. Is this disciplinary method effective in achieving cooperation?
2. Is this method the most loving?
3. What does this method really teach my children?
4. Does this method ultimately improve our relationship?

TAKING AWAY PRIVILEGES

Of the parents who responded to the survey, 79 percent said they disciplined their children by taking away privileges. They probably said things like this:

- "If you don't get your homework done, you can't watch TV."
- "If you don't stop arguing, you can't use the phone for a week."
- "If you don't put away your dishes, no Nintendo for a week."
- "If you don't stop arguing with your sister, you can't sleep over at Matt's."
- "Quit picking on your brother, or you will have to go to bed early."
- "If you aren't home by ten o'clock, you will lose your allowance."
- "If you sass me one more time, you'll be grounded for a week."

What's wrong with all these threats? The punishment has nothing to do with the offense. There is no connection between the crime and the punishment. In order for children to learn what not to do, they have to associate the punishment with their misbehavior. They have to connect the "crime with the time," so to speak. If they don't associate the two things, they will just think of you as a mean person who takes their favorite things away. You want your children to learn from the natural consequences of their behavior. This truth teaches that when we do A, then B happens. (I will discuss this in more detail later.) We need to make sure that our children learn from their mistakes. There is a better way to gain cooperation than trying to find something we can snatch away from our children.

What is the point of all these statements? It seems to be this: Find out what means the most to the child and then use that as a weapon.

This method doesn't seem loving to me. Whenever possible, we want our children to feel that we are on their side. You want to be in the position of being the person who rewards rather than takes away. Wouldn't you rather play the role of the cheerleader and encourage them?

Privileges are rewards for positive behavior. *Giving* privileges works much better than taking them away. Sleepovers, pizza parties, sporting events, a new outfit, story time, staying up late, playing a board game, or an hour of watching television are all great rewards for good behavior. Children need motivation to obey. Privileges are to be earned by working for them. Once they are earned, they are theirs to keep and should not be taken away. If they earn a privilege, don't threaten to take it away. You want your children to trust you. You don't want them to fear that you will take back things you have already given them. You will seem more loving when you give to them. They feel warmer toward you. Those ingredients will make a strong relationship.

Is taking away privileges effective in achieving cooperation? Sure, it can be. Taking away privileges certainly gives parents some power to make children obey. Your children will most likely cooperate the first few times you threaten to take the privilege away.

I'm concerned about more than just effectiveness. Taking away privileges could be teaching your children some things you may not want them to learn. It may teach them to not get too attached to anyone or anything for fear you will use it against them. They might learn to keep their distance from objects of their affection (including people).

"Jenny, if you don't come here right now, you won't play with Sara the rest of the week." The issue is between you and Jenny. There is no reason to bring Sara into it at all. You don't want Jenny to distance herself from her friend to avoid the pain of your keeping them apart as a punishment. You want to encourage healthy friendships for your children. You don't want your children to think of people as pawns in your battle to get them to obey you.

The other thing taking away privileges may teach them is to try to keep secret what they like for fear you will use it to hurt them by taking it away. When your favorite method of discipline is to remove objects of affection, your children may try to hide their pleasure out of fear of losing it. That's just human nature. We always try to protect ourselves from pain. We want to encourage our children to attach themselves to people and their favorite things. It gives them a sense of safety and security.

We certainly want to encourage our children that it is safe for them to reveal themselves to us. We don't want them to fear that we will use our intimate knowledge of them to hurt them. We don't want them to live in self-protective armor. We want them to trust us to protect them from unreasonable harm.

So even though taking away privileges may be very popular

and fairly successful, I think there are some persuasive reasons to doubt the overall effectiveness of this method. Besides, what happens if you have already taken everything away? What do you do then?

CONFINING CHILDREN TO THEIR ROOMS

Of the parents who responded to the survey, 59 percent disciplined their children by sending them to their rooms. I have several concerns with this popular practice. We usually go to great lengths to make our kids' rooms as comfortable and inviting as possible. What sense does it make to banish a child to a safe, enticing, desirable room? As George Carlin says, "I have to go to my room? Great! That's where all my cool stuff is!" In other words, that is supposed to be a punishment? I realize kids will usually resist this discipline, but that is more likely because they would argue about anything, even what kind of ice cream you would offer them.

Children's bedrooms should feel like desirable places to be. They should not be places to isolate them. Someone recently told me that as a child, he was sent to his room so often that he just automatically went there as soon as he got home from school. He got so accustomed to it that he preferred to be alone. That response is probably unusual, but it illustrates the tendency to deal with problems by isolating people rather than working toward resolution. Do we want to use a disciplinary method that by nature separates us from our children? We want to build a strong relationship with our children. We want them to experience the relief of resolving problems rather than running from them.

Let's make sure their bedrooms are places for safety and self-expression. They should give them fond memories. Children's rooms should be thought of as sanctuaries, not prisons.

Another reason this tool should be challenged is that it has nothing to do with the problem in the first place. Life's lessons are best remembered when the painful consequence is easily connected to the behavior. If we touch the hot stove, we get burned. If I get cold, I'll remember to bring my heavier coat next time. Natural or logical consequences are great teachers. Confining children to their rooms usually has nothing to do with their offense. Unless you confine them to their rooms until they clean them up or finish their homework, I can't think of any other reason that restricting them to their rooms would fit the situation. I will talk about this more in the next chapter.

When you confine your children to their rooms, do you honestly think they are taking advantage of the time to ponder the error of their ways? As today's kids would say, "Not!" Most likely they are distracted with their "cool stuff" or pouting. We can be pretty sure they are not in there thinking, *Well, let's see. I hit my sister because she took my ball. But I probably shouldn't have done that because hitting is wrong. I know I don't like to get hit. Hitting is violent, and if I'm not careful I might grow up with an anger problem. I don't want to get arrested for assault and battery when I'm older, so I need to learn some other forms of expressing my displeasure when she bothers me. What could I do? Hmmm.*

Thoughts like those are not running through their heads. If they are thinking anything at all, it is probably how unfair we are as parents or how they can get even with whoever got them in trouble.

Confining children to their rooms has probably served the purpose of allowing their negative feelings some time to fester. The adrenaline may be out of their system, but they may still have some animosity in their hearts. The discipline has probably not taught them what we want them to learn. Something more needs to be done.

At this point most parents would say it's time to have a talk with the child because everyone has calmed down. The assumption is that the child is eager to learn from what the parents have to say. Is that what happens? Are your children excited to hear your words of wisdom? Children know how the drill works. They let us make our speeches, and then they say, "OK, now can I go?" After it's over, it leaves us with a sense that something isn't quite right. It feels incomplete. But what is wrong? Everyone is calm now. They listened and said "OK." What's missing is the unmistakable sense that the children truly understood what they did wrong and why it is wrong, felt sorry for what they did, and had the relationship restored to what it should be. Confining children to their rooms most often isn't adequate to accomplish that goal.

Another reason to discourage confining children to their bedrooms is that it could be damaging emotionally. The separation may feel like a subtle kind of rejection. The message they could get from this tool is, "I must be really bad because my own mom and dad don't even want me around!"

Your children may be wondering how much you still like them. They may begin to worry about the endurance of the relationship. The message we should send to our children is that we can be counted on to pursue the relationship no matter how disobedient they become. Avoid the risk of even hinting that your children's behavior or attitude could threaten your love for them.

My other concern with this tool is that I think there is a better way to model managing frustration and anger. Instead of having people separate when emotions get intense, harness that energy to do the necessary work of altering attitude or character. Should we talk to each other only when we are calm? Can't we talk to each other without inflicting damage when we are passionate, hurt, scared, or angry? Childhood is the best time to learn how to handle intense, powerful emotions. We should do our best to model this for them.

Granted, this takes a lot of maturity and self-control. But if we expect our kids to show some restraint when they are expressing their feelings, then we should also. The family should be the best place to learn how to work through conflict. Negotiating is a valuable tool to learn. It will serve our children well throughout their lives. What better time to teach them than when they are young? Conflict provides valuable teaching opportunities. Will we use it to help them work through conflict, or will we use it to isolate them and teach them an unhealthy pattern of avoiding disputes?

When parents send children to their rooms, they have the best intentions of talking about it later, but how many times does that really happen? It takes more effort to return to the problem at a later time than it does to stick with it and work it out. Those intense feelings supply the energy to help you get over the hump of the problem. Harness the energy of those feelings to help work out a solution. Everyone is motivated to work. Do it.

In summary, confining children to their rooms as a method of discipline isn't as effective as it first sounds. Similarly, two related methods of discipline—time-outs and groundings—also have some weaknesses.

Time-out

The term *time-out* is an abbreviated form of the phrase "time-out from positive reinforcement, i.e. reward." It means that the child is psychologically or physically isolated, or both, so that no reinforcement in any form is given. The term originated from a school of psychology called behavior modification, which focuses exclusively on what its name suggests: behavior.

When the time-out originally became popular, it was a great help in controlling students in a classroom setting. The behavior-modification specialists even had helpful guidelines for how time-outs should be used. For example, they suggested that children should not be left in time-out for more than three or four minutes, and they reminded adults that time-outs were teaching devices for children, not rest periods for adults.

If time-outs are always used this carefully, they can have some value in discipline. Time-outs provide some time and space for everyone to calm down, think, and act appropriately.

However, I usually see time-outs being misused. Children are told to sit in a chair indefinitely. "You stay there until I say you can get up!" "You sit on the step until you decide you can behave!" How do children figure that out? Time-outs are too often overused as well as misused by well-meaning parents and teachers. The more often they are used (and especially when they are misused), the more I have concerns similar to the ones I expressed about confining children to their rooms.

I think one reason for the popularity of time-outs is that they are great for crowd control. One can easily put offending children somewhere and keep an eye on them. Also, time-outs require very little time or energy from the adult. In other words, time-outs aren't much work. Just put children in chairs, and leave them there as long as necessary.

My concern with this approach is that teachers don't have the same motivation as parents. I would expect parents to have more of a commitment to their children's growth and development. I'm not saying anything against teachers and their commitment to their students. It's just that when you have a class of students, you can't afford the same time and energy that parents can give to their children. I would expect parents to make more of an effort with their own children.

My other concern is that parents and teachers don't always have equivalent values. I would also expect parents' standards for their children's values and morals to be somewhat higher than a teacher's. Therefore, I suggest that a method that may accomplish the goal of crowd control may not be the best method for parents to use at home. If our commitment and standards are higher, then shouldn't the methods we use also be better designed for our purposes? Discipline should fit into our higher goals of building loving, respectful relationships with our children, who possess positive attitudes and strong character.

Grounding

Grounding seems to be a favorite way to discipline older children. It helps ensure that your children will not get into any more trouble because they are home all the time. It keeps them confined to your vicinity. The assumption is that they wouldn't dare do anything foolish while at home.

Grounding your children is similar to denying privileges because older kids are usually more interested in going out and seeing their friends. Grounding prevents that privilege.

Grounding is popular because we know it hurts children. They almost always groan when they are grounded. We hope that it teaches them a lesson and motivates them to not disobey the next time. Sometimes it does, and sometimes it doesn't. Grounding is also a popular tool because as children get older, most parents feel that they don't have many other effective methods to use. Parents get desperate to find something that works.

I have the same concerns about grounding that I do about the previous methods. However, I would add two more concerns. The biggest problem with grounding is that it lasts too long. Effective discipline should last only as long as necessary. When discipline goes on too long, it feels unfair to children. And if it feels unfair, children don't internalize any lesson from the discipline.

Remember that returning to a harmonious relationship is the point of discipline. You want to repair and restore the relationship as soon as you can. The goal is to be able to enjoy your relationship with your children. You don't want to have to endure each other for a week or so, which is what often happens during a grounding.

A problem with grounding is that it is too easy to not follow through with the punishment. Children may try a couple of tactics to escape the full discipline. One is to turn into angels so we feel guilty or forget why they were grounded:

"Oh, honey, you've been so good lately. Of course you can go out with Bethany tonight. Just be sure to be home on time."

"You mean I'm not grounded anymore?!"

"Well, no, I guess not. We'll let it go this time."

A precedent has been set. Leniency will be expected next time, even if it is not deserved.

The other tactic is for our children to turn into pouting grumps. They can make life miserable and wear us down so we give in to their emotional blackmail:

"Oh, just take the car. I'm tired of having to drive you everywhere."

"Yes, you can go to Sandi's. You've been pouting around here all week."

Children will look for our Achilles' heel, and if it is exhaustion or guilt, they won't hesitate to use it. Grounding then becomes as much of a burden on the parents as it is on the children. The temptation to shorten the discipline can overwhelm our better judgment. When that happens, the threat of grounding loses its power. The next time parents need to discipline their children, they are left with two options: a really long grounding or no disciplinary tool at all. That's a scary thought.

In summary, if you like to use confining children to their rooms, time-outs, or grounding, then please consider the risks to the relationship and to the children's sense of self-worth. Are these methods really effective? Do they teach effective conflict-resolution skills? Are they the most loving methods? What are your children really learning when you use these methods? What message do these methods send to your children? You may arrive at different conclusions than I did, but you will at least know why you are using those methods.

SPANKING OR HITTING

Almost half of the parents surveyed indicated that they spanked or hit their children. I classify spanking and hitting as two different responses. Because spanking is such an important subject, I have reserved a whole chapter for it in part 3. For now, let's look at hitting.

Hitting includes such actions as slapping your children across the face, plunking them on the head with your finger, pulling their hair, yanking on their earlobe, pinching them, or anything else that inflicts pain.

Hitting children is not appropriate. Hitting tells your children that you are frustrated and don't know what to do with your frustration. Your children learn to handle their own feelings in the same immature manner: When you don't know what else to do, hit.

I recently had a mother of six children, five boys and a girl, tell me that she shocked herself by slapping her ten-year-old daughter for sassing her. This person is an extremely intelligent, kind, soft-spoken, mature, Christian mother. She is one of the last people anyone would ever expect to slap her daughter. We discussed the incident, and I advised her to apologize to her daughter for her rudeness. She did, and later as the mother thought about the incident, she remembered how her father would slap her on occasion when she was a young girl. She had completely forgotten those times, only to have them come back to her after she had done exactly what she hated her father for doing to her so many years ago.

The only things accomplished by hitting are that your children will know you are stronger than they are and that you are out of control. It is strictly a power play—using power for power's sake. Hitting only tears children down and involves no building up. There is no hint of self-discipline with hitting. By hitting, you lose any shred of dignity. Your children will not respect you. They won't fear you; they will be terrified of you. In the end, they will only resent you. They may begin to shy away from you like a dog that has been mistreated by its master. You don't want your children to cower when you walk by.

The only time hitting (and I am using the term in the broadest sense of the word) may be appropriate is when you are trying to train very young children about physical dangers such as playing with electrical outlets, touching a hot stove, or running out into the street. A quick slap on the hand or rear end, along with a forceful *no*, is all that should be necessary to get across your message. Of course, you should also put plastic covers in your electrical outlets, turn the pan handles inward on top of the stove, and keep close watch when your children are playing near a street.

INSULTING OR SWEARING

Almost half of all parents who responded to the survey admitted to insulting or swearing at their children. Words have great power and far-reaching effects. Words are like a hammer. They can be used to build children up or to break them down.

Words can encourage children. "I know you missed that fly ball, but I was sure proud of the way you ran so hard to try to get it. You gave 100 percent and almost caught it. When we get home, I'll hit you some fly balls so you can make that catch more easily next time. How about it? There is one thing I know about you—you are a hard worker. You always try your best."

Words can build up children's character. "I know you don't like to do the dishes, but you are an important member of this family. That's why we feed you every day. And since you eat off of these dishes, it's important that they be clean. Everyone does a part in preparing the meal, and we need you to do your part; otherwise it wouldn't get done. You are an important part of this family because you are the dishwasher. Now, let's get to work."

I wouldn't give that little pep talk every time, but I would let them know that even menial tasks are vital. Dishes, dusting, and laundry may be boring, but they are important.

Like a hammer, words can also break someone down. A friend of mine says that even after thirty-five years, she can still remember the phrase her father called her when she was in trouble. She rattled it off her tongue as if she had heard it yesterday. He insulted her by calling her a "selfish, spoiled, inconsiderate brat." When he said those words to her, she would cry. He would later apologize, but by then it was too late. Her father's insulting words are still branded on her heart and have left her scarred for life. Children have an uncanny knack for living up to or down to the names we give them.

Parents' words have measureless influence on their children. Children have no choice but to believe what parents tell them. Children take parents' words and use them to form their identity and self-worth.

When you use words, be careful not to use them as weapons. Using insults or swearing to discipline your children is like using a knife. Those words cut and slash, causing a lot of pain. The intent may be to correct behavior, but the result is hurt and shame. Parents who insult or swear at their children intend to wound not teach. Don't even use G-rated names such as "lazy," "deaf," "stupid," or "slow."

If you found your children cowering in a closet because they were afraid, would you call them brave? Probably not. But when an angel of the Lord found Gideon hiding from the invading Midianites in a winepress, he called him a "mighty hero" (Judg. 6:12). What was the angel doing? The angel was challenging Gideon to be all he could be. He was planting a seed inside Gideon's head. The angel of the Lord could see Gideon for what he would someday become. It was quite a process for Gideon to grow into a mighty hero. Gideon's self-image was very low. "My clan is the weakest in the whole tribe of Manasseh, and I am the least in my entire family!" he said to the angel (Judg. 6:15). Gideon lived up to the angel's expectations of what he could become—a hero. When we tell our kids they are "helpful" and "good workers" rather than "lazy," they will try to live up to our expectation of them.

Sometimes we need to confront our children with the truth. We can do that without calling them names. When I sense that my children are not telling me the truth, I don't have to call them liars. They already feel the guilt of lying. They are afraid of the punishment. However, I do let them know how angry I am about their lie. I want them to know that lying is seriously wrong.

When you confront your children, keep the focus on their behavior ("Take out the trash") or attitude ("Don't talk to me with that tone of voice"). Do not attack their character ("You are a lazy slob") or identity ("You are good for nothing"). One of the goals of discipline is to move toward repentance. This allows children to feel the freedom of forgiveness as soon as possible. Then they won't have time to develop the identity of liars or lazy kids. If you confront the behavior each time it happens, the poison of the sin does not have sufficient time to fester into an infectious wound.

When we confront our children about their misbehavior and compliment them on their noble deeds, they will learn their strengths and weaknesses. In Christian terms, they will know that even though they are sinners, we love them as if they were saints. That is what God does for us.

Don't call your kids names except when you praise them. You are trying to shape their identity, so call them "honest," "respectful," and "likable." Say things such as "You are a hard worker. Thank you for mopping the kitchen floor" or "Thank you for being so honest about accidentally breaking that picture. I know I can trust you" or "Thank you for being such a good helper by bringing in the groceries" or "You are so pleasant and such a joy to be around!"

Let's give our children a catalog of names we've called them. This may help them combat the list of names others call them throughout the rest of their lives. Let us all say to our children the same words that God said to his Son, "You are my beloved [child], and I am fully pleased with you" (Mark 1:11). What a great inheritance that would be for our children.

Summary

Simply because these disciplinary methods are so popular doesn't mean they are the best ones to use. In fact, I've argued that we shouldn't be using some of them at all. Hitting, insulting, and swearing do not belong in our tool-box.

We may find value in denying our children certain privileges, confining them to their rooms, giving them time-outs, or grounding them. But for the most part those methods are primitive and shortsighted when it comes to building strong character, positive attitudes, and cooperative behavior in children. Even more important, those strategies could do more damage than good in the long run. They may handle the immediate behavioral problem with some degree of success, but they may damage our children's sense of self-worth and our relationship with them.

I believe that all these methods can have more negative than positive results because they do not address the foundational issues of attitude and because they do not bring parents and children together. In part 2 we will look at some powerful tools to use in reaching the goals of adjusting attitudes and bringing parents and children together to live in harmony.

■ ■ ■ Reflection Questions

Take a few minutes to think about these questions. If possible, discuss them with your spouse, another parent, or a group of parents. Write down your observations, feelings, and goals in a journal.

1. Which of these disciplinary methods do you usually use?
2. What are your children's attitudes after you use any of these strategies?
3. What has this chapter caused you to reevaluate?
4. Will you continue to use any of these methods? Why?
5. Are these methods effective in achieving cooperation? a good attitude?
6. Are these methods loving?
7. What do these methods teach your children about relationships? about themselves? about you?
8. Do these disciplinary methods improve your relationship with your children?

Assembling the Power Tools

*Repeat [these commandments] again and again to
your children. Talk about them when you are at
home and when you are away on a journey, when
you are lying down and when you
are getting up again.*

— D e u t e r o n o m y 6 : 7

6

Setting Expectations

My kids loved the movie *The Lion King*. They especially love
to walk around the house singing one of the movie's songs,
"I Just Can't Wait to Be King." I bet your kids loved that song
too, and I think its popularity is due to more than just the
clever melody. The lyrics of the song tell the story of every
child's fantasy. The young lion, Simba, thinks he knows all
he needs to know about life and doesn't have to listen to the
adults anymore. He dreams of doing whatever he wants. That
attitude gets him and his father, Mufasa, into big trouble.
Simba's rebellion ends up costing Mufasa his life. Sound
familiar?

When I was four years old, my dad used to let me sit on his
lap and drive the car in a big U-turn in front of our apart-
ment. I had to sit on his lap so I could see over the steering
wheel. That was before power steering was available on most
cars, so I would have to turn the wheel with all my strength.
Although my dad and I were traveling at the "breakneck"
speed of 3 mph, it was a thrill for me. I would beg him to go
faster, and he would punch the accelerator for a split second.

I would feel the rush of adrenaline as the car lurched forward. I loved it. But I also felt a rush of panic that we would crash. But then dad would apply the brakes so we wouldn't drive over the curb. Fortunately, my dad was right there, closely orchestrating everything. It was both comforting and frustrating that I couldn't have total control. The power of driving was thrilling.

Children think they know much more than they really do. Life seems so simple to them. They have no concept of how challenging life can get. Most of their worries are taken care of for them. From the time some children are old enough to reach the "steering wheel" and "gas pedal" of their lives, they want to put the pedal to the metal. They think they are old enough to drive.

This may come as a surprise to some people, but children are not little adults! Children do not think like adults; they think like children. Children focus primarily on their own wants and needs.

Parents have to teach children the rules of the road—societal and family norms. Simple things such as using the brakes and paying attention are vital parts of safe driving. Many children don't understand the consequences of their actions. They just want to drive.

Parents want children to develop personal integrity and character. Loving parents take the time and energy to teach their children what to do and how to be responsible with their freedom. Loving parents steer their children's attitudes toward submitting to their leadership.

William Damon, director of the Center for Human Development, says: "Children need to be held to consistent standards, firmly enforced, in order to develop respect for persons other than themselves. Children must learn to cope with stubborn realities that will not change as the children's moods and feelings change, and that will not vanish when the children's complaints grow loud enough. Failing to give children firm rules and guidelines is a sure way to breed arrogance and disrespect."[1]

In the next few chapters we will move beyond the questions of what a good attitude is and why it is important. We will begin outlining the steps toward lovingly yet firmly turning children's rebellious attitudes into yielding ones.

In this chapter we will explore a basic tool in discipline: setting expectations for our children. In chapter 7 we will look at the tool of enforcing logical consequences. Many of you will already be using these two tools, and these chapters will help you focus your skills. In chapters 8–11 we will discuss some power tools that may be new to you. But I think you will find them very effective.

Setting Expectations

The first step in discipline is setting expectations, letting our children know what we want them to do. Setting expectations is critical. Children need to be taught. Often they need to be shown what to do and how to do it. We should never punish our children for disobedience unless we are sure that they knew exactly what was expected of them in the first place. Punishment will not work unless the expectations are clear.

Stop for a minute and think: Do you know what you expect from your children? Can you list five or seven things that are your top-priority expectations? If you don't know what your expectations are, then is it any surprise that your children are not meeting those expectations? Does your spouse expect the same things that you do from your children? If not, then you may be confusing your children.

This question may be even more important: Do your children know what your expectations are? That may seem like a silly question, but it is really an important one. When children know what you expect, they feel secure. The framework of their lives is stable. When they know what to expect from you and what you expect from them, their lives become predictable and safe. They can relax.

There are hundreds of big and little expectations to teach our children, including:

- Personal hygiene and grooming
- Mealtime etiquette
- Restaurant etiquette
- General social manners
- Meeting and greeting skills
- Introducing others
- Making requests
- Handling requests from others
- Responding when someone wrongs you
- Responding when you have wronged someone else
- Responding to criticism
- Relating to authority figures
- Handling anger
- Working cooperatively in a small group
- Becoming involved in group activities
- Respecting others' property
- Respecting social distance and touching
- Respecting private topics
- Relating to someone from a different culture[2]

Physical Expectations (Household Chores)

Over the years Sharon and I have used various ways of communicating to our two children what we expect from them in terms of household chores. When our kids were too young to read, we took pictures of their daily chores: brushing their teeth, making their beds, taking a bath, giving their mom and dad a hug (an easy one everyone liked). Instead of saying, "Go clean your room," we could hand them a picture of a clean room and say, "Make your room look like this." (You may also want to include a picture of their closets so everything doesn't get thrown in there.)

After they completed these jobs, they would put the pictures in a little pouch and tell us they were all done. Then we would inspect their work. The main purpose of the inspection was to tell them what a great job they did and how proud we were of their effort. But when they were ready and when it was necessary, we would take this time to teach them how to do the job better. The praising is far more valuable for future compliance. Younger kids usually like to do what pleases parents.

As our children got older, we added more jobs. Our rule of thumb was that if our children were physically capable of doing a task, they were expected to do it. Our friends were amazed that our two-year-old daughter would sort her own laundry. When she was three, her older brother (six years old at the time) would help her put her clothes in the washer and dryer. After the clothes were dry, she would fold them and put them away. Our kids do the dishes the old-fashioned way—in the sink. We don't have too many cereal bowls left, but our children are learning the skills of housekeeping. Do they like it? *No!* But then, who does? We like the results but not the work.

An important part of setting expectations is showing your children what the finished job should look like. Demonstrate how to do the task. As they grow up and their abilities develop, raise the standards. They should be able to do the work faster, without reminders, and to a better degree of expertise.

Social Expectations

We need to communicate our expectations of how we would like our children to act in social situations. It is important that we do that *before* the situation; make the expectations very clear. When our children were younger, we would frequently remind them what we expected from them: "Do not run in the house" or "Say please and thank you" or "Call them 'Mr.' and 'Mrs.'" When we went shopping, we gave them similar instructions: "Don't touch things on the shelf unless I ask you to pick them out for me" or "Stay by my side and don't play hide-and-seek games."

Our son, Dugan, is fourteen years old. We still continue this practice with a few modifications. Instead of talking to him as if this is new information, we assume he already knows it. I was talking to him about a new social club we are starting. Many of the kids already know each other, but some are coming in new. Since Dugan is one of the founding members and knows everyone, I told him he had a little more responsibility than the others. Dugan has some leadership ability and loves to make others laugh, so he often finds himself in the center of the social activity. Therefore I challenged him to make sure that the new members feel welcome and included in the conversations and activities.

Before leaving a friend's home, Sharon reminds the kids that it's "eyeball" time. This is a code word meaning "look our hosts in the eye and tell them 'Thank you for your hospitality and for inviting us over.'" Sure, they see us doing it, but they still need reminding that this a very important social custom. We want it so ingrained in them that they would feel that something important was missing if they forgot to do it.

When our children were younger, Sharon and I would say things like, "Greet everyone with a handshake, eye contact, and a smile. Speak politely. Include everyone in your play and conversation. Wait until someone is done talking before you talk. Ask us if you are not sure you should be doing something" (our kids still call us on the phone to make sure they can watch a movie while staying overnight at a friend's house). Now that our children are older and don't need the warning talk so much, we sometimes ask them later, "Did you help clean up?" or "How did you get along with everyone?" I don't just settle for the "fine" nonanswer. I say, "So, tell me what you did." I can usually read between the lines if there was a problem.

When our children have been with other adults, we always check with the adults later to see if they detected any problems in our children's behavior or attitudes. We want to know if we need to do some more teaching in any area.

It is a challenge to teach children your expectations for their behavior in tough situations in relationships. These situations include learning how to respond when someone wrongs them or when they have wronged someone, how to respond to criticism, how to show respect to others' property or person, etc. These skills require sensitive and specific instruction.

When training your children in these skills, remember two key components. The first key is to tell them exactly *what* to do. Keep in mind that children may be ignorant about how these particular social skills should be handled. Patiently tell them what they did poorly and what they should do differently when it happens again. Don't let them sidetrack the conversation onto how it wasn't their fault. Help them focus on what they can do, even if the other person is clearly in the wrong.

The second key is to teach them *how* to do it. This includes tone of voice, volume of voice, and body movement and posture. My favorite way to teach this is by role-playing. Younger kids love to pretend, so use that ability in their favor. Tell them to play the other person in the conflict, and you play your child so they can see how to handle things differently. Let them play out all their "what if" scenarios, with you responding in an age-appropriate, realistic manner. It can actually be fun for both of you. After a while, switch roles. This will give them practice responding in some of the ways you just modeled for them. It gives them a chance to add their own style. This "play" tool is exactly what children do with each other or by themselves. Listen to them sometime, and you will hear them reenact situations from their real life.

Older children may not enjoy the role-playing as much, but I would not give up too easily. Call it a "verbal quiz" to test their ability to think on their feet. Then you could throw them a few curves to see how they handle them. The strong point of the role-playing with children of any age is that it is usually lighter and more fun in nature. Role-playing is also very powerful because your children will remember what they practiced much more than what you said.

Even if you can't get your older kids to act something out with you, at least get them to tell you how they plan to handle the situation the next time. Challenge them to put themselves back into that situation mentally and tell you exactly what they would do differently. It isn't quite as powerful, but it is much better than having them just listen to us lecture them.

Setting expectations for teenagers covers very important matters, including how to relate to the opposite sex, how to face serious temptations, and how to negotiate freedoms and responsibilities. Parents, whatever you do, don't abdicate your authority to teens. Your teenagers are not adults. They still need some guidance from you. As you face their growing independence, you want to loosen up on the reins somewhat, but don't let go of them. Let them know which expectations are not negotiable such as maintaining sexual purity, not using drugs, and showing responsibility for a growing number of things. By fulfilling these expectations, teenagers demonstrate that they are ready to handle the many freedoms "all their friends" have.

Attitude Expectations

The difficulty with expectations about attitudes is that attitudes are hard to measure because they are an internal posture. Matters of the heart are private, even from ourselves many times. How do we determine someone's true attitudes?

The only way to assess someone's attitude is by what we see or hear. We have to look at the evidence and draw some conclusions. In chapter 2 is a partial list of positive attitudes we expect from our children. Any one of them can be defined by specific behaviors.

Having a cooperative attitude is one expectation Sharon and I focus on a lot. This can be measured many ways. I'll break it down into a list of Do's and Don'ts.

DO:
- say OK when asked to do something
- have a pleasant tone of voice
- work at an appropriate, reasonable speed
- the request to the best of your ability

DON'T:
- whine ("Why?" "Do I have to?" "Ah, come on.")
- make excuses ("I'm too tired." "I did it last time.")
- delay or put it off ("Can I wait until after this is over?" "I'll get to it later.")
- make any disparaging sounds (grunting or sighing)
- make faces or roll your eyes

- have a commentary on the request ("Whatever" "What am I? A slave?")

I tell Dugan and Breeze, "You don't have to be excited and overjoyed about the work I expect you to do. But I also don't want to hear the complaining about it. Just do what I ask with a cooperative attitude. Thank you."

The minimum attitude we should expect from our children is *respect*. Respecting others is something all children should be taught. They don't have to be best friends with all people or even like them all, but they should always to be cordial and polite. Some of the ways to express respect are to

- answer people when they ask a question
- look at them when they are speaking
- wait until someone is done talking before you start talking
- shake someone's hand when you are introduced
- refer to adults as "Mr." or "Mrs."

With older children, you can raise the standard of what a good attitude looks like. Because Dugan is now a teenager, we are trying to teach him to have an attitude of thoughtfulness. We want him to have some initiative when it comes to daily responsibilities. I tell him to look around the house and yard for things that need to be done and then do them. We want him to develop an attitude of serving others. Sometimes he surprises us with his thoughtfulness, and other times he focuses only on himself. I wonder where he gets that from?

Tone of voice speaks volumes about a person's attitude. I don't expect to hear sweetness all the time. But I definitely don't want to hear grumpiness either. Our voices betray our attitudes much more accurately than our words do. You can use that insight when assessing your children's attitudes.

Now please don't get the idea that my kids are angels. If they were, I'd have no material or motivation to write this book. We still have to remind them of how to respond to us. We give them a chance to correct their slips without pouncing on them. I don't want to get pharisaical with this either. Children need guidance and direction, but they should not be treated with legalistic rigidity. Kids need some room to breathe.

Verbal Repetition

Wouldn't it be nice if we could say something only once and be assured that our children would remember it? Dream on, right? Children seem to have some sort of automatic "delete key" when it comes to expectations. I wish I had a nickel for every time I've heard "I forgot" or "I never heard you say that." I get tired of reminding them about things I've already told them.

A helpful tool to counteract this tactic is verbal repetition. It is very simple to use. If you have the slightest inclination that your children may not be listening very closely, then have them repeat what you just said to them:

"Susan, after we get home I want you to clean up the dog messes in the yard."

"Huh? Oh, sure, Dad."

"What did I say?"

"Umm, something about the dog. You want me to let him out."

"No. Try again."

"I don't know."

"I want you to clean up the dog messes. Now say it back to me."

"You want me to clean up all the dog messes."

"Thank you."

"You're welcome."

■ ■ ■

When I have to use verbal repetition with our children, I have them repeat the instruction three times. I may do that if I've already reminded them once, if they just have a habit of "forgetting" an unpleasant chore, or if they argue with me a little bit:

"Breeze, I want you to sweep your room, make your bed, and take out all the trash."

"OK, Dad. I will in just a minute," Breeze responds from the sofa, where she has curled up with a book.

"What will you do in just a minute?" I ask.

"What you said."

"What did I say?" I persist.

"Something about my room."

"Breeze, what did I say?"

"I don't know. I forget."

"I'm going to tell you again, and then you will repeat it so I know you understand it. I want you to sweep your room, make your bed, and take out all the trash in the house."

"You want me to sweep my room, make my bed, and take out my trash."

"What trash?"

"My trash."

"No, all the trash."

"OK, all the trash."

"Now say it correctly three times."

"You want me to sweep my room, make my bed, and take out all the trash in the house. You want me to sweep my room, make my bed, and take out all the trash in the house. You want me to sweep my room, make my bed, and take out all the trash in the house."

"Thank you. Get started now, and let me know when you are done."

"OK, Dad."

■　■　■

This tool would have been appropriate for Michael, the little boy who couldn't keep his hands off the Christmas tree. If he had repeated, "I will obey my mommy by moving away from the tree," he may have been able to resist touching it.

This verbal repetition would also have been useful with Christy before she went to her friend's house. Her dad could have had her say, "I will be back in this house before one o'clock." It becomes a verbal promise. With verbal repetitions, you know that they know what is expected. And also, they know that you know what they have to do. It may help prevent an argument over what was expected. It clears up any confusion.

When children are younger than five years old, it is often necessary to have them repeat, "I will obey my mommy and daddy." This is just the kind of "brainwashing" children need. Sometimes their brains are just too full of their own ideas. They need to have an injection of obedience (don't we all).

"Kara, it's time to come inside now and wash up for dinner."

"But, Mom, I'm not hungry."

"It's time to eat. Now come inside."

"Mo-o-m. I don't want to."

"Kara. Come here right now." She comes very slowly. "I want you to repeat this after me. 'When Mommy calls me, I will come right away.'"

"But, Mo-o-m."

"Say it."

"When Mommy calls, I'll come right away."

"Good. Now repeat this. 'I will obey Mom.'"

"I will obey Mom."
"Will you?"
"Yes, Mom."
"Good. Now go wash up."

■ ■ ■

The verbal repetition also serves as a test to gauge how well your children accept your expectation.

"Alex, will you please sweep the driveway this morning?"

"OK." He never looks up from the TV.

"What did I say?"

With what sounds like his last ounce of energy, he says, "You want me to sweep the driveway."

"Say it three times, please."

"I will sweep the driveway. I will sweep the driveway. I will sweep the driveway."

His tone of voice isn't joyful, but it is cooperative. I give him the benefit of the doubt and trust he will follow through.

Verbal repetitions are a handy tool. No one needs to yell or have tempers flare. It is just a simple "pop quiz" to test your children's attitudes. If they pass the simple test, life goes on more smoothly.

GUIDELINES FOR SETTING EXPECTATIONS

When you set your expectations and communicate them to your children, keep in mind these guidelines.

Make the Expectations Positive

Has anyone ever told you, "Whatever you do, *don't* think of an elephant! Do *not* picture an elephant in your head"? It's impossible. Our brains are wired to picture an elephant before we can even try to erase it.

When we are trying to instill certain values or behavior in our children, it is better to have them focus on doing what's positive rather than avoiding something negative. This sets the expectation and focuses the children's minds on what you want them to do rather than on what you don't want them to do.

Instead of telling them "Stop talking rudely to your brother!" tell them "Please talk kindly to your brother." If they act up in a store, get them to look you right in the eye and ask them "What did we say in the car?" If they don't remember, remind them of the expectation and have them repeat it a couple times right there in the store: "I will stay by your side and put my hands only on you and the cart."

Instead of saying "Stop making a mess," you can say "After you are done playing, you have to clean all this up." Rather than saying "Be quiet!" you can say "Use your inside voice." Rather than crabbing "Don't bounce the ball in the house," say "Balls get bounced only outside." Say "Be sure to drive the speed limit" rather than "Don't drive like a maniac." Encourage kids with "Play hard, and be sure to pass the ball. I know you will do well," rather than "Don't be a ball hog like you were last time."

I could give my kids a whole job chart of things not to do, and they could check them all off without actually doing anything. But they also would not learn anything that way. If I make the goal positive, they will practice doing something good.

I realize it is necessary to also have some "do not" rules. Certain things are so dangerous we have to instill a certain fear about specific behaviors. "Do not use drugs." "Do not have sex before marriage." "Do not run out into the street." However, if we can keep our children doing what they should, they have less time to get into trouble. If they are busy doing the "do's," they won't have time to do the "don'ts."

Inspect Your Children's Work

It's discouraging to do a good job on something and not have anyone notice it. Kids are always saying "Watch me!" or "Look at what I did." Older kids are not quite so obvious, but they still want to be noticed.

Whenever I give my kids an assignment, I add, "Let me know when you finish." This gives me a chance to praise them for how well they did. I want them to know that I know they worked hard. I see several benefits of inspecting our children's work: They will know that someone thinks they are capable; they will feel the pleasure of successfully completing a challenge; they will feel that someone is proud of them; they will know there is a payoff for submitting to expectations. All this contributes to their being able to tackle bigger challenges as they grow up.

Words of praise help children feel nourished. Your words are sustenance for your children. Inspecting their work gives us an opportunity to give them some nourishment. After your children have completed a tough job of cleaning, you can say, "Wow, look at this! I hardly recognize it. And you even got this part clean. Good job! You are a great worker." On the ride home from visiting a friend, you can say, "I was proud of the way you looked Mrs. Rogers in the eye and said thank you. That was a very gracious thing to do."

I'm sure there will also be many times when the quality of the children's work leaves something to be desired. This is where you have to use your judgment. Is their poor work the result of a lack of ability or experience, or is it the result of a bad attitude? If it is because they lack ability, give them grace and praise what they were able to accomplish. Then take the time to show them how to do it better. If it is because they lack experience, give them more time to practice and a challenge to "be sure to do it like this next time. I know you can do it." This wisdom and discernment come from knowing your children's tendencies as well as from experience. Learn from what works and doesn't work with them. I'll discuss how to deal with the attitude part later.

Clearly Teach What You Expect

When setting expectations with children, do not assume anything. Be very specific. Show them what to do and how to do it. Watch them do it. Leave no room for misunderstanding or misinterpretation. Rather than telling them to "be good," say "I want you to listen to your teacher and do exactly what he tells you to do." Rather than saying "Don't stay out too late," tell them "I expect you to be home before ten o'clock."

My eleven-year-old daughter, Breeze, and her friend Briana asked me if they could go to a store to buy some candy. Instead of telling her to be careful, which is vague, I gave her some concrete directions. I gave her a whistle to wear to blow if she got scared or lost. In case some kids or adults bothered her, I had her practice yelling real loud, "I don't know you! Leave me alone!" I gave her special permission to yell inside the house. She enjoyed that. I will still have a slight degree of worry about her safety, but I don't want her to feel caged up in her house either.

I make my expectations something I could either watch them do or hear them say. We should be able to capture on videotape what we expect them to do.

When trying to identify how to make your expectations clear, ask yourself, "What do I want? What is the goal?" After you have identified that, ask, "What will that look (or sound) like?" It may help to discuss some of your expectations with your spouse. He or she can help you get a clear picture of what you expect. If you can make it clear to yourself and each other, then you can clarify it to your children.

Most of us would like to communicate expectations when we are calm and the climate is right for teaching and explaining. This "classroom atmosphere" is usually a fantasy. We aren't always that organized, and we can't anticipate all the wonderful surprises children throw our way. What usually happens is that a problem occurs, and then we explain what we want. Learning comes by living. As problems arise, figure out what the expectation is and patiently teach your children accordingly. A little grace sprinkled in goes a long way when training children.

How God Sets Expectations

As our heavenly Father, God explains his expectations to us. The Bible is full of examples of what God expects from his children. In the Garden of Eden, God explained his expectations to Adam and Eve. When his children grew into a large nation, God reiterated his expectations in the form of the Ten Commandments. Later on, he gave them all the dietary, sacrificial, and social laws.

God wanted his expectations to be well known to his children; he didn't want any doubt regarding what he expected. "And you must commit yourselves wholeheartedly to these commands I am giving you today. Repeat them again and again to your children. Talk about them when you are at home and when you are away on a journey, when you are lying down and when you are getting up again. Tie them to your hands as a reminder, and wear them on your forehead. Write them on the doorposts of your house and on your gates" (Deut. 6:6-9).

Later God had all his children practice their verbal submission to his expectations. "Then the Levites must shout to all the people of Israel. . . . " The next eleven verses list all that God wanted his children to remember. After each proclamation, the entire nation would reply, "Amen" (Deut. 27:14-26). Everyone clearly knew God's expectations.

PROGRESSION OF DISCIPLINE

Setting expectations is one of the first, most basic tools we can use in disciplining our children. If our children do not respond to this tool, then we progress to the next level and use the next tool. Seeing discipline as a progression helps us determine what tools to use in certain situations.

The Progression of Discipline chart illustrates how this progression develops at the beginning. As we discuss other tools, we will see how they fit into this progression of discipline.

Progression of Discipline

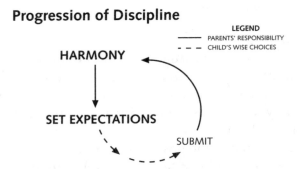

LEGEND
—— PARENTS' RESPONSIBILITY
– – – CHILD'S WISE CHOICES

HARMONY

SET EXPECTATIONS

SUBMIT

Harmony is the goal of discipline. Relational harmony is characterized by a relaxed, warm, open feeling between family members. Everyone feels safe. Secrets are unnecessary. Everyone is welcome to join in the conversation. Trust is evident. Playfulness happens spontaneously and frequently. Work is an opportunity to serve each other, not a drudgery to endure. Remember, this is the ideal, not necessarily an everyday situation. But it should at least be the direction the family is heading.

In order to achieve harmony, the parents set and communicate their expectations. At that point the children have a choice: They can obey the expectations, or they can refuse to obey the expectations. If they make the wise choice to obey the expectations, they reap the rewards of relational harmony. Parents should make sure their children see tangible rewards for their wise choices. It doesn't have to be something major. It could be as simple as a hug, a thank-you, a kind word, a cookie, reading a story, etc.

However, if your children choose not to obey your expectations, they take a detour and do not return to relational harmony. Instead you take them on a different path, using the next tool of discipline in the progression of discipline—enforcing logical consequences. That will be the subject of the next chapter.

Summary

We cannot expect our children to meet our expectations of them if we don't let them know what we expect. The first tool in disciplining our children, then, is setting and communicating clearly what kinds of behavior and attitudes we expect from them. We need to phrase the expectations so that we ask them to do something positive rather than not do something negative. If our children respond by submitting and meeting our expectations, everyone is happy. If they do not, then we take up the next tool.

Reflection Questions

Take a few minutes to think about these questions. If possible, discuss them with your spouse, another parent, or a group of parents. Write down your observations, feelings, and goals in a journal.

1. Do your children know what you expect from them?
2. If you have more than one child, make a list of specific things you expect from each one. Think of these categories:

   - household chores
   - personal hygiene
   - attitudes toward family members
   - attitudes toward other people
   - social behavior

3. What can you do to make your expectations more clear to your children?
4. How can you use verbal repetition and practice to help your children learn obedience?
5. How can you demonstrate submission to God and other authorities in your life so that your children will have a model of what it is like to submit to you and other authorities?
6. Do you and your spouse agree on the expectations you have for your children? How can you work toward agreement?

My son, obey your father's commands, and don't
neglect your mother's teaching. . . . For these
commands and this teaching are a lamp to light the
way ahead of you. The correction of discipline
is the way to life.

— P r o v e r b s   6 : 2 0 - 2 3

7

Enforcing Logical Consequences

The last chapter explained how we set expectations and communicate them to our children. This is the first stage in disciplining our children. Without it, any sort of discipline would be unfair to our children. And if the discipline is unfair, our children will not learn anything positive from it. The result will be bitterness and a damaged relationship.

If your children always cooperate with your expectations, then you can close this book. You don't need to read any further. In fact, I'd like to read your book on how you do it.

But if you are like the rest of us, you know that children don't always live up to our expectations. In fact they exercise their will against us and often do not do what we have asked them to do. They disobey us. I've even had the distinct feeling that sometimes my children disobey me in order to test me. It's as if inside they are saying, "I'm not going to do that, and what are you going to do about it?"

So, now what do you do? Is this where you lose your cool and start yelling or taking away privileges or calling your children names? I hope not. Let's look at another important tool in your possession: enforcing logical consequences.

The Bible approaches discipline from a positive and a negative aspect. The positive approach involves teaching (giving information and demonstrating) and training (coaching). Negative discipline is reproof (blame assigned) and punishment. Enforcing logical consequences is the backup tool when the positive approach fails.

God used consequences as a way of responding to his children's wrong choices. The entire chapter of Leviticus 26 details the consequences of fulfilling or not fulfilling God's expectations. Take a look at that chapter. My translation even has the heading "Blessings for Obedience" for the first thirteen verses and "Punishments for Disobedience" for the last thirty-three verses. God, our Father, is the one who originated the concept of rewards and punishments.

Some people refer to rewards and punishments as the "carrot and stick" approach. In order to get a stubborn mule to move, the farmer would dangle a carrot in front of its face to entice it to pull the cart. Every so often, the farmer had to give the mule the carrot as a reward. That was the easy way to get the mule to work.

When that approach wasn't successful, the farmer would use a stick to sting the mule's rear end or legs. The mule would then start walking to try to avoid the pain. The farmer wasn't being cruel. After all, he needed the mule to work. He simply used the stick prudently in an effort to motivate the mule to pull the load.

Like mules, some people can be motivated by the rewards of obedience while others need the tight structure of painful consequences. Most of us are motivated by a combination of striving for the rewards of obedience while trying to avoid the pain of rebellion.

REWARDS AND PUNISHMENTS

Not only are there two kinds of consequences—rewards and punishments—there are also two subcategories of consequences. These are natural and logical consequences. Natural consequences are enforced by natural law. As adults we know that if we leave a shovel outside in the rain or snow, it will get rusty. If we eat more food than we need, we will gain weight. If we don't put gas in the car, we will be stranded somewhere.

Logical consequences are enforced by people. If we leave on a water faucet for a week, our water bill would increase dramatically. If we drive twenty miles an hour over the speed limit, the police may stop us and make us pay a fine. If we don't pay our mortgage payments for a year, we will lose our house.

Our children also understand rewards and punishments. Let's look at what some natural and logical rewards and punishments may look like in their lives.

Rewards and Punishments

Natural Rewards

- Learning to walk leads to the joy of mobility.
- Learning to ride a bike leads to the thrill of speed.
- Learning to drive a car leads to the excitement of seeing more of the world as well as the freedom from depending on parents to drive you.

Natural Punishments

- Touching the hot pan leads to burned skin.
- Racing down a steep hill and falling may produce bruises or worse.
- Driving fast on ice may lead to an accident.

Logical Rewards
- Potty training leads to the freedom to sleep over at a friend's house without fear of embarrassment.
- Mowing the yard leads to a few extra dollars at allowance time.
- Doing your laundry means your favorite outfit is clean for that last-minute party.

Logical Punishments
- Teasing your sister leads to writing her a letter listing her admirable qualities.
- Not cleaning your room when asked to leads to cleaning it right now even if it means staying home from a friend's party.
- Running stop signs results in expensive tickets and an angry parent.

The important thing to remember here is not the label for each category. The reason to distinguish all four possibilities is simply to help us see the different kinds of consequences.

PARENTS ARE THE ENFORCERS OF LOGICAL CONSEQUENCES

Parents should be their children's first enforcers of logical consequences. If parents do their job, society or the judicial system would not have to impose more severe consequences.

Children don't need much help with the *natural* rewards and punishments. Kids don't need lectures on the advantages of walking versus crawling. They are naturally excited to try out their developing limbs and muscles. They fall down several dozen times until they master the skills needed for balance. Parents will scold kids when they try to touch the top of the stove, but it usually takes only one burned finger before their brain screams *no* if they make another attempt.

But when it comes to *logical* rewards or punishments, parents play the essential role. To be most effective, the consequences must be linked to our expectations. For every expectation we set up for our children, we need to set up corresponding logical consequences, both positive and negative. Just as it is vitally important to communicate our expectations to our children, we must also tell them what the rewards or punishments are connected to those expectations.

USING REWARDS TO MOTIVATE

Whenever possible, use rewards to motivate children. Children get excited about rewards. Parents can use this God-given tendency to teach children many things. Potty-training techniques are well known for using candy to motivate kids to use the toilet. Or what parent hasn't said, "If you finish all your vegetables, then you can have some dessert"? I know of a family who promised a new doll to their daughter if she slept in her own bed rather than come into their bedroom in the middle of the night.

When we knew our daughter, Breeze, was physically capable of sleeping through the night without wetting her bed, we rewarded her with the privilege of wearing a dress that day. At that time, she just loved dresses, and within about a week, she woke up every morning in a dry bed. If she had wet the bed several times and become discouraged, then we would have waited for a while. Her discouragement would have told us that she was motivated but perhaps not physically ready to stay dry through the night. We would have just waited for a few more weeks or months until we thought she was ready to try again. And we would have let her wear dresses in the meantime.

Older children are rewarded with privileges. They like to

stay up longer, stay out later, and borrow the car. Money is also a popular reward. It works for me.

In our family we use spending time with friends as a reward. We consider that to be a privilege. That particular reward is dependent on how well our children treat each other and us parents. Our thinking is that if our children can't treat their own family with respect, then they have not earned the privilege of spending time with other people. Relationships start in the home. We don't want our kids thinking they can be rude at home and then enjoy a good time with their friends.

Giving rewards is so much more pleasant than giving punishments. Parents get to be heroes when they give rewards. The nice thing about giving rewards is that parents can be their children's cheerleaders. It is much nicer to say, "I know you can finish raking the yard so we can enjoy an ice-cream cone together" than to say, "If you don't finish raking that yard, you can't have an ice-cream cone." The latter sounds like a threat and makes the parent seem like Scrooge. The former makes the parent sound like Santa Claus.

If you aren't sure what motivates your children, ask them. "What would it take for you to want to _____?" This is the beginning of teaching them negotiating skills. It helps them to identify what they like and form their preferences.

The most effective rewards are tied to the expectations. The link between rewards and expectations is sometimes difficult for children to make, especially if the reward is intangible. The reward for brushing and flossing their teeth is not to have to endure the pain of having a filling put in. The reward for making their beds every day is the character trait of thoroughness and orderliness. Young children cannot make that long-term connection between those causes and effects. Older children may not *want* to make that connection. Parents have to be the extension cord between cause and effect until children can complete the circuit themselves. Parents can help make that connection by giving simple, tangible rewards immediately after their children comply with their expectations.

Some examples of rewards that are tied to expectations include the following:

- dessert after eating a healthy meal
- more time for play after jobs are finished
- an extra book at bedtime because they got ready for bed early
- being trusted to go play with a neighbor because your children left the neighbor's house last time when the neighbor put an R-rated movie in the VCR while the parents were gone
- riding their bikes to the store because they could successfully lead you there and back without needing directions
- staying up later than usual because they had been polite the day after they stayed up late the last time
- playing with friends after demonstrating that they could play respectfully with their siblings
- getting a base hit after having practiced hitting the ball
- later curfew for children who have continually obeyed the current ones
- fewer parental questions for children who have repeatedly demonstrated open, honest communication, even about subjects they were scared to talk about
- more freedom and responsibility after the successful demonstration of current responsibility

It can be a challenge to tie the reward to the expectation, but the better we can make that connection, the more likely the desired behavior or attitude will follow.

Sometimes rewards for obedience aren't enough. When rewards don't work, God has provided another option.

USING PUNISHMENTS TO MOTIVATE

Punishment can also be a powerful motivator. The key ingredient to punishment is pain. As the saying goes, "You can either do it the easy way or the hard way."

When it comes to disciplining children, sometimes parents are the necessary pain activators. The first level of pain is natural consequences. But after children learn about hot stoves, needles, knives, sunburn, and not wearing long pants while sliding into second base, parents have to step in and administer the logical consequences.

Pain doesn't necessarily have to be physical. Losses can be very painful. As a result, they often make a lasting impression. Consider these kinds of losses:

Loss of autonomy:

- "You will have to keep quiet for two minutes for interrupting our conversation."
- "Since you talked rudely to your brother, I want you to make it up to him by doing his paper route today."
- "You may not ride your bike for the rest of the day for riding it in the street."
- "I'll have to comb your hair since you don't want to take the time to do it right."
- "I'm sorry you got a speeding ticket, but give me your car keys for one month so you learn the importance of driving the speed limit."

Loss of free time:

- "Come in here and take care of your dirty dishes right now."
- "It's time for you to go to bed. You've been rude and cranky (i.e. tired) ever since lunch."

Loss of money:

- "You'll have to use your allowance to buy them a new squirt gun since you threw it down and broke it."
- "That 'little fender bender' will probably cost you about eight hundred dollars. I hope you are more careful the next time you back out of a parking spot."

Loss of nursing a grudge:

- "I know she didn't let you have a turn on the swing, but that doesn't make it right for you to call her a name. Now I want you to sit here and think of three things you like about Karen and then tell her what they are."
- "I'll take care of Mark, but you cannot hit him for that. I want you to caress him softly until you can let go of your anger."

All these examples illustrate the principle of making the punishment fit the crime. Effective discipline always tries to connect the offense with the punishment. Sometimes this takes some creative definitions of exactly what offense was committed. Sometimes you may define arguing as talking rudely. Other times you may consider it talking too loudly. Usually, arguing reveals a bad attitude. Each definition would require a different consequence. You have some leeway in how you define the problem. Use your judgment as to what the real problem is. I'll give you some suggestions as to what to do in the very next section. Attitude will be addressed in the next chapter.

Not only do you want to make the consequence match the expectation, you also want to match the intensity of the punishment with the expectation. The severity of the punishment should closely match the severity of the offense. For example:

- Going to bed without supper is too severe a consequence for children who did not eat their beans; not getting dessert is a more appropriate logical consequence.
- Writing multiplication tables twenty-five times is too severe a consequence for children who fail a math test; saying the tables aloud to you two or three times is a more appropriate logical consequence.
- Not being allowed to play outside all day is too severe a consequence for children who did not hang up their coats; practicing hanging up their coats is a more appropriate consequence.
- Being sent away after a meal is too severe a consequence for children who spilled their water; wiping up the spill is a more appropriate logical consequence.
- Being ignored is too severe a consequence for children who talk rudely to you; telling them how they offended you and teaching them how to not do that again is a more appropriate logical consequence (see next section for details).

For those of you paying very close attention, you may have noticed a slight similarity between some of these logical consequences and the consequence of denying privileges (discussed in chapter 5). Let me make an important distinction about logical consequences. Having privileges taken away is the direct result of those same privileges being misused. Children are losing the privilege—but not arbitrarily or capriciously. The privilege lost is the same privilege being abused. It makes sense to children. It is connected with what they did wrong. By misusing the privilege, they lose it for a brief time.

Practice or Repetition

The practice or repetition tool is one of my favorites. It is extremely effective. It is the perfect tool for making the consequences match the offense. It motivates children to cooperate and serves as a powerful reminder to them for next time. I can scale it to match the intensity of the situation. I can make it as light as possible (sometimes almost a game) or as painful as necessary. Plus it gives me a good barometer on children's attitudes.

The practice tool is a first cousin to the verbal repetitions discussed in chapter 6. Practice takes it the next step so that children's bodies actually do what is expected. Practice is an effective way to teach. You can actually witness how well your children understand your expectation and can coach them further if necessary.

Practicing the right way to do whatever they did wrong is a logical consequence of their not having done it right the first time. It makes sense to children. I usually get very little argument about it being "unfair." When I present this idea to children, I say something like, "Since you didn't put away your dishes the first time I asked, I figure you must need some practice. I would like you to practice putting your dishes in the sink five times. You can start right now."

If your children have neglected to put their clothes away in the dresser drawers, there is no need to lecture, yell, or take away television privileges for a week. The problem is simply that they did not put their clothes away. Have them practice the task three or four times. Practice should help cement the expectation in their head and motivate them to do it right away the next time. It may even get to be a habit. Wouldn't that be nice!

Practice works well for many tasks children often "forget" to do, such as brushing their teeth, hanging up their coats, putting away the breakfast cereal, closing the back door, and (my personal favorite) turning off the light wa-a-ay up in their bedrooms. Once they "practice" it several times, they usually remember for at least a while.

This tool would have worked well for Derek, the boy who kept "forgetting" to put his bike away. Derek's dad could have had Derek practice putting his bike in the garage several times, at a rate significantly faster than a snail's pace. Ashley's mom could have had her practice putting away her toys. Samantha could have practiced doing her chores so she wouldn't wait until the last minute and get into a big argument. These conversations might have sounded like this:

"Derek, since you are having such a hard time getting motivated to take care of your bike, I want you to practice putting it away. Get on your bike, ride it to the corner and back, and then put it away in the garage. I want you to do that three times. Maybe this will help you remember to put it away. Any questions?"

"Why do I have to do all that?"

"I just told you."

"But that won't help me remember."

"Do you have any other ideas?"

"Well, no."

"OK, then we'll try this one to see if it works. Now get going."

■   ■   ■

This is how things might have gone for Ashley.

"Ashley, it looks like you need some practice putting your toys away. I'm going to help you put everything away, and then I want you to show me how you can do it all by yourself. Come on, help me. Let's do this together."

"I don't want to."

"Ashley, you can choose to help me, or you can choose to do it all by yourself. What is your choice?" Ashley comes over and starts putting things away. That first step is the hardest one to get her to take. It should be a little easier from here on out.

"Good job, Ashley. We did it. Now let's take these toys out again." They take some toys out and scatter them around the room again. "OK, now it's your turn to show me you can do this all by yourself. I know you can do it because you are such a big girl."

"But, Mo-o-om—" Ashley whines.

Mom doesn't even let her finish. "If you don't get started right now, I will take some more toys out and have you put those away also."

Ashley pauses for a brief moment. By her mom's tone of voice Ashley can tell she really means it. She starts to put them away, slowly.

"Good job, honey. Come on now, let's move a little quicker." Mom wants to push her a little bit.

After Ashley finishes, her mom says, "Good job, honey. See how nice it looks? Now do you think you can do that the next time without arguing or whining?"

"Yes, Mommy. I'll remember."

"Good. Now we can read some more of your book. Where were we?"

This example was the first time Ashley had been introduced to this tool. It went fairly easily this time. Next time her mom may not be so patient since Ashley would be familiar with this tool.

Ashley would also benefit from practicing verbal repetition of submitting to her mother. Her mother could have her repeat "I will obey you, Mommy, and put away my toys" four times before they started putting the toys away. Sometimes the verbal practicing greases the gears of the behavioral practicing.

■ ■ ■

Samantha's scenerio might have sounded like this:

"Samantha, remember yesterday we had that big argument about going over to Bethany's house?"

"Yeah, what about it?"

"Well, I have an idea that might help us avoid having it again."

"You mean you'll just take me next time without making me do those stupid chores?"

"No, not exactly that. In fact, I'd rather help you remember to do your chores. If you had done that yesterday, I would have been able to take you to Bethany's and still had time to do the things I needed to do. So this is my idea. One of the things you didn't do was the laundry. There are a few more loads to do this morning. I'd like you to do them. I call it the 'practice makes perfect' drill. I figure if you practice doing your chores, they won't seem so hard and you can remember to do them when you have more time so you won't get so frazzled when you want to do something."

"Oh, Mom. That sounds silly. I don't think it will help."

"You may be right, but we're going to give it a try. Now get started."

"Oh, all right."

This practice tool raises the standard of cooperation. You are giving your children another chance to do it right, but the expectations have gone up a little bit. The fact that they don't like it means you have their attention. Your hope is that slight pain will motivate them more next time. If they complain about it, all you need to say is, "Then next time do it the first time I ask you." You are subtly telling them that you will enforce what you expect. You say what you mean, and you mean what you say.

Making your children practice sends a message regarding your commitment to their training. You are saying, "This stuff is important. Not so much the dishes or whatever. But your being responsible and cooperative is key to your moral and social development. You are a capable person, and I expect you to do your part in this household. I am committed to helping you be the best person you can be. Count on it!"

HOW GOD USES LOGICAL CONSEQUENCES

God uses logical consequences quite often. In Genesis 3, we read how God used logical consequences with his children. God loved Adam and Eve; kicking them out of the Garden did not make him happy. But God is definitely a God of justice. He knows the importance of enforcing consequences. He is keenly aware of how costly and painful those consequences are for his children. It cost him the life of his Son.

The tool of practice is seen in all the rituals that Israel

observed. Rituals were an integral part of their daily life. Through them the people of Israel practiced and practiced obedience in their observance of the rules for food preparation, work, social life, sacrifice, and worship.

DETECTING ATTITUDE PROBLEMS

If your children start whining, complaining, arguing, "forgetting," or refusing to do what you have spelled out for them, they are starting to reveal their underlying attitudes. This is significant. You want to see the status of their attitudes by observing their behavior. You are testing their submission and cooperation.

Practice is an effective tool when children simply don't want to do the task. If they buck you hard about putting their dishes in the sink, a logical consequence would be to have them put everyone's dishes in the sink. If they whine about your reminder to shut the garage door, have them run from the kitchen to the garage and open and shut the door five times so they won't complain about the original request. As the saying goes, "If you don't like the time, then don't do the crime."

Warn your children that if they accept the "practicing" consequences, the matter will end. But if they insist on arguing, then the stakes will continue to rise. Strongly suggest to them that it would be in their own best interest not to push it any further than they already have. Warn them that they can do it the easy way or the hard way. It's up to them. They have the choice.

Let's see how all this looks on the Progression of Discipline chart. The relationship starts with harmony and stays in the first loop as much as possible. But when kids make foolish choices and take a detour into rebelliousness, parents are ready to intervene with the logical consequences. If children respond to logical consequences with a wise choice—to submit and have a good attitude, for example—the situation returns to harmony, and the minor adjustment is complete.

Progression of Discipline

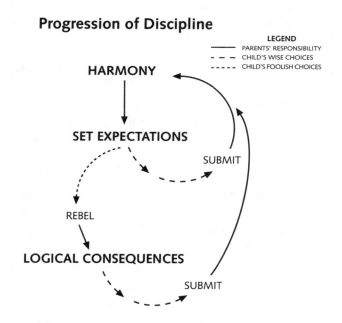

LEGEND
—— PARENTS' RESPONSIBILITY
– – – CHILD'S WISE CHOICES
----- CHILD'S FOOLISH CHOICES

HARMONY

SET EXPECTATIONS

SUBMIT

REBEL

LOGICAL CONSEQUENCES

SUBMIT

By using the tool of enforcing logical consequences, parents give their children the opportunity to make a wise choice and loop back up into relational harmony.

Using Consequences as Tools
Natural consequences (administered by nature)
Positive consequences—the thrill of mastering a task like walking or skiing
Negative consequences—the pain of physical injury

Logical consequences (administered by parents or other authority figures)
Positive consequences—receiving affirmation, privileges, money
Negative consequences—a slightly "painful" inconvenience of learning a lesson (including verbal and behavioral repetition)

One other suggestion: *Make sure that your children follow through on the consequence you enforce and that they do the job well.* Inspect their effort according to their age, experience, and ability. Do not let them do a halfhearted job. If you let them do a poor job, then you are sending a message that you don't care much about them. They begin to think they are not very valuable or capable. They may not put forth much effort in other things. If you don't care, why should they?

Keep in mind that mastering skills is one of the building blocks to a healthy self-image. If we let our kids get by without mastering basic living skills, they will miss out on realizing that they can accomplish almost anything they put their effort into. We want them to have numerous success experiences. Accomplishments are revealed not just on the stage or the athletic field but also at home with mundane tasks. Your children can go to bed feeling good about themselves simply because they did a good job at everything they needed to do that day.

ENGAGE IN THE BATTLE

"Your own actions have brought this upon you. This punishment is a bitter dose of your own medicine. It has pierced you to the heart!" (Jer. 4:18). Those are the Lord's words spoken to his disobedient children, the people of Israel. They were enduring the suffering their rebellion brought on themselves. I'm sure it was very painful.

But the pain is not limited to the children of Israel. God is anguished by all his children's rebellion. Listen to his heart as it is expressed in the prophecy of Hosea:

> When Israel was a child, I loved him as a son, and I called my son out of Egypt. But the more I called to him, the more he rebelled. . . . It was I who taught Israel how to walk, leading him along by the hand. But he doesn't know or even care that it was I who took care of him. I led Israel along with my ropes of kindness and love. . . . For my people are determined to desert me. . . . *Oh, how can I give you up, Israel? How can I let you go? . . . My heart is torn within me, and my compassion overflows.* No, I will not punish you as much as my burning anger tells me to. I will not completely destroy Israel, for I am God and not a mere mortal. I am the Holy One living among you, and I will not come to destroy. For someday the people will follow the Lord. I will roar like a lion, and my people will return trembling from the west. . . . I will bring them home again (Hos. 11:1-11, italics added).

Does the phrase "This hurts me more than it hurts you" seem apropos here? Logical consequences may seem quite severe at times. If your children have not finished their report for school, they may have to miss out on the sleepover party. If your children have not cleaned their rooms, they may miss out on enjoying a movie with their friends while they clean their room. You can play the "sad cheerleader" role: "I'm so sorry you didn't get to go with your friends. You knew you had to get that report done, but you chose to do something else. I really wish you could have gotten to go. It would have been a lot of fun. I sure hope you remember next time."

It is up to parents to enforce the logical consequences. It's not always easy. We hate to see our children suffer. When we clean out our children's scrapes and cuts, they cry because it hurts them. But we know that if we don't, the cuts will get infected. Children don't care about the risk of infection. They just want it to stop hurting.

This is where parents can demonstrate their strength and leadership. Children often need someone to do for them what they cannot do for themselves. If they cannot or will not follow through with our expectations, then it is up to us to help them. Parents have to be willing to step in, set the standards, and enforce them.

Last year Dugan went on a camping trip. He knew about the trip for weeks. He knew it was his responsibility to find a substitute for his paper route for those three days. He's had to find a substitute before, and he often has trouble finding someone to fill in for him. On the night before the camping trip, just as Sharon and I were getting ready for bed, Dugan asked me if I would do his paper route for him. I asked him what he had done to find a substitute, and he named a few people he had called. I asked him if he had called Mike back. Dugan said he had not because he had been too busy. He was "busy" sleeping over at Tyler's house and then forgot to take care of it.

I considered making him stay home to do his papers, but I decided that would be too severe a consequence, at least this time. He said he would call Mike in the morning, but he didn't know if he would be able to connect with him. I told Dugan I would do his route for him, but it would cost him $10 per day (he earns $4 per day). He didn't like it one bit. I told him he has to take care of his responsibilities and when he doesn't, it costs him. This time the pain was in his wallet.

I didn't need the $30. It's not about the money. But Dugan had to remember this lesson. Our previous reminders to find a substitute hadn't motivated him to plan ahead. But the punishment was hard on me too. I didn't like seeing my son suffer. And I especially didn't enjoy enforcing this suffering. The risk was that he would stay angry at me and would not learn anything from this. I confess I was very tempted just to serve him by doing the papers. If I had done that, maybe he would have learned how to be a gracious servant when someone has a need. It was a tough call. Parenting is never easy, is it?

But that time I decided that he needed to suffer some consequences for his procrastination. I wanted him to learn that someone will not always bail him out, and even if someone does bail him out, it costs something. I prayed that he would learn this mildly painful lesson now rather than a very painful one later on. Thankfully he did. Since that incident he has worked hard to find a substitute for his route well in advance. He also thanked me for helping him out, and he told me that he would be more responsible next time. I was relieved.

Sometimes parents have to be the bad guys. We have to risk our children's anger if they are to learn some of life's lessons. When parents don't enforce logical consequences with their children, they cripple them socially. Relationships will be adversely affected by children who have seldom suffered logical consequences. I'm sure you've all had to endure someone else's unruly child. But what makes those times truly unbearable is when the parents do nothing about it. They make excuses like "Johnny is always so energetic. I like to encourage his playfulness. I hope you don't mind his jumping on your couch." Or "Susie is just so curious. I hope that wasn't a valuable lamp she knocked over." When parents are not willing to enforce logical consequences (reasonable limits), children are at greater risk of becoming social outcasts. Who wants to play with kids who have to have their own way all the time?

Remember Tommy, the six-year-old who gave his baby-sitter a hard time? Tommy refused to pick up his toys or go to bed and tore Laurie's coat after she had asked him to leave it alone. Those three actions clearly revealed his rebellious attitude. His external posture of refusing to cooperate exposed his internal posture of rebellion. If Tommy's dad were to follow the guidelines from this chapter, this is what the situation could have sounded like:

"Hey, Tommy. What are you doing up?" Bob Hoyt asked their six-year-old son when he and his wife returned home from an evening out.

"Miss Parker let me stay up," answered Tommy.

"Laurie, we asked you to have him in bed by 8:30. What happened?"

"Mr. Hoyt, I'm sorry. I tried but Tommy wouldn't go to bed when I told him to. He refused to pick up his toys, and he 'accidentally' tore my coat," Laurie responded.

"Tommy, you should have obeyed Miss Parker. You were wrong for not doing what she asked you to do," said Mr. Hoyt.

"But, Dad, I was going to."

"But you didn't, Tommy. Now we're going to try it again. When Miss Parker asks you to pick up your toys, you say, 'OK, Miss Parker, I will pick up my toys now.'"

"But, Dad—"

"That's fine, Mr. Hoyt. I put them away," Laurie interjected.

"But it's not fine, Laurie. This is very important. Please stay.

I will pay you for your extra time unless you need to get somewhere."

"No, I can stay," Laurie responded, a little uncomfortable but curious to know what was about to happen.

"Good." Turning to Tommy, Mr. Hoyt said in a calm voice, "Son, Miss Parker is going to ask you to pick up your toys again, and I want you to repeat what you are supposed to say to her three times. Go ahead, Miss Parker."

"Tommy, will you please put your toys away?"

"OK, Miss Parker, I will pick up my toys now. OK, Miss Parker, I will pick up my toys now. OK, Miss Parker, I will pick up my toys now," responded Tommy obediently.

"That's better."

"One last time, what will you do the next time Miss Parker asks you to pick up your toys, Tommy?"

"I'll put my toys away like Miss Parker told me to."

"Good. Now go up to bed." Tommy went upstairs with his mother.

"Laurie, I'm very sorry Tommy gave you such a hard time. It's not your fault. Tommy should obey you. I will have him practice picking up his toys tomorrow. The next time you come, I will make very clear to Tommy that I expect him to follow your instructions."

"Thanks, Mr. Hoyt. That makes me feel better. I wasn't sure if I wanted to baby-sit for Tommy again, but now I think I do."

"Well, I'm glad. I know you want to do a good job, but it's up to me to make sure Tommy cooperates with you. Send me the repair bill for your coat. Tommy doesn't have any money, but I will find him some jobs to do around here. Anyway, thanks again for coming. We'll call you about next weekend."

"Thanks, Mr. Hoyt. Good night."

■ ■ ■

With just a little help from his dad, Tommy handled that pretty well. Tommy got the message that he has to respect Laurie as much as he has to respect his mom and dad. Tommy had to humble himself in front of Laurie so that the next time she baby-sits him, he will be much less likely to test her. Laurie also got the support of Mr. Hoyt. She has confidence that Mr. Hoyt will not let Tommy ignore her reasonable requests.

Most important, Tommy has not been alienated from Laurie. Like a broken bone, the damaged relationship has been set in place. The healing will occur the next time Laurie comes over to baby-sit.

Mr. Hoyt is working on removing his son's rude attitude before it takes root in his behavior. He is pruning back Tommy's insolent behavior as part of his responsibility to shape Tommy's attitudes. If the father didn't do this, the only "friends" Tommy could attract would be other negative kids. Birds of a feather do flock together. We want our children to associate with positive kids. In order to help make that happen, we must make sure that our children have positive, friendly attitudes.

Summary

When the first tool (setting expectations) in the progression of discipline doesn't work, we move to the next tool—enforcing logical consequences, both positive and negative. Two effective methods to use in enforcing consequences are practice and verbal repetition. If our children respond to the enforcement of logical consequences with wise choices, we return to relational harmony. If they still choose to continue in their stubbornness and bad attitudes, we must move to the next level in the progression of discipline—assigning work.

Reflection Questions

Take a few minutes to think about these questions. If possible, discuss them with your spouse, another parent, or a group of parents. Write down your observations, feelings, and goals in a journal.

1. What kinds of consequences do you use with your children?
2. How are these consequences related to the expectations you have set for them?
3. What are your children learning from the consequences?
4. What are your children's most frequent offenses?
5. What logical consequences could you use for these offenses?
6. What must you do to be willing to follow through on these consequences?

I will test them in this to see whether they will
follow my instructions.

— E x o d u s   1 6 : 4

8
Assigning Work

God's children have had a tumultuous history with their
Father. In fact, the name *Israel* reflects the struggle God has
had with his children.

Have you ever wrestled with anyone? I love athletics, but I
find wrestling an exhausting sport. I only had to do it in gym
class, but that was more than enough for me. Every muscle
would be sore for days after only three or four minutes of
wrestling—and I was an athlete! I could only imagine the
pain if I hadn't been in halfway decent shape. Could you
imagine wrestling with someone all night long?

Jacob did (Gen. 32:22-32). He wrestled all night with the
angel of the Lord. At the end of the battle, the angel changed
Jacob's name to Israel, which means "One who wrestles with
God."

God wrestled with Jacob, and he sometimes wrestles with
us too. He gets involved with us. He engages us.

Is it any wonder that our own children do the same with
us? Whether literally or figuratively, our children want to
engage us. They want us to interact with them. They need us

to test their strengths by comparing theirs with ours. They want to know how they measure up. And to the extent that we meet them face-to-face, we leave our impression on their lives.

When we physically wrestle with our children, not only do our arms and legs get intertwined, so do our hearts. Not only do we have skin-to-skin contact, we also have heart-to-heart contact. Even when our "wrestling" is more relational than physical, the process still knits our hearts together and draws our children out to the point where we can leave an impression on them. That is exactly what we want to do as parents, as long as the impression is positive. One critical place we want to leave a long-lasting impression is on their attitudes. We want to shape their attitudes into positive ones.

Until this point in the book, you may not have heard much that you haven't heard before. Many authors and child-rearing experts talk about setting expectations and enforcing logical consequences. But very few talk about how to change children's bad attitudes, and even fewer would suggest using the tools I will discuss.

Once we begin to see a pattern of noncooperation in our children, it becomes obvious we are dealing with more than just behavior. We are seeing a bad attitude. Children's refusal to cooperate exposes their bad attitudes. This is the time to take discipline to the next level and fully engage them and their attitude problem.

Children's attitudes are like the steering wheel of a car. Their attitudes determine whether or not they stay on the road and what direction they go. We don't want them to end up in a ditch or head in the wrong direction. Some driver-education cars have two steering wheels, accelerators, and brake systems. As long as the student driver makes good decisions about how and where to drive, the instructor leaves the power connected to the student's side of the car. However, when the student's decisions or behavior endangers people or the car, then the instructor can flip a switch that gives him or her immediate power over the car.

We need to maintain that level of authority over our children until they have consistently demonstrated their ability to steer their attitudes. If our children are weaving back and forth, then we need to suggest verbal steering corrections. If our children do not listen to our instructions, then we should ask them to slow down. If our children ignore these warnings, then we should use our authority to switch control to our steering wheel so we don't end up in the ditch or possibly hurt someone else.

We don't hesitate to stop our children from harming themselves physically. We spank them when they disobey us and run out into the street or sternly warn them about the dangers of electrical outlets. We talk to them about the dangers of using drugs. We cook healthy meals for them. We steer them toward friends we think are a positive influence. We enroll them in worthwhile activities so they have opportunities to develop their interests and strengths. All this guidance is possible because parents have the power and authority to provide it.

Just as parents have the responsibility to help children grow, we also have the responsibility to prune some of their growth. When their budding spirits sprout off in the wrong direction or with unbridled passion, parents need to step in and prune them back.

The attitude of the parents does not have to be harsh or critical when doing this necessary work. In other words, parents don't have to be authoritarian. But parents who really love their children do not hesitate to use their authority to protect and to guide them.

So how can we steer their attitudes in a new direction?

WORK IS A LOGICAL CONSEQUENCE

When the simple tools of setting expectations and enforcing consequences are not effective enough, it's time to unveil some of the "power tools" of discipline. Work is one of those power tools. That's right—good, old-fashioned manual labor.

How is work a logical consequence for children who have bad attitudes? If a bad attitude is a defiant internal posture, then the best tool is one that will alter that rebellious attitude into a compliant one. Work is the most effective, loving, gracious way to do that.

Take Tommy, the six-year-old who argued with his babysitter. Some parents would define Tommy's problem as misunderstanding: "Tommy just didn't understand. That's why he didn't put away his toys." If parents have clearly communicated their expectations and if Tommy has verbally repeated the expectations, then understanding is not the problem. Tommy's problem was that he didn't want to do what Laurie asked him to do.

Take Christy, the sixteen-year-old who wanted to stay out later than her parents thought she should. Some parents would say of Christy's behavior, "Christy just wanted to be with her friends. Give her a break." The truth is, Christy simply didn't want to come home when her father told her to. Her attitude was, "I'm old enough to make my own decisions. I don't have to listen to you!"

What about Samantha, the teenager who hadn't finished her chores in time for her mother to drive her to her friend's house? Was her problem that she just couldn't get everything done that her mother expected her to? No. She had plenty of time to take care of her responsibilities. She wasted her time and then expected her mom to be lenient and let her go out. Samantha's problem was her selfish attitude. Not only did she not want to do her chores, but she also expected her mom to reorient her schedule at the last second to drive her to Bethany's house.

What about Derek, the boy who left his bicycle in the driveway again? Was his problem his dad? Should his dad lighten up and stop nagging Derek? Derek knew he had to take care of his bike, and he knew what had happened to the last bike because he had not taken care of it. Derek pushed by arguing and trying to put off his dad, hoping his dad would forget.

The real problem in each of these cases is the children's attitudes, their internal posture. They are resisting their parents' reasonable requests. Their argumentative, uncooperative behavior reveals their bad attitudes. Don't engage your children in verbal battles about your reasonable expectations. When children dig in their heels, they need practice submitting their attitudes to you. Their bad attitudes are now fully exposed. They have raised the stakes a notch or two by their persistent resisting and arguing. This is when we parents have to match that level of strength to prevent a runaway bad attitude. Work is a power tool that gives them practice submitting to you until their attitudes have become cooperative.

Tell your children what kind of attitudes you expect. Tell them you expect them to say OK when you ask them to do something. They don't have to be excited about responsibilities. I don't expect them to say, "Oh, boy!" when I ask them to do something. But I need them to know that I will not accept their grumbling and groaning. I could even accept,

"Boy, that sure is a drag, but I'll get right to it." They have expressed their feeling of hating to do the job, but they have done so without rebellion. They haven't whined or argued by saying, "Do I have to?" They have submitted to the task with a cooperative attitude.

Expect that your children will test the limits. Like Derek, they will want to see what happens when they don't give in right away. Be ready to match their strength and meet their challenge. Their internal posture says, "I'm feeling pretty strong and energetic right now, so let's see you make me! Let's see how strong you really are!"

When your kids push the limits, you need to match their strength by holding them back. You can lovingly and firmly answer, "I'm glad you feel strong and energetic, but you are just a little too big for your britches right now. I'm going to help you bring your attitude down just a notch or two so you still know how to be respectful as well as strong." There is nothing wrong with being strong. But there is a big difference between strength and rebellion. Children need lots of guidance to learn how to harness all their energy and willpower. When your children are standing up to you, externally or internally, and daring you to get them to cooperate, you have to accept that challenge.

An insolent internal posture is a refusal to budge. Work forces your children to budge. It involves the exertion of energy. Just by getting our children to move their bodies, we have already won half the battle. Then it just becomes a question of how long it will take for them not only to change their attitudes but also to admit that their attitudes have changed. This point will be explained more fully in the next chapter.

You can assign work to your children as a logical consequence in several ways as you will see in the following paragraphs.

"Since you refuse to hang up your coat without arguing, apparently you need an attitude adjustment. You need some practice obeying me. We've tried practicing and verbally promising to do it, but those don't seem to be working. So we're going to take it to the next level. In addition to hanging up your coat, I want you to put away the dishes. You need some practice helping to keep the house neat. Now get started."

"Since you continue to argue with me about going out with your friends, apparently you need an attitude adjustment. You need some practice accepting what I say. I want you to take out all the trash in the house and put it in the garbage cans outside. If you can accept the conditions of being with your friends after doing that, we will talk. If you still want to argue, then I will have another job for you to do. And before you leave to do the work, I want you to say, 'OK, Dad. I will take out all the trash in the house.' When you are done, find me and ask me to check your work. Not only do I want to see clean trash cans, I want to see a clean attitude! Now get going!"

"Since your attitude while making your bed was very pouty, you need some help changing your attitude. I will not let you hang on to that attitude. We will 'work it out' of you, literally. If you are going to argue about doing your jobs around here, then you will practice doing several jobs until you accept your responsibility to do them well. You will be doing jobs until your attitude is cooperative and pleasant. I want you to start by cleaning the bathtub. Go ahead."

"We've been getting too many reports from school about your getting into arguments in class. That is not the way to treat people. Apparently you do not remember what it means to respect others. You need an attitude adjustment and some practice treating others with consideration. Since your teachers and classmates are not here, you get to practice treating other people with respect with me and your family. Your mom and I are going to give you as many chances as we think are necessary for you to serve us. I will be watching your attitude. I expect a positive one, not the one I see on your face right now. I want you to start by sweeping and mopping the kitchen floor. Then come back and tell me when you are done."

You may have noticed how I end the quick speeches in the above examples with "Now get started" or "Now get going" or "Go ahead." I usually say something like that because I feel it stops the arguing. The longer children can hang on to their bad attitudes, the stronger the attitudes get. Your children are trying to wear you down. Even though we may be stronger than they are, they have an advantage in energy and time. They can usually outdistance us when it comes to arguing. After they have stated their case to try to change your mind, it turns into a battle of who will win. Telling them to get started on the work now should end the conversation.

I understand you wouldn't normally end a request to your children in this way, but this time is different. They are challenging your authority, and you need to respond with an increase in strength. Words such as *now* and *go* should sound final yet not harsh.

The work tool fits into the progression of discipline process in much the same way that setting expectations and enforcing logical consequences do. Remember that you use the work tool because your children have not responded with wise choices after you have used the first two tools. Indirectly they have forced you to progress to another tool. At this point, work is a very effective tool.

Progression of Discipline

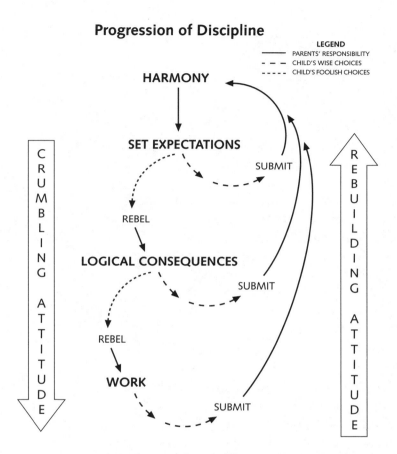

LEGEND
— PARENTS' RESPONSIBILITY
– – – CHILD'S WISE CHOICES
······ CHILD'S FOOLISH CHOICES

HARMONY

SET EXPECTATIONS

SUBMIT

REBEL

LOGICAL CONSEQUENCES

SUBMIT

REBEL

WORK

SUBMIT

C R U M B L I N G   A T T I T U D E

R E B U I L D I N G   A T T I T U D E

So what does the work tool look like? What kind of work would be effective in adjusting your children's attitudes? Let me make some suggestions:

- rake the yard
- weed the garden or yard by hand (not with chemicals)
- turn over the dirt to mix the mulch
- pick up sticks
- pull grass in sidewalk cracks

- sweep the deck
- sweep the driveway
- sweep the garage
- clean the bathtub
- clean the toilet
- clean the sink
- clean the shower curtain
- vacuum the house
- clean out the garbage cans
- sweep and mop the kitchen floor
- scrape rust off the fence in preparation for painting
- scrape paint off the garage
- wash the kitchen walls or floor
- scour the oven without chemicals
- shovel the snow off the sidewalk
- wash the car
- wash windows
- chop and stack firewood

GUIDELINES FOR ASSIGNING WORK

How you assign the work and what you expect from your children are important issues. Here are a few suggestions to make this tool most effective.

1. *Match the degree of work difficulty with the level of the bad attitude.* Work is definitely a power tool. As with any power tool, caution should always be used. Be careful not to use too much power—or too little—for that matter. The amount and difficulty of work should be determined by the level of your children's resistance. The stronger the negative attitude, the harder the job should be. Try to give enough work to subdue the out-of-control attitude but not too much to overwhelm your children. This is where we have to know our children.

Some children need more work assigned to them in order to work out their bad attitudes. Others may need only a few small jobs to do it.

Last year our entire backyard needed to be seeded. We could have used shovels to turn over all the dirt, but that would have taken all week and given me a lot of blisters and a backache. I suppose we could have brought in a truckload of dirt, hired an earthmoving truck, or just dynamited the backyard to start over. But those options seemed too extreme. I borrowed a rototiller, which was just the right amount of power necessary for the size of the job.

If your children need just a little help with their attitudes, give them a job they can complete in ten or twenty minutes. If their attitudes still seem negative, then give them a little harder job to do. But if you can tell from the start that their attitudes are intensely negative, then start right off with the hard jobs like raking the entire yard or scraping the paint off an entire side of the garage.

If you aren't sure how much work is necessary, err on the side of not assigning enough. I always add this statement to the end of the work assignment: "And when you're done, we'll see how your attitudes are. If they still aren't positive, then you will have more work to do." This serves as a warning to the child. By saying something like this, my children feel as if I am being fair. They only have themselves to blame if they still have bad attitudes and get more work assigned. I try to give them every opportunity to change their attitudes.

2. The job should use liberal amounts of elbow grease, not chemicals or power tools. Children should use their muscles to do the work. Physical exertion is crucial in making this tool successful. It requires them to put their whole heart into it and not rely on anything else.

3. The standard for work assigned as a disciplinary tool is higher than the standard for daily chores. The white-glove test is the standard for attitude-adjusting work. If you tolerate dishes that are not completely clean in normal chores, set the standard higher for dishes cleaned as part of an attitude-adjustment assignment. You want to bring up your children's attitude as high as you can, knowing it will not always maintain that level. It will slip slightly, but not down into the pit it was in before. You can live with some normal disappointment, but continued whining, complaining, and arguing are not acceptable attitudes.

You may notice that all of the listed jobs involve cleaning. The subliminal message is this: "Just as you are cleaning up the garage [sidewalk, car, yard, sink, etc.], you need to clean up your attitude. I want a clean, fresh attitude, not a messy, rotten one."

4. Make sure your children are physically capable of doing the work you assign them. Assign tasks according to your children's ability level; your work assignments for your five-year-old will be different from the assignments you give your ten-year-old. You may have to teach your children what to do and how you want the job done. When you assess their work, keep the age factor in mind. You don't want to dishearten them, just soften their hearts. Remember the ultimate goal is to improve the relationship. But don't be afraid to challenge them either. Push them just a little bit harder than they are pushing you.

5. Attitude-adjustment work is not a substitute for regular chores. Explain to your children that this work is assigned as a logical consequence of their choice not to obey you or their choice to have a sour attitude. You still expect them to do their daily jobs. When they have demonstrated that their attitudes are clean, they will be done with their work. The next chapter will explain more about how to decide when the attitude adjustment is complete.

THE DUGAN STORY

Let me walk you through an example from our own family of how we have used work as a tool to adjust our son's attitude. First I must explain that this is an example of a fairly intense use of the work tool—a situation I would call an attitude-adjustment session. Sometimes we give our kids a fairly quick work assignment because that's all we think the situation needs. However, in this case, the bad attitude came after Dugan had resisted recent opportunities we had given him to straighten out his attitude in other areas. It was time for a real attitude adjustment.

I came home one day and found my wife, Sharon, and our then-nine-year-old son, Dugan, in the midst of a battle about his math assignment. I could tell from the frown on Sharon's face and scowl on Dugan's face that this had been going on for a while. I asked Sharon if she needed my help, and she gave me the yes-I-can't-take-it-anymore look. I could tell from Dugan's pout that he was determined not to cooperate.

I had several choices. I could have played newspaper reporter and asked a lot of questions about what happened. I didn't do that because I trusted that Sharon wasn't asking Dugan to do anything unreasonable, and I know that she doesn't overreact. If I had asked a lot of questions, Sharon might have felt insulted by my second-guessing her, and Dugan might have thought he could excuse his disobedient attitude. Neither result was desirable.

I could have tried to play peacemaker and get them to calm down and get along. This would have required that Sharon

revoke her expectation that Dugan do his math in a cooperative way. If I had chosen this option, I would have looked like
a hero to Dugan at the expense of making my wife look like
the villain. That's not a good idea at all. Not only am I supposed to love, honor, and respect her, but I also want to continue eating her cooking and sleeping together at night. I'd
much rather have my wife's gratitude than my son's. Besides, I
trust my wife's ability to parent, and when my son is having a
battle with her, I know which one needs to back down.

I could have just dismissed the whole thing and told Sharon
to handle it herself because I was too tired or too busy to deal
with it. I could have dumped it all on her and said, "You got
yourself into this mess, so it's up to you to get yourself out of
it." But that would not be honoring to my wife. We are a parenting team, and this was a case in which we needed to operate
as a tag team. Sharon was worn out, so I was on.

I could have assigned more math problems to make Dugan
practice. I could tell by the exasperation on Sharon's face and
the scowl of defiance on Dugan's that this would have been
like trying to put out a forest fire with a water pistol. I could
have told Dugan to verbally practice saying, "OK, Mom, I'll
do the math problems." Or I may have even been able to get
him to write that phrase a few dozen times. But it just didn't
seem like enough to tackle the intensity of the situation. It
was time to bring out a power tool.

I decided it was time for an attitude adjustment that
involved work. I asked Sharon if she had any jobs for Dugan to
do, and she said no. I told Dugan to go into the basement to
get the old screwdriver and hand broom, put on his winter
gear, and meet me by the front door. He knew something was
up.

I should tell you that we live near Chicago, and this was

early February. Chicago is not quite the North Pole, but we can sometimes see it from here. We had just endured a week of alternating snow and freezing rain. I was learning how to "ski" my car to work. No other family member had ventured outside for the last few days, and our mail carrier would just wave as she passed by our personal glacier covering our unshoveled sidewalk.

I told Dugan that since he was refusing to do his math assignment with a good attitude, he would clear the ice off the sidewalk until I thought his rotten attitude was gone and would not return anytime soon. I took him to the sidewalk and showed him how to chip off the ice with the screwdriver and then sweep it off. I cleared off about a three-inch square to show him exactly how I expected the finished task to look.

To say Dugan was not happy with this development would be an understatement. He was crying. He was angry at me for making him do the work. He was yelling at me, "This isn't fair. I can't do this!" His anger wasn't the problem. The anger only confirmed his rebellious I-don't-want-to-and-you-can't-make-me attitude. I just let his angry comments slide off my back.

I was not concerned about Dugan's anger during the attitude adjustment. My main concern was to keep his body working. As long as he is moving, I'm not concerned with such statements as "I hate you," "I'll never do what you want," etc. In fact, those sorts of feelings indicate that he was engaging with me. We were bonding in a way. Those intense feelings would eventually make the connection between Dugan and me stronger. He will feel purged.

A cleansing occurs when children can eradicate those feelings from inside them. A word of caution: I never allow vulgar, repulsive, or truly insulting language. Plus I would not let him go on and on about his feelings. Saying something once or twice is sufficient. As long as I focused on the task at hand and not on Dugan's words, he would do the work. I knew that if I had entered into a debate, he would have accomplished his goal of delaying and possibly getting out of the work by engaging me in a verbal volleyball match.

Dugan's mutinous attitude was my main focus. I would not allow him to go back to the warmth of the house and his mother's arms until he had proven his radical change of heart. I calmly warned him that he would be working on the ice until his attitude was clean and he was extremely cooperative. I didn't have to yell. I wasn't even angry. I knew what would eventually result after the next hour or so. His attitude would be cooperative. However long it took, Dugan would be a "new boy" by the time we were done.

Dugan predictably attempted the OK-I-promise-I'll-cooperate-with-Mommy-now battlefield conversion. I didn't argue with him. I simply said, "Great, I'm glad to hear that. But first you have to work on the sidewalk until I say you can stop." I know better than to believe those shallow-soil promises. From past experience I know they sprout up quickly only to die off all too soon. Dugan then displayed another crying and pouting tantrum in a last-ditch attempt to get me to drop this work project. I didn't argue with him. I simply told him to get to work.

Dugan began the task with minimal effort. He limply jabbed at the thick ice as if to prove that he couldn't do it. I reminded him that he had no choice as to whether or not he cleared it off. His only decision was how long it would take him to change his attitude. I told him to work faster and put more umph into it. He began to turn a corner by putting out a minuscule amount of energy. After about five minutes of watching him, I encouraged him to keep up the effort. I told him I would be back soon to check on his progress. I went inside. I wanted to leave him alone to deal with his own heart for a while. He needed to realize that the battle is also with himself, not just with me or his mother. I wasn't sure he would come to that realization this time, but it was worth a shot.

Leaving him alone was a tough call and may sound contradictory to what I've said about time-outs and confining children in their rooms. Leaving him alone in this situation was different because I was leaving him alone as a reward for his progress, not because I was rejecting him in any way. I was subtly saying, "I am going to trust you to keep on working without my breathing down your neck every minute. I hope you prove me right."

Leaving children alone is *not* a critical element of this work tool. You may want to spend the entire time with them. The only reason I mention it now is because that is what happened and I thought it may be helpful to explain why I did it.

First of all, this was not Dugan's first attitude adjustment. He knew the drill. He knew he had no choice at this point. I didn't need to stay right with him as I had done in previous situations. Second, I knew he was not a risk to run away. If he had threatened to do that or if he had tried it before, I would have stayed with him to supervise. Third, sometimes kids will purposely work very slowly in an attempt to aggravate you into yelling. This gives them some satisfaction knowing you are sharing in their misery. My leaving Dugan left him alone with his misery. He had no one to share it with. It began to dawn on him, *Hey, this stinks. I'm out here doing this stupid work all by myself. This isn't worth it.* Thoughts like these were the first steps toward his change of attitude. He was beginning to see that it was his choice. He has the choice and therefore the responsibility for what he did or didn't do.

Since Dugan already knew this path, I didn't have to remind him. That lecture he had already heard. If he hadn't, then I would have remained with him and periodically salted the time with quiz questions such as "Do you remember why you are doing this work?" The first few answers are ideas like "Because you are making me" or "Because I can't do my math" or "Because you hate me" or "No. And this is stupid. It won't help!" This is when I would have done some critical corrections to his thinking by reminding him, "No. You are doing this work because you kept refusing to do your math assignment. This work is to help you work on your attitude by giving you some practice submitting to me and your mom." Don't get sucked into another argument here. Refuse to debate the issue. Let the work change the heart. It will be more effective than your words.

If you leave your children alone to do the work, use these guidelines:

1. *Do not leave your children alone until they are making progress with their attitudes.* The hardest part of this process is getting the change started. Don't leave them alone until you see some changes starting. If you leave too soon, it will only delay the change.

2. *Leave your children alone for only a short time.* Generally, a few minutes is plenty. This is not like a regular household job. They should be closely scrutinized. Make them feel the heat of your gaze.

3. *The older the children, the more you can leave them alone.* Younger children need closer supervision, teaching, and encouragement. The quality of their work will quickly deteriorate when you leave. The goal with older children is to

encourage their independent ability to work and change their attitude without your help. Tell them you are testing them to see how well they continue with their work while you are gone.

4. *As their attitude improves, you can leave them alone for longer periods of time.* Giving them some space is their reward for taking a small step toward an improved attitude. The opposite is also true. If their work performance slips, they need you to stand over them to make sure they work harder.

5. *Sneak looks at their effort level when they don't know you are looking.* This is how you can tell if they are just acting when you come into view. Make a judgment of their attitude by how much effort they are putting into the work.

6. *Praise even the slightest improvement.* Encourage their progress. As eager as you are to confront their bad attitudes, be just as eager to applaud their successes.

During my attitude-adjustment time with Dugan, I checked on him frequently to encourage his progress or push him harder, whichever he seemed to need. His tears began to dry up. I imagine it was painful to have them freeze on his cheeks. He seemed to be resigning himself to the task.

I gauged how long the job should take and then set a reasonable goal for him. "If you can get this section from here to here (about ten feet) done in thirty minutes *and* if your attitude has changed, you will be done and you can return to your math assignment. But if not, you will have another section of sidewalk do to. I think you can do it." I wanted to give him a challenge and goal so he could sprint toward the finish line. I felt that if I gave him a light at the end of the tunnel, he would begin to feel hopeful.

After about fifteen minutes I checked on him again. I asked him how he was doing, and he said he was OK. I asked him how his attitude was, and he said, "Good. I feel bad for treating Mom that way." I noticed the change in his tone of voice. It was softer and calmer. The biting edge was gone. I asked him if he wanted to apologize, and he said he did. I allowed him to come in the house to apologize to his mother.

Then I told him to go back and finish the job. When he went out after apologizing, he really put his heart into his work. His actions had changed his feelings, and he was able to overcome his stubborn attitude.

Some of you may be wondering, *Why did you send him back out for more work? Do you enjoy watching children suffer?* No, I don't. It was tempting to think that because my son had apologized, it should be over. Having him finish the work served two very important purposes.

First, it was one final test of whether he had truly experienced a change of heart. If he had made a plea that he had already apologized and that he shouldn't have to finish the sidewalk, he would have been telling me that some root of the bad attitude was still inside him and that he needed more work to pull it out. If he had complained that sending him back to finish the job wasn't fair, I would have reminded him that the work was to finish the job assigned with a good attitude. I was glad that he wanted to apologize to his mom, but that didn't mean that he could avoid the work assigned to him. I would have told him that his resistance indicated a lingering evidence of a bad attitude. His arguing with me would have proved that he was not finished yet. Arguing and whining do not go with a good attitude.

Second, by sending my son back out to work, I witnessed a profound thing. He demonstrated that he had made a great deal of progress. He had turned around his attitude, and he had an opportunity to put significant mileage between his pouty attitude and his new, clean, proud self. He felt good about himself because he was succeeding at a difficult task—not just the icy sidewalk but his internal attitude as well. He was cleaning away not only the ice on the sidewalk but also the remorse he felt for having been so rude to his mom.

He probably took credit for this change, but that was fine with me. In fact I wanted him to take the credit because then he would be more likely to change his attitude sooner the next time. I was relieved to be back in harmony with him. The time and energy it took me to clean up his bad attitude were worth every second.

When Dugan went out to finish chipping the ice, he plowed into it full force. He wanted to express the joy of being forgiven and his gratitude for returning to harmony. Dugan eventually came back into the house to report that he had finished. He was very proud. We all went out and praised him for the job he had done. At this point he was enthusiastic and pleasant. His attitude was clean. He felt good about himself, and he felt good toward us. We shared a time of hugs. He even let his little sister, Breeze, hug him. (That's when we really knew he had a good attitude.)

The only thing left to do was finish his math assignment, which he did willingly. That was the final little test to ensure the change of attitude. The ordeal had come full circle. He finished his math with enthusiasm.

The family had not simply returned to harmony; the family had defined a new harmony. We had all been through a battle together. Even Breeze had felt the tension during the ordeal and could now enjoy the elation of renewed relationships.

You may be wondering how often to use this work tool.

The quick answer is, as often as necessary. Keep in mind that as with any discipline, there is a range of work intensity. As I indicated earlier, this was what I would consider a major adjustment session. Most children probably won't need a major adjustment any more than once or twice a year (as long as you are keeping up with the daily attitude adjustments). As a point of reference, let me rate the intensity of this ice-chipping example. On a scale of 1–10, I would rate the work in this story about an 8. Chipping ice off our sidewalk is a fairly difficult, tedious task in tough work conditions. Plus it took Dugan almost an hour to begin to change his attitude. But once he started to change, it went fairly rapidly and smoothly, and it ended on a great note. If he had tried to run away or if he had balked at finishing the job, it would have been at least a 9. The total time it took was about two and half hours from the time I came home until we celebrated as a family.

Use the work tool as rarely as possible but as often as necessary. You may have to use it more in the beginning—maybe even daily during critical periods when kids are testing the boundaries—until your children get used to it. They need to be convinced that you are committed to the goal of a clean attitude. Then they will begin to see the wisdom of not testing your strength and resolve as much.

After things settle down into a more normal routine, you probably won't need to use the intensive (7–9 category) work tool more than two or three times a year. Usually, if the minor attitude adjustments are administered consistently, the major ones are rare. *A bad attitude is just like any other problem: the more you put it off, the bigger it gets.*

I think one of the biggest hurdles for parents to overcome is the time it takes to administer the work tool. These attitude-adjustment tools do take considerable time. I can't argue about that. It is an important commitment and sometimes a major sacrifice. For parents, it may mean being late to a meeting, canceling an appointment, not getting to relax, or interrupting a project. That may seem extreme at first, but if your children were having physical problems, you probably would not think twice about taking the time to help them. *Treating their sick attitudes is just as important as treating their sick bodies.*

You may be wondering how this tool is "short and sweet." In comparison to things such as no television for a week, being grounded for a weekend, or no phone calls for a month, a couple of hours is quick. The common disciplines get dragged out for hours or days. They often prolong the agony of a strained relationship. But more importantly, the results with this work tool are much more dramatic and effective. Work doesn't just stem the flow as other discipline methods attempt to do; work changes the direction. It restores the relationship to even better than it was before. (I'll talk more about that in chapter 11.)

SOME ADDITIONAL GUIDELINES

Let me offer a few more guidelines in using the work tool with your children.

1. Stay involved. You may need to stand over your children while they do the work to make sure it is done well. Don't get sidetracked by other things. You may want to give them some space as discussed earlier, but don't stay away very long. Make sure your children know you are keenly aware of what they are doing.

2. Your goal is submissiveness. You are looking for a complete eradication of your children's poor attitudes. If they want to push it this far and if you are going to invest that much time and energy into them, then you want to get the maximum out of this investment. Stop at nothing less than total cooperation. At times when my son is doing extra work to change a bad attitude, he asks me how much more he has to do. That question tells me he still has the attitude of trying to do the minimum. After all this effort, I don't want just the minimum. I want the maximum return for all the time and energy both he and I spend in adjusting his attitude. If you were getting your car repaired, wouldn't you have the mechanic make all the repairs at once to save you the hassle of taking the car in for minor repairs every other week? The extra time it takes to transform a bad attitude into a good one is worth it. Don't settle for a lukewarm change of attitude.

3. *Use variety.* Try to have several different work assignments available when your children need an attitude adjustment. Always using the same one may lose its effectiveness by becoming too familiar. They may not dislike it enough to want to change their attitudes.

4. *Use the tool as early as possible.* Sharon and I began to use work as an attitude-adjustment tool when our children were three years old. When they were toddlers, some of their attitude-adjustment work involved things like putting away the silverware, separating the dark from light laundry, and cleaning the toothpaste out of the bathroom sink. It was more the idea that they had no choice but to obey. It was not real labor intensive.

We would supervise and inspect their work and ask them if they had a better attitude when they were done. It didn't take much pressure to get them to have a complete change of heart. We would sometimes watch their eyes fill with tears and their lips quiver in sadness. Sometimes we would feel our hearts begin to break, but our children understood what it meant to have a clean attitude and how important it was to us.

5. *Invest the time.* Raising children takes lots of time. Our society is beginning to wake up to that crucial fact. Disciplining our children well is a part of the commitment we make to them. Let me warn you, these tools will take more time and effort than the popular tools of discipline. But disciplining our children effectively is just as crucial to their development as reading them bedtime stories or giving them nutritious meals.

When I am helping our children with their attitude problems, they sometimes try to sidetrack me by reminding me that I should be leaving for my office. I answer, "My other work will wait. I'm working with you right now, and I'll be here until we are finished." I am sending a very important message to them: "You are more important to me than anything else right now."

6. *Later is better than not at all.* Ideally, the sooner you can address your children's bad attitudes, the better. I realize that is not always possible. Sometimes we don't even hear about their attitude problems until we get a note from their teacher or a phone call from their friend's parent. These situations still demand some action even though it may be later than we would like.

When these situations arise in our family, I sternly tell our children the facts of what I learned from the other source. I tell them this sort of thing will not be tolerated and that obviously they need some practice submitting to my expectations of how to cooperate when they are in the company of other people. I then assign them a medium-sized job to test whether they will submit to this discipline. If they cooperate,

I can just remind them of my expectations when they are with others. If a similar problem occurs again, I am then on solid ground to confront them with what I see as a pattern of rebellious behavior with others. This may require more work at home as well as for the other person involved. In any case, if you smell the smoke of a bad attitude, assume there is a fire somewhere inside. It may just be smoldering by the time you catch a whiff of it, but don't hesitate to explore to see if you can expose any burning embers that need extinguishing.

WHY IS THIS TOOL EFFECTIVE?

Think of some project in which you have invested significant time, energy, or money (money is tangible time and energy). Maybe you got a college degree, remodeled an antique car, trained to run a five-mile race, or lost some weight. Whatever it was, you had a lot of feelings about that project. While you were in the midst of it, you may have felt frustrated or overwhelmed and questioned why you started it to begin with. You may have almost quit several times, but thankfully you didn't. Maybe it took other people to encourage you to finish the valuable project. But chances are, when you completed it, you felt proud of it. A significant part of you was in it. You cared about it.

That's what is happening when your children do the work assignment. You are "encouraging" your children to invest themselves in having good attitudes. It goes without saying that they are not the least bit interested in that investment. Their self-centered human nature is screaming at you to stop. But when you get them to do the work, they will have those same exhilarating feelings you had with your accomplishment. It doesn't matter that you had to do 90 percent of the work by pushing them. They will experience the success of overcoming their own bad attitudes. They like the feeling of having good attitudes.

When my son chipped the ice, he gradually started to feel good—first about the task and later about himself. He was experiencing the fact that he could make a good choice. He truly was in control of himself. He realized that he could do something even when he didn't feel like it. He began to believe in himself. His character was strengthened, and he was learning how to change his attitudes.

Work is so effective for a very simple reason: it makes kids move. External movement will eventually change their internal posture. It is hard for them to maintain a hard, rebellious internal posture while their external bodies are cooperatively moving. They may be able to do it for a while, but not for long. The work will wear them down until they are softer inside. When they are soft, they can be remolded like clay. That is what you want. Movement—work—forces their internal posture to change.

Does it matter that they had to be pushed into this? No. Even though they didn't have a lot of choice in the matter, what little choice they did have blossomed into something beautiful. Let them take all the credit for what they did. It doesn't matter. They get to enjoy the fruit of all the work, even though we did the majority of it. (We were all in the same dilemma with our heavenly Father. He did all the work through his Son's death.)

In C. S. Lewis's *The Screwtape Letters*, Screwtape, the senior devil, counsels his protégé on how to neutralize someone who has just decided to follow Christ. Screwtape offers this insightful admonishment: "At the very least, [human beings] can be persuaded that the bodily position makes no difference to their prayers; for they constantly forget what you must always remember, that they are animals and that whatever their bodies do affects their souls."[1]

WHAT DOES GOD THINK ABOUT WORK AND DISCIPLINE?

God used the attitude-adjusting work tool several times in his interactions with the people of Israel. God used slavery (work) as a discipline for Israel's continued disobedience and rebellious attitude. "The Israelites did what was evil in the Lord's sight. They forgot about the Lord their God, and they worshiped the images of Baal and the Asherah poles. Then the Lord burned with anger against Israel, and he handed them over to King Cushan-rishathaim of Aram-naharaim. And the Israelites were subject to [slaves of] Cushan-rishathaim for eight years. But when Israel cried out to the Lord for help, the Lord raised up a man to rescue them. His name was Othniel" (Judg. 3:7-9).

After Othniel died, the Israelites rebelled again, so God allowed them to become slaves of Eglon, king of Moab, for eighteen years. Then the Israelites repented of their disobedience and asked the Lord to save them. He gave them another deliverer—Ehud (Judg. 3:12-23).

But after Ehud died, the Israelites once again became rebellious and disobeyed God. So the Lord sold them into the hands of Jabin, who cruelly oppressed the Israelites for twenty years. Once again they came to their senses and cried to the Lord for help (Judg. 4:1-3).

I could go on, but I think you get the picture. God's children would rebel. God would punish them with slave labor until they cried out for help. God would deliver them and restore the relationship. This cycle repeated itself several more times (Judg. 6:1-6; 8:33-34; 10:6-16; 13:1). Children are slow learners aren't they, even when the "children" are adults.

I do want to be clear about one point—children are not

slaves. I am merely pointing out that God would subject his own children to the rigors of work so they would soften their rebellious attitudes. Their attitude adjustments would take years to be complete. The attitude adjustments we use with our children are very brief in comparison.

God used work for the benefit of his children. His example demonstrates for us the value of this powerful tool. It effectively leads children to changing their attitudes and restoring the relationship. Pray that we use it wisely, governed by our love and commitment to our children.

WHAT IF MY CHILDREN WON'T DO THE WORK?

Probably the most frequently asked question regarding this tool is this: "If my kids won't do their regular chores, why would they do this extra work?" Great question. I don't have a full explanation. But I do know that kids will do the work we assign them as part of an attitude adjustment. It doesn't seem logical at all to us, but we are not dealing with logic. We are dealing with kids' unbridled attitudes and emotions.

I will offer a few thoughts on why they do the work even when they refuse to obey the original request. First of all, I think they respond to the determination in your voice. Children can tell when you really mean something, and deep inside they know they are no match for your strength.

Second, I think kids know when they are wrong. They know that they are on shaky ground and don't feel confident in challenging your authority. Children know when you are right, and they don't want to fight a losing battle.

Third, I believe children take great comfort when parents demonstrate their moral strength and leadership. They can breathe an internal sigh of relief knowing their parents care enough about them to make them obey.

However, at times children will stand their ground to see what you will do next. Be prepared for that contingent because it will happen. When your children simply refuse to carry out the work assignment, you have two options.

The first option is to physically assist your children in the work project. If Dugan had persisted in limply jabbing at the ice, I would have taken his hand in mine, held it firmly with the screwdriver in his hand, and chopped at the ice for a few jabs. I would have held it firmly but without trying to hurt his hand. He probably would have complained that I was "killing him" or some other exaggeration. I am aware of my own strength and know when I am hurting someone.

I have held my children's hands and arms to "help" them rake for a while until they were ready to do it on their own. I've had to do the same thing with helping my son shovel the dirt in the garden. After indicating to your children that you are serious, you can give them a choice: "You can do the raking by yourself, or I will help you until your attitude starts to change." The time for explaining and arguing is over. It is time to move. If they refuse, then help them. You don't need to resort to screaming or roughness at this point. Simply let them know the conversation is over.

Helping should be done only for five to ten seconds at the most. Making them submit to work is humbling; manhandling them feels humiliating. I use this only as a last resort. I don't want to humiliate my children; I just want to humble them. That is why I stop after only a few seconds and tell them to do it on their own now. If they don't, then I help them again for a few more seconds. I again tell them they can do it on their own. I've never had to do this more than two or three times before they decide that they would rather move their bodies themselves.

If you don't like this option, the other option is taking an attitude adjustment to the next level, which is discussed thoroughly in chapter 11.

Another question I am frequently asked is, "Won't kids hate doing regular chores if they have to do extra work for punishment?" At first I was flabbergasted by this question. I didn't know what to say. Does *anyone* enjoy household chores? I know I like the result of having the chores done, but I rarely enjoy doing them.

I've talked to several people who tell me their children enjoy working. But when I ask the children if they enjoy cleaning their rooms on their own or putting away their toys by themselves when they would rather watch TV, I get a different story. What is usually happening is that children enjoy working alongside their mom or dad. That is great. They are learning a skill directly from their parents. That's how learning should be. But there are times when they have to do chores on their own, whether it is fun or not. Some chores are simply tedious, but they still have to be done.

Assigning more work to adjust their attitude is a motivational tool. If they do the chore with a positive attitude the first time, they won't have more work to do. Kids are smart enough to learn that if they have a bad attitude about regular chores, they will be assigned more work.

Summary
When the first two tools in the progression of discipline don't get the job done, you can choose to use the power tool of work. Physical work helps children work their rebellious inner posture out of their bodies. If children respond to the work tool and make wise choices, they return to relational harmony. If they choose to stay in their rebellious attitude, you have another power tool to use—exercises.

But before discussing how to use exercise as a disciplinary tool, I want to be very sure I've been clear about the goal of these disciplinary tools. Let's take some time in the next chapter to see what a positive attitude change will look like in your children and how you will know when your children's attitudes have changed.

Reflection Questions

Take a few minutes to think about these questions. If possible, discuss them with your spouse, another parent, or a group of parents. Write down your observations, feelings, and goals in a journal.

1. Have you ever worked hard on an unpleasant task and then looked back on how valuable that was for you?
2. Make a list of jobs your children can do for attitude adjustments.
3. What will be hard about making your children do work to improve their attitudes?
4. How do you think your children will respond to doing work?
5. How will you respond to your children's reactions?

A heart at peace gives life to the body.

— P r o v e r b s   1 4 : 3 0 ,   N I V

9

Recognizing a Changed Attitude

"All right, I'm sorry! I didn't mean to push her. She got in my way."

"No, Alex. Your sister did not get in your way. You walked into her. You have to walk around her," said his dad.

"Fine. I'll walk around her. Now can I go? The guys are waiting for me."

"Oh, I suppose. Just be home by ten o'clock."

"Yea, whatever."

Was Alex treating his sister and his dad with respect? Does he have a clean heart? I hope by now you can pick out a bad attitude when you see one. Alex's attitude is rotten. He carelessly knocked into his sister, blamed her for it, talked sarcastically to his dad, didn't want to take any responsibility for his action, wanted to avoid repairing any hurt he had caused her, was more concerned with spending time with his friends than his family, had no appreciation of the privilege of going out, and wouldn't commit to being home on time. I think Alex has a few attitudes to improve.

What would a clean attitude look like? How do you know for sure when the discipline is complete?

CLEAN HEARTS

When we get to this level of discipline with our children, we are looking for what I call a clean heart. In biblical language, it would be described as a "circumcised heart." More recent translations describe it as a "cleansed heart." A clean heart is characterized as soft, warm, open, cooperative, and submissive. That's how our children should be after an attitude adjustment. But what exactly does that look like?

"This is what the Lord says to the people of Judah and Jerusalem: 'Plow up the hard ground of your hearts! Do not waste your good seed among thorns. Cleanse [circumcise] your minds and hearts before the Lord, or my anger will burn like an unquenchable fire because of all your sins'" (Jer. 4:3-4). In this passage God is pleading with and warning his people to change their ways. God wants soft hearts, hearts that will allow seeds of love and truth to grow in them. God wants workable, teachable hearts.

Parents are in the role of plowing up the soil in children's hearts when those hearts get too hard. We don't want "thorns" (rebellion and arrogance) growing in the hearts of our children. We have to help our children keep their "soil" soft.

"The Lord your God will circumcise your hearts and the hearts of your descendants, so that you may love him with all your heart and with all your soul, and live" (Deut. 30:6, NIV). God is pleading with his children to submit to his purification so they can enjoy loving relationships for a long time.

UNCIRCUMCISED HEARTS

In contrast to the cleansed heart is the "uncircumcised heart." The Bible warns against uncircumcised hearts. "[The Lord says,] 'But if [Israel] will confess their sins and the sins of their fathers—their treachery against me and their hostility toward me, which made me hostile toward them so that I sent them into the land of their enemies—then when their uncircumcised hearts are humbled and they pay for their sin, I will remember my covenant with Jacob'" (Lev. 26:40-42, NIV). Passages in the New Testament also use the image: "You stiff-necked people, with uncircumcised hearts and ears! You are just like your fathers: You always resist the Holy Spirit!" (Acts 7:51, NIV).

The phrase "uncircumcised heart" is synonymous with arrogance. People whose hearts were not "circumcised" disobeyed God and had broken relationships with others. They fought back and argued with others.

Did you ever think about why God might have chosen the procedure of circumcision to seal a relationship with him (Gen. 17:11)? Is this ritual a haphazard decision? What was God thinking? What message was he sending?

I don't think God is capricious. He knew exactly what he was doing. He always does. When he instituted the practice of circumcision with his children, he did it with a purpose. His message seems to be, "I want you to submit the most private parts of yourself to me. And when you do that, there will be pain. Blood will need to be shed if you want to be associated with me. People should know that you are mine."

A circumcised heart is a clean heart. God wants us to have an attitude characterized by tenderness, a willingness to listen, an openness to receive truth, and a trust to love others. God wants us to reclaim some of our being created in his image, to reflect his innocent, trusting, vibrant heart. "True circumcision is not a cutting of the body but a change of heart produced by God's Spirit" (Rom. 2:29).

Now that we have some idea of what a clean, circumcised heart looks like, how do we know when our children's hearts are circumcised, clean? What will that look like in them?

SEEING A CLEAN HEART

Measuring a change in attitude is like trying to measure a change in the barometric pressure without a barometer. The only way to do it is by looking at the signs. A change in the air pressure can be detected in subtle ways. You have to know what to look for. A change in barometric pressure will be evidenced by different kinds of clouds, changes in wind speed or direction, or a change in temperature. Some people can even detect air-pressure changes by pain in their joints. Farmers are usually pretty good at noticing barometric changes because their lives often depend on the weather. They learn to read the signs.

We parents don't have a gauge to measure our children's attitudes, their internal posture. We don't have a little window to see into their hearts. So if we cannot precisely measure our children's attitudes, how can we tell when they have changed from rebellious to submissive? How do we know when the attitude-adjustment session is over? What instruments can we use to measure attitude change?

The only way to judge our children's internal posture is by what is external. The key to reading your children's changed attitudes is in learning to read the external clues given off by their bodies. This includes everything we can see, hear, or touch (taste and smell would not be relevant). Studies have shown that more than 80 percent of what we communicate to others is nonverbal; it is done with our bodies. Learn to read your children's body language.

The Bible also suggests that our bodies express our attitudes. God describes people with bad attitudes as "stiff-necked." This term gives a perfect physical description of an arrogant person. God describes people whose internal posture is stubborn as "hard-hearted." God gauges our hearts by what we do. A loving heart expresses itself in being kind to strangers (Matt. 25:35). A submissive heart is measured by how far we are willing to go to help people (Matt. 5:41). Our attitudes are revealed by what our bodies do in various situations.

I worked many years in child care, and I learned a phrase that I have added to my vocabulary. When staff members were talking about a student who was doing well, we would say, "Yeah, he's doing well. His face is clean" or "She's really come a long way. She's a lot cleaner now." We all knew exactly what was meant by that, and it didn't have anything to do with whether the students had washed with soap and water that morning. We use a similar image when we say that people have "cleaned up their act."

When your children have a good attitude, you will know it. It should be fairly obvious, especially when you compare the attitude to the "dirty," rebellious attitude. Instead of being grumpy and complaining, they will be happy and joyful. Experience has taught me to look for these following external clues.

SIGNS OF AN EMERGING POSITIVE ATTITUDE
In the midst of an attitude adjustment, you will eventually see some good signs surfacing in your children's bodies and voices. Keep your eyes, ears, and hands open for these signs that will help you determine if your children's attitude is softening.

1. *Tone of voice.* This is probably one of the easiest gauges of attitude. The tone of your children's voices reveals a lot of unspoken information. About 25 percent of what we communicate is done with our tone of voice. That may be part of the reason why your children do not want to say much during an attitude-adjustment session. They may not want you to know that they are still holding on to some of their bad attitudes. Listen closely for sarcasm, impatience, irritation, arguing, whining, anger, or anything that suggests they are still harboring something against you. Ask them questions. Listen not only to what they say but also to how they say it.

Sometimes when I am working with my children on a bad attitude, they talk in a monotone, robotic tone of voice. It's as if I am listening to a space alien saying the right words, but something crucial is missing. They are saying the right words, but their hollow tone of voice betrays the truth of their heart. They are saying only what they know I want to hear. There is no energy in their voices. Their lips are moving, but their hearts are immovable. When I see this lack of emotion, I know the attitude adjustment is not yet over.

When children have a gentle internal posture, they will speak in a soft, tender tone of voice. Their tone will be polite and respectful. It will have some energy and enthusiasm in it.

2. *Words.* Words are probably one of the least reliable ways to measure your children's attitudes. They can quickly and easily learn what words you want to hear and parrot them back to you. And sometimes I do tell them exactly what to say when they are practicing how to respond politely.

During the work session, I don't listen too much to what they say because I don't want them talking too much anyway. I want them working and thinking. After everything is over, I listen more to what they say. Most often I listen for how many words they use. The more words they use, the more open and vulnerable they are.

3. *Energy level.* One way to judge your children's internal posture is by the effort with which they do the work. How hard are they trying? How much elbow grease are they really using? Don't just listen to their cries of pain. Listen for their grunts of effort. Look at the speed and quality of their work. If you challenge them to work a little faster and they argue, you are hearing a bad attitude.

Give them a short goal: "Let's see if you can get this amount done in fifteen minutes with a good attitude." If you see them work very hard, you will know that their posture is moving toward cooperation and submission. They may look tired, but they should not look apathetic. If their bodies seem limp or lifeless, they are probably not putting much effort into the work. Their bodies should look connected. They should not act like rag dolls hanging together by a few threads. If they seem lethargic on the outside, they are probably listless on the inside as well. They should have some energy.

4. *General body posture.* Their movements should appear fluid. A body holding on to a bad attitude appears stiff and jerky. They need more work if they appear like that. A tense body is either fearful or angry. They have not yet let go of their rebellion.

5. *Hands and arms.* If, when I am talking to my children during an attitude-adjustment session, my children twirl their hair, rub their eyes, pick their teeth, fidget with their fingers, pick their ears, or fiddle with their shoelaces, it indicates that they are not paying attention to me. I usually ask them to put their arms down or keep their hands still. By doing so, I am removing a barrier between them and me. I'm trying to have an influence. I don't want them being distracted from me.

When they are at peace inside, their arms and hands will fall
calmly by their sides.

6. Eyes. The eyes are most definitely a "window to the
soul." Looking into my children's eyes is my favorite way to
read them. I usually don't have to say anything. I can usually
tell their attitude by taking the time to look into their eyes.

If your children won't look at you, they are probably trying
to hide something. If they are looking at your face, then they
are paying attention to you. You want them to be engaged with
you. When they have a good attitude, their eyes will look soft
and warm. They will not have any trace of that icy stare. They
should be looking at you, not through you. When their attitude is good, their eyes will appear open rather than squinty.

Your eyes need to communicate how you feel about them.
Let them see your strong and determined love. Let them see
your resolve to know them inside and out.

7. Face. Check your children's faces. Are they frowning? Are
their lips tight or relaxed? When they talk, do they barely
open their mouths? Is there even a hint of a smile? Or is it a
smirk? Are you able to make them laugh? If you can, they are
well on their way toward having a good attitude. After you
have a good laugh, you should also be able to return to the
serious matter at hand with equal ease.

8. Touching. Touching is usually very accurate in revealing
your children's attitudes. If you touch them and they pull
away from you in any way, they still want to fight you. If they
cringe at your touch, they are not yet ready to submit to you.
If they react that way, they may need more work to do.

Touching them can be more than just a way to gauge their
attitude. It can also be a tool to help them change their attitude.
Reaching out and gently touching your children on the shoulder or head is a powerful message of love for them. Touch can

sometimes melt away that last little bit of resistance. They may have some ambivalence about your touching them; this is where you need to know your children. It takes some discernment to know when they are ready to be relieved of their bad attitude and when they truly want nothing to do with you yet. If you can approach them cautiously and gently, you may be able to help them overcome their reluctance to trust and submit to you. You could even try to make it a playful moment. Sometimes some gentle tickling can break the ice.

If you touch them and they melt like butter, you know their hearts are ready to be soft, submissive, and loving. You also know they were just waiting for you to touch them. Touching has a way of helping them release any vestiges of fear or hurt. Touching helps siphon off any remaining rebellion.

I was recently touring a private boarding school for boys. The director was remarking that staff members never touch any of the boys for discipline. They will never spank or even restrain a child. He was proudly implying that touching an angry child was bad. I understand that a school has to be concerned with accusations and lawsuits, but the director seemed to be taking it further than that. He was suggesting that to touch a child during discipline was wrong.

Touching children, especially during discipline, can communicate volumes to them. Touching is a powerful, nonverbal tool to send multiple messages instantaneously. Touching can say: "I am reaching out to you. I will not let you get away. I will not let you go too far with this attitude. I am strong enough to stop this behavior, and I will if necessary. Your rude behavior and attitude do not scare me away. I love you even when you don't love me. I can control myself, and I will help you get in control of yourself."

Many times children will pull away from these sorts of

messages. Strangely, they may not want to hear them. They may like feeling angry and not want to let go of their anger. When you touch them, they feel themselves surrendering to you, and a part of them doesn't want to do that.

They may feel embarrassed that they have been so rude to you. They may be afraid that if they admit that they treated you wrongly, you will rub it in by lecturing them. Feeling humble makes us feel small. Children don't like to feel small even though they are small. That is why it is so critical to build your children up when they humble themselves. Breaking down their resistance is a big test for parents. It is a test of whether your children can feel safe with you to protect their dignity when they are weak. If they feel humiliated rather than humbled, they will fight you even harder next time. If your children do their part by humbling themselves, you have to do your part and honor them with your love. If you fail this test, you may lose their hearts. I will talk about this further in the next chapter.

When you begin to see some of these signs emerging during the attitude-adjustment process, it can be tempting to settle for the slight improvement shown. It is easy to think, *Oh, finally. They are starting to let go of this rotten attitude. Thank God! I better stop so they don't get mad again. I don't want to jeopardize their progress by pushing too hard.* Friends, that is a *big* mistake! Don't stop!

Attitude adjustment is like the birth process. Just because the baby's head is out doesn't mean the process is over. Sure, maybe the hardest part is over and the rest should come more easily, but don't quit prematurely. Finish the process. The attitude-adjustment process isn't completed until you see several signs of a new attitude. Don't settle for just one or two. Go for all the changes you can get using this tool.

When trying to ascertain whether your children have changed their attitudes, use this general rule of thumb: If you aren't sure whether you are seeing a changed attitude, you probably aren't. A new heart is usually unmistakable. You will know one when you see one.

THE TEST

When I feel as if my children and I are nearing the end of an attitude-adjustment session, I often give them a test. I ask them to do a small job to gauge the depth of the changed attitude. It may be as simple as saying, "Honey, I left my book out in the car. Would you please bring it in for me?" or "Dugan, I noticed the trash in the kitchen needs emptying. Will you take care of it for me?" If this simple request triggers another angry outburst, then you have exposed a remnant of a bad attitude. Or the request could cement the change in their hearts into a solidly positive attitude.

Another test is given in spending some time together. Sometimes I say, "I need some help washing the car. Will you help me?" or "I have to run to the store. Come with me." This gives both of us some time to get beyond the strain of the attitude adjustment and reconnect with each other.

God tested his children to determine the depth of their commitment to him. "I did this to test Israel—to see whether or not they would obey the Lord as their ancestors did" (Judg. 2:22). Testing a positive attitude is not a sign of disbelief. Testing creates a signpost of a restored relationship.

FACING THE FUTURE

The change in your children's attitudes should last for a while. In fact, the hours—and sometimes days—after the attitude adjustment may feel like a honeymoon. However, eventually the good attitude will fade because that's human nature. But if it seems to be fading rather abruptly, you may have missed something.

If your children claim they have good attitudes, promise to cooperate, and give every impression they truly have changed but the change lasts for only an hour, then they got away with it this time. You don't have to dredge up the old battle. Just deal with the current one. Warn them that you will not tolerate the return of their bad attitudes. Remind them that there are still plenty of jobs that need to be done around the house. They may think they can wear you out, but you must persevere.

If the changed attitude doesn't last very long, consider these adjustments.

1. Make sure the expectations are clear. Review the specific expectations with your children. Have them state those expectations to you several times so you know that they know what you want them to do. It may be necessary to practice them again.

2. Make sure no one is supporting your children in their rebellion. If your children are hanging on to their bad attitudes far longer than you would reasonably expect, they may have an ally from whom they are garnering strength to resist your efforts. Obvious people to consider are their friends or maybe even a teacher or television character. But do not forget the possibility that they may have found an ally in an aunt, uncle, grandparent, or a sibling. You may need to take steps to reduce or even cut off their supply line of negative influence. It could be as simple as having a heart-to-heart talk with the other person. A commonly overlooked place for children to acquire an ally is in the other parent. This will be discussed further in chapter 14.

3. Assess whether you stopped the attitude adjustment prematurely. You may be letting your children off the hook too early with their attitude adjustment. It will take time and experience for you to develop a sense for knowing when their attitudes are as good as they should be. If you are too lenient at first, that is all right. Leniency can work for you. It makes you seem more than fair if you have to get tougher next time. You can in all honesty say, "When we quit here last time, it didn't last too long. We are going to take this attitude adjustment further this time so we won't have to do this so often." This is where the "tests" after the sessions may come in handy.

Summary

Discerning when your children have changed their attitudes is very important. Your children's external bodies will reveal their internal posture. You should see a "clean" demeanor and feel the warmth and friendliness in their bodies. You should hear respect in their voices. If you pay attention to these signals your children give off, you will get a fairly accurate reading on their attitudes.

Adjusting your children's attitudes can be difficult. It will take a lot of practice. We all know how deceptive and wicked the human heart can be (Jer. 17:9). Kids will throw a lot of curves at us. Don't get discouraged. Your children are worth the struggle.

I do have one last power tool to present to you. But before I get to that, I want to discuss the key part of this whole process: restoration of the relationship between you and your children. Returning the relationship to harmony is the whole point of these power tools, but if we just focus on the tools themselves, the process is unfinished. Not restoring the relationship would be like running twenty-five miles of a twenty-six-mile marathon. You don't want to quit right before you finish what you've worked so hard to achieve.

■ ■ ■ Reflection Questions

Take a few minutes to think about these questions. If possible, discuss them with your spouse, another parent, or a group of parents. Write down your observations, feelings, and goals in a journal.

1. Attitude adjustment takes time. Are you willing to stay with it until your children's hearts become clean?
2. What are you willing to sacrifice?
3. Describe the signs that will indicate your children have clean hearts and good attitudes.
4. Describe the signs that will indicate your children have dirty hearts and bad attitudes.
5. Who are your children's negative allies? What can you do to minimize the negative influence and increase your influence?
6. What do you expect to be the most challenging part of discerning a positive attitude?
7. What test will you use to see if your children's attitudes are cooperative?

*You would not be pleased with sacrifices, or I would
bring them. If I brought you a burnt offering, you
would not accept it. The sacrifice you want is a
broken spirit. A broken and repentant heart,
O God, you will not despise.*

— P s a l m   5 1 : 1 6 - 1 7

10

Restoring Intimacy with Your Children

"You make me sick." Mandy's words could not cut more if
she used a knife.

"You seem pretty angry," says her mom, trying to salvage
this conversation.

"No kidding, Sherlock."

"Mandy, now calm down. Stop being so nasty. Let's talk
about this."

"Why bother? You never listen. Besides, I'm sixteen. I don't
have to listen to you anymore." Her venom is getting dead-
lier. Her mom is reeling from the sting.

"Mandy, please . . ."

"Just forget it. I've been planning on leaving anyway. I
might as well do it now. I'll come back in the morning to get
my stuff." Her venom is poisoning herself too.

"But where will you go?"

"Anywhere I want to! Somewhere where I won't have to listen to you anymore." Mandy's parting words clang endlessly
in her mom's head.

■ ■ ■

You can just feel the ripping and tearing in the relationship between Mandy and her mom. You can hear the unmistakable sounds of a relationship dying. It is painful to listen to. We've all been through it. Sometimes words like those rattle around in our heads for a lifetime. We try to drown them out or calm them down, but they never seem to go away.

We long to hear different words. Our ears strain to pick up that voice saying, "I miss you. I know I hurt you terribly. I'm so sorry. Can you ever forgive me? I love you." These sincere words can hasten the healing of most wounds.

The purpose of all this disciplinary work is not just to win the battle of the wills. We want to win our children's hearts. We want to live in harmonious relationship with each other. We need to show our children that respect and submission are prerequisites to harmony. Attitudes of rebellion and selfishness tend to subvert these goals. When children have a bad attitude and are disobedient, relationships get very strained. If the tension lasts too long, the relationship runs the risk of being broken. Our goal must be to restore the strained relationship before it becomes a broken relationship. Let's repair the minor tears before the fabric is completely torn in two. The goal of any attitude-adjustment session is not only a softened heart but also a restored heart—restored to cleanliness, restored to God, and restored to you.

This chapter is the "heart" of the book. This is where you get your ROI, "return on investment." This chapter will give you the ingredients necessary to restore the relationship with your children after a disciplinary session with them.

Restoring your strained relationship involves seven

stages—pain, brokenness, remorse and sorrow, repentance, forgiveness, reconnecting, and celebration. Each instance of reconciliation will be different, but varying amounts of these ingredients will be involved in every occurrence.

Restoring the relationship is a process. By identifying these seven factors, I run the risk of making it sound too easy. Sometimes it's a little more complex than simply combining these seven things to have a good relationship. The process is more mysterious than can be explained in one chapter or book. My intent in identifying and discussing these ingredients is to give you something to look for when you are in the midst of this process.

The apostle Paul confronted the new church in Corinth about several things. You can read all about that in his letter called 1 Corinthians. Apparently Paul got some criticism for the pain his words caused in that young church. In his second letter to those same people he said, "I am no longer sorry that I sent that letter to you, though I was sorry for a time, for I know that it was painful to you for a little while. Now I am glad I sent it, not because it hurt you, but because the pain caused you to have remorse and change your ways. It was the kind of sorrow God wants his people to have, so you were not harmed by us in any way. For God can use sorrow in our lives to help us turn away from sin and seek salvation. We will never regret that kind of sorrow. But sorrow without repentance is the kind that results in death" (2 Cor. 7:8-10).

From the tone of this letter, it sounds like Paul felt bad for hurting their feelings with his first letter. Then he realized that his sharp words had served their purpose. It is that way with disciplining children. The painful journey is necessary to achieve the goal.

Pain

Whenever I use the words *pain* and *children* in the same sentence, I cringe. Pain is something we usually protect our children from. We all try to avoid pain.

But pain is not the enemy. Pain is an effective tool that warns us of danger. It is designed to wake us up. C. S. Lewis says, "Pain is God's megaphone to rouse a deaf world." When nothing else works, pain will help you get your children's attention.

God used pain to motivate his children. The people of Israel were so stubborn that God had to use it quite often. Pain was not God's first choice in disciplining his children, but he was not hesitant about using it. For several illustrations of God using this tool, read the entire book of Judges. It shows how severely and often God used pain to discipline his children.

At times, parents have to use pain in order to prevent further harm to their children. The general principle is very simple: *The pain of disobedience has to be greater than the pleasure of rebellion.* When children disobey, the consequences of their disobedience have to be stronger than the payoff. With each level of discipline, the pain level slightly increases. Instead of rewards for obedience, they need to feel the pain of disobedience. The greater the disobedience, the more painful the consequences need to be.

That's why the pain tool is definitely "For Mature Adults Only." This tool in the wrong hands can do needless damage. Parents are the most qualified to use the tool because they know their children.

Don't assume that pain is always just physical. Pain could also be emotional or relational. My youngest brother didn't need a lot of discipline. All my mom had to do was look at him sternly, and he would get tears in his eyes. He was a very tenderhearted boy. Unfortunately, not all children are quite so easily corrected. Some kids need firmer measures.

BROKENNESS

Pain should eventually bring children to a point of brokenness. Being broken doesn't mean that children will be shattered into pieces. In Hebrew the word *brokenness* literally means "to rub together." The image is that of stones rubbing together in a stream so they eventually become smooth. That is a good description for what an attitude adjustment is like. It rubs the rough edges off attitudes that are stubborn, argumentative, selfish, and disrespectful. An attitude adjustment makes our children's attitudes smoother.

Brokenness is a close cousin of submissiveness, but it is a state that isn't arrived at easily. The "rubbing together" generates some friction and heat. As you know by now, the method of being broken is not for the fainthearted. It is intense both for the person doing the rubbing and the person receiving the rubbing. Sometimes it takes a lot of rubbing to get the fight out of children.

Sometimes brokenness is not always easy to detect. Often it is inferred from the absence of negative outbursts. One minute your children may be yelling or crying but shortly thereafter, they are sitting quietly or doing what they were asked to do. You may be tempted to poke them to see if they are still alive. If they are truly broken, there will be no more fight in them. This is where testing them will confirm that they are broken.

God says brokenness is a vital component in restoring a relationship to health. Scripture reminds us, "The sacrifice you [God] want is a broken spirit. A broken and repentant heart, O God, you will not despise" (Ps. 51:17). Sacrifice was the Old Testament system used by the children of Israel to restore their relationship with God. Without their sacrifices, their relationship with God would be permanently severed. This verse says that the sacrifice God desires is our broken spirit and heart. When we are broken, we are like soft, malleable clay, which God can mold and use (Jer. 18:6).

REMORSE AND SORROW

Remorse is a gnawing ache stemming from the guilt of past wrongs. It is the pain we feel in the pit of our stomachs when we realize we have done something terribly wrong. If your children feel remorse, it means that they realize the impact of what they did, and they feel ashamed for the hurt they caused.

Sorrow is a feeling of deep grief or sadness. Feeling bad for disobedience is a necessary part of restoring a damaged relationship. That goes for any age, but especially for children. Their sorrow should be evident.

When your children express sorrow, they will probably cry. That's common. Children can't hide their feelings as well as adults can. Give your children the freedom and safety to express their emotions without any shame whatsoever. Tears help a great deal to cleanse their hearts.

Not all children will cry. If your children seem tender, that is all that is necessary. Of the six stages, this one is probably least important. Feeling remorse or sorrow is more evidence of a deeper change, but their future attitude and behavior are what you really care about.

Your children may express their sorrow or remorse primarily with their words and tone of voice. You may hear them say things like "I'm so sorry" or "I feel really bad now" or "I feel sick like I might throw up." These words are evidence of sorrow and mean that your children are turning the corner from the darkness toward the light. As Paul says in 2 Corinthians, sorrow should lead to repentance (2 Cor. 7:10).

REPENTANCE

Repentance involves a change of direction. It is more than just a decision to turn *away* from sin; it also means deciding to turn *toward* a positive attitude and behavior. Repentance means turning from disobedience to obedience, from a negative to a positive attitude. It is a change of heart.

Since repentance is a decision, the evidence of it initially is found through words. Repentant children will have to tell you that they want to change their direction. Their words will manifest their thoughts. Speaking their thoughts aloud is just like writing them into a contract. Most of us call this conversation an apology. The apology is one of the ingredients you have been working so hard for, one of the fruits of your labor.

An attitude adjustment without an apology would be like having a wedding without the vows. The entire ceremony culminates with the bride and groom speaking their vows to each other. Everyone strains to hear them speak their words of love and devotion. The past has brought them to this point, and their future will never be the same. Their entire relationship is captured in a few sober moments of deep meaning.

As with any vows or words, only time will tell if those words are lived out. The sincerity of an apology can be tested only by what your children do in the future. In order to make this apology as meaningful as possible, take your time with this process.

Some parents are very uncomfortable with an apology. They think that requiring an apology is rubbing in the offense. They don't want their children to feel bad, so they just quickly fly by the apology. They would just as soon forget the issue and pretend it didn't happen. Please don't abort the process at this point or rush through this phase.

Many children are very uncomfortable with apologizing. It brings to the surface everything in this entire process. It is somewhat painful to have to face the truth about what they did. They would just as soon avoid their responsibility to deal with it. But this aspect of restoring the relationship is crucial.

Many times children have to be taught exactly how to apologize. You may have to walk them through an apology until they have done it a few times. It is another of the many expectations they need to learn from you. Take the time to teach them well.

Teach Your Children to Apologize

An apology has four ingredients, each one critical in making the apology complete. An effective apology will encompass these four vital statements:

1. *"I was wrong when I . . ."* Apologies need to be very specific. An apology should identify a particular offense. Your children's apologies should arise from one of four possible scenarios:

- They *did* something they should not have done.
- They *didn't do* something they should have done.
- They *said* something they should not have said.
- They *didn't say* something they should have said.

When your children say, "I was wrong when I . . . ," they indicate that they know that what they did was wrong. They have no excuse for what they did. They admit their responsibility for the action. This statement is a confession of guilt.

A true apology will *not* include any hint of excuses like these:

- "But I didn't mean to!"
- "I couldn't help it."
- "It was an accident."
- "He did it first."
- "She started it."
- "Why do I always get in trouble? She never does."

If your children offer these kinds of excuses, they are revealing an internal posture that is still resistant. If your children cannot say, "I was wrong," they are unrepentant. Your children should continue on with the attitude-adjusting work until you see more evidence of true repentance.

"I was wrong when I . . ." really says, "I admit that I am accountable for my actions. No one else is to blame for what I do." Wouldn't that be refreshing to hear in today's world? Let's teach children the importance of standing up and assuming responsibility for their actions.

2. *"I'm sorry for . . ."* This statement expresses the sorrow your children feel about their offense. An apology is not just mumbling, "Sorry." They should say the entire phrase so the other person knows exactly what they are sorry for.

Even if your children don't have much sorrow, they should still say they are sorry to the offended person. It should be more than perfunctory, but it doesn't have to be tearful. Saying it to the offended person's face is a humbling experience, especially if it is a sibling. Feeling humbled may help motivate your children to avoid doing it again.

Your children should have at least some feelings of remorse. If you don't sense many of those feelings, you may have to help them remember a time they got hurt. By reminding them of their pain, you are teaching them how to have some compassion for others. They should be able to appreciate the seriousness of the hurt they caused the person they are apologizing to.

3. *"Next time I will . . ."* This statement is the essence of repentance. It indicates a turning away from the offense, a change of heart. This statement implies a new direction in their future behavior. Ask your children to state in a positive way what they will say or do the next time. Help them visualize what a changed direction will look like. Repentance is a promise to try to do better.

4. *"Will you please forgive me for . . . ?"* Each of the four statements is important, but this one is critical. It is the clincher. An apology without asking for forgiveness would be like saying the wedding vows but without the final "I do." Something crucial would be missing without hearing those words. Asking for forgiveness is the "Yes, I do" of an apology. It is what everyone came to hear. Unless your children ask to be forgiven, their internal posture is still not completely submissive.

Asking for forgiveness is a humbling experience. It should be. They should feel the discomfort their behavior has generated in the relationship. Their offense has introduced a wound or debt. The debt is incurred because the offensive behavior took something from the offended person. More than likely it took away some of the person's respect or dignity. That's what rudeness or insults do. Seeking forgiveness is asking to be released from debt. Forgiveness is an unmerited favor, a gift. Seeking forgiveness is asking to be set free from the fear of retribution. It is asking that this incident never be brought up again. That may be overly optimistic, but your children should be able to expect that you will not seek retaliation. Revenge is not an option once forgiveness is asked for and granted. That is true freedom.

Usually at least one of these four statements is very difficult for children to say aloud. However, insist that they say it. If you avoid the awkwardness of the moment, you will miss one of the most tender, intimate moments in human relationships. Take it slowly. Do not rush through this experience. Whatever you do, do not forgive them until they have asked you to forgive them. Saying the phrase "Will you please forgive me for . . ." is an integral ingredient of this whole phase.

Practically speaking, at first you may have to tell your children exactly what to say and how to say it. Spell it out for them. Have them repeat what you say. Teach them. Don't worry about getting too detailed. God likes the details. Just read through the book of Leviticus. God is explicit in what he wants Israel to do, when to do it, and in what order he wants it done. No, God is not controlling. He just knows what is best for us. He knows what needs to be done for our own good. He knows how foolish we can be, and he doesn't want to leave anything to chance.

Learning how to apologize may be the most important relational skill you ever pass on to your children. Without it, they will be crippled in their ability to repair the inevitable damage they will inflict on others. This inability may develop into a pattern of unresolved damage to relationships that will alienate them from others and even from God.

FORGIVENESS

When God confronted Adam and Eve in the Garden of Eden, he did not leave them feeling ashamed in their nakedness. God did not make them endure the humiliation of vulnerability any longer than was necessary. After God pronounced their sentence, he restored their dignity by replacing their flimsy leaves and clothing them with durable, more adequate animal skins (Gen. 3:21). He reassured them that he still cared for them by covering them up so they wouldn't live in a constant state of shame. We need to reassure our repentant children of our love for them so that they don't live in shame.

Granting forgiveness is the best part of this entire process. You have humbled your children by confronting their disobedience, breaking their rebellious internal posture, and leading them through repentance. Your children's tender hearts are ready for you. The process of forgiving them will now restore your relationship to harmony.

Forgiving your children is one of the most simple yet profound experiences you will ever have with them. When you say those three special words "I forgive you," you are performing a miracle. You are breathing life back into your relationship with them. You are freeing your children to live without guilt and fear.

Don't forget your own need for forgiveness. If you have lost touch with your own sinfulness, you run the risk of treating your children harshly. You are to be like the Old Testament high priest to your children: "[Every high priest] is able to deal gently with those who are ignorant and are going astray, since he himself is subject to weakness" (Heb. 5:2, NIV).

Always forgive your children—*always*. You will crush them if you do not forgive them. Not forgiving your children is abusive. It leaves them emotionally crippled, far worse than if you had hit them with your fist. They will be starving for your love. If they don't get enough from you, there are others who will offer them a mirage of love. Give your children the real thing.

RECONNECTING

Administering an attitude adjustment is similar to performing a medical operation. They are both radical and should be pretty rare. They are invasive procedures and involve altering or removing something from inside the body. Surgeons repair defective tissue, and parents repair defective attitudes. Surgeons remove diseased organs while parents work to remove a diseased attitude.

In Luke 11:24-26 Jesus talks to his disciples about evil spirits living in a person. Jesus says that when an unclean spirit is eradicated from a person, something else needs to fill the void left behind. If the space is left empty, it will just fill up again, but with even more evil than was there originally.

I think this principle also applies to parents when they extract a bad attitude from their children. I am *not* saying that a bad attitude is an evil spirit (in the way Jesus was using the term). I am saying that we parents need to replace that rebellious attitude in our children with a positive attitude. If we don't, then we are inviting that negative attitude back again. You have spent considerable time and energy breaking down your children's resistance. Now is the time to build them up and put them back together.

Practically speaking, celebration and reconnection look like this. Your children need four tangible things from you at this point: words, touching, looks, and time. These ingredients are critical because they reassure your children how loved they truly are.

Words

The words you speak build your children's sense of worth. Just as children need to confess their shortcomings aloud, you need to fill their heart with words about their value to you. Refresh their memory and spirit with their significance by telling them how important they are to you.

Tell them how talented they are. Tell them specifically what you love about them. List the specific attributes you find most appealing about them. Remind them of times when they have shown their admirable qualities. Tell them specifically what makes them so unique and special. Fill them with praise until they are full. And whatever you do, don't use this as a time to lecture. Lecturing will only alienate your children. This is a time to replenish and give nourishment with your words.

Touching

When you forgive your children, take them into your arms and say, "Yes, I forgive you. I love you very, very much." Touching your children in a tender manner is an absolute must if you want them to *feel* forgiven. It doesn't matter how averse you or your children are to touching; if you don't touch them, you will lose this golden opportunity. You can express tender touching to your children any way possible: holding hands with them, holding them on your lap, rubbing their forearms, stroking their hair, etc. Something physiological happens with touch. Touching changes the body's chemistry and helps your children relax much quicker. They can literally feel your tenderness. You will see an appreciable difference after you touch them. They should be willing to be close to you. By this point, they should be relaxed and friendly.

If you are holding your children, do it for as long as they will let you. The feelings of intimacy between you and your children at this moment will rival every other loving moment you can have with them. You and your children are in the afterglow of your intense encounter. The feelings of openness, closeness, and trust after a successful discipline session are about as sweet as it gets. Both you and your children will come out of the attitude adjustment feeling physically tired but relationally refreshed, renewed, and reconnected in a new way. This is a bonding experience like no other.

Forgiving your children and holding them on your lap helps your children draw nourishment from you. They are like sponges, absorbing your love and strength through your closeness. You don't want to miss it.

Some children may be a little hesitant to allow you to touch them. Playful tickling or wrestling may break that last bit of hesitation to being close. It may help them bridge the gap between you. Hesitating to move near you may mean that they have some residual pain or that they may be harboring some resentment. If you think they have something to say, give them a chance. Listen to them.

Whatever you do, find a way to make the atmosphere feel friendly again. If you sense that there may still be a problem, it's too late to return to any of the power discipline tools, but you could try one thing. Spend some time together. Have them join you in your errands or work around the house. Then that last bit of "fog" may evaporate into the air. Don't let them avoid you. Stay together until things feel right between you.

Looks

Forgiving is a time to send some messages by the look on your own face. Let your eyes say, "I will always love you." They should be as soft and tender as possible. Whatever you do, do not look away. Hold their gaze for as long as they want to. They want to bask in your warm attention.

They are also scrutinizing you, looking for your approval. Their primary question is, "Do you still love me even though I messed up?" If your eyes say you love them, they think, *If you still love me, then I must be OK.* Be sure they receive that message clearly from your eyes. The message you send at this moment will last a lifetime.

This is also a time for you to look deeply into their eyes,

down into the depths of their innermost being. You can shine the spotlight of your gaze down into their depths. It is like one final sweep of a searchlight.

Time

Nothing else is more important than reconnecting with your children at this moment. Everything else can wait. Don't interrupt this time for any reason. Your relationship is bonding together; give it sufficient time to let the glue dry. This reconnecting moment is one of the most intense, intimate moments you will have with your children. Make forgiveness a memorable occasion for both of you. Restoring a relationship is deeply rewarding. Don't rush it.

Whether your children want to sit on your lap for thirty seconds or thirty minutes, let them. They will let you know when they are ready to get up. They will tell you when they are full of your love. Don't frustrate or disappoint them by leaving them hungry for more. Study your children's face and body closely. This is what innocent, loved, loving children look like. This is how they should appear the majority of the time.

Capturing this moment is like writing both of your initials in the cement before it dries. You want to help them remember the moment as a fond memory. They will soon forget the pain if you can cement these good feelings nice and deep. Devoting sufficient time to this process protects your children from feeling like another chore on your to-do list.

Some Final Thoughts

This intimate, winding-down time is a perfect time to offer amnesty. As long as you are both "cleaning house," you might as well try to do as thorough a job as possible. You could say, "You know, as long as we're doing this, you may want to take this opportunity to confess anything else. I'm in a very forgiving spirit right now. Plus I think you would feel a whole lot better unburdening yourself of any more garbage." It should go without saying that amnesty means just that—no reprisals or lectures, just forgiveness (Prov. 19:11). If you try to do anything else with this confession, you will never get another one like it.

Take special care not to minimize this moment. Do not say things like "Oh, that's all right. It was no big deal. Don't worry about it." If you treat this moment casually, your children will not appreciate the importance of being forgiven. If you don't take it seriously, you run the risk of belittling them. Forgiveness in never a trivial event. Don't treat it lightly.

You want your children to feel loved. If you don't give them the words, touch, looks, or time necessary, you leave them feeling vulnerable and naked. They have nothing to counteract their feelings of self-doubt. Don't focus anymore on how they disobeyed. You want them to remember how much you love them. You want them to know that they are worth all this effort.

Examples

Before I move on to the section on celebration, I want to give you a couple of sample conversations showing how the process of restoring a relationship might sound. The frustrating part is that I cannot convey the tone of voice, length of pauses between comments, eye contact, facial expressions, how touching might look, and how to respond to your children's nonverbal messages. Help me out by imagining a tender love scene. Bring that image and those feelings to these dialogues.

Five-year-old Kurt has just been disciplined for refusing to put his toys away—even when his mom offered to help—and having a temper tantrum when his mom wouldn't let him go out and play. Kurt's dad offered to help with Kurt's attitude, so the mother invited him to take over since she was exhausted. Dad made Kurt sweep off the deck until every single leaf and twig were on the grass. It took Kurt a good hour to finish that to his dad's satisfaction. Then Kurt came in and put all his toys away perfectly. His heart had grown softer as evidenced by his calmer tone of voice, quicker response time to his dad's requests, and generally subdued, cooperative attitude.

This is how an apology might sound:

Dad: "Are you ready to apologize?"

Kurt: "Yes. I'm sorry."

Dad: "What did you do wrong?"

Kurt: "I yelled at Mommy."

Dad: "Yes, you did. But that isn't why we disciplined you. What did you do wrong?"

Kurt: "Umm . . . I dunno."

Dad: "What happened when Mommy asked you to put your toys away?"

Kurt: "Oh, yeah. I didn't want to."

Dad: "And what did you do?"

Kurt: "I yelled."

Dad: "You argued with Mommy. You said you were not going to do it because you didn't want to. Isn't that right?"

Kurt: "Yeah."

Dad: "Yeah, what?"

Kurt: "I argued with Mommy and said I wouldn't put my toys away."

Dad: "Is it all right to argue with Mommy?"

Kurt: "No."

Dad: "What are you supposed to say when Mommy asks you to put your toys away?"

Kurt: "I dunno."

Dad: "You are supposed to say, 'OK, Mommy. I'll put my toys away.' Now try it."

Kurt: "OK, Mommy. I'll put my toys away."

Dad: "Good. That's what I want you to say next time."

Kurt: "OK."

Dad: "Are you sorry you argued with Mommy?"

Kurt: "Yes."

Dad: "Yes, what?"

Kurt: "I'm sorry I argued with Mommy."

Dad: "What do you need to say to Mommy?"

Kurt: "I'm sorry."

Dad: "And what else?"

Kurt: "I dunno."

Dad: "Do you need to ask Mommy to forgive you?"

Kurt: "Yes."

Dad: "Are you ready to ask her?"

Kurt: "Yes."

Dad: "OK, I'll get her." (Kurt's dad calls the mother into the room.) "Kurt has some things to say to you."

Kurt: "I'm sorry for arguing with you, Mommy."

Dad: "And what else?"

Kurt: "I forget."

Dad: "What did you do wrong?"

Kurt: "I was wrong for arguing with you, Mommy."

Dad: "And what else?"

Kurt: "Da-a-ad . . ." (He whines.)

Dad: "Kurt, you know what you need to say."

Kurt: "But, Dad. I said I was sorry." (We are seeing some reluctance for this painfully vulnerable process.

This is good. It will help remind Kurt the next time
he is tempted to argue.)

Dad: "Yes, but we are going to do this right. You need to
tell Mommy what you did wrong, that you are
sorry, that next time you will say 'OK', and then ask
her to forgive you."

Kurt: "I was wrong for arguing with you about putting my
toys away. I'm sorry, Mommy. Next time I'll say OK
when you ask me, and . . ." (Kurt pauses. Tears are
forming in his eyes. Tears are also building in his
mom's and dad's eyes, but they let Kurt struggle
with getting these next critical words out himself.)
"Will you please forgive me?" (Kurt is staring at the
floor. Tears are falling.)

Mom: (pulling Kurt near to her) "Yes, I forgive you."
(Now the tears really flow—from everyone. No one
talks for a long time. Mom just cradles Kurt; Dad
rubs his back. Finally Kurt sits up straight and looks
at his mom. Mom looks deep into his eyes with
tenderness and smiles. Kurt looks at his dad. Dad
also looks back softly.)

Dad: "We love you, Kurt." (Kurt just smiles.) "You know,
I'm really proud of you, Kurt."

Kurt: "Why?" (He sounds confused but interested.)

Dad: "A lot of boys wouldn't have the courage to apologize the way you just did."

Kurt: "Really?"

Dad: "No. They would have kept arguing and sweeping.
But you decided to admit you were wrong. That
shows me you have good character."

Kurt: "Well, my arms were getting tired of sweeping."

Dad: "That's true. But even that doesn't stop some boys. They just keep on arguing."

Kurt: "Well, I'm not going to do that again."

Dad: "I'm glad. I don't want to have to make you do that kind of work again."

Kurt: "You mean I won't have to sweep the deck again?"

Dad: "No, that's not what I mean. But you won't have to sweep it because you were refusing to cooperate with Mom. You will sweep it because you are being helpful."

Kurt : (thinks for a minute) "Yeah, and when I do it that way, everyone will be happier."

Dad: "That's right. Everyone will be happier."

Kurt: "Especially me."

Dad: "That's right. How about being helpful right now and setting the table for supper?"

Kurt: "OK. Can I set the silverware?"

Dad: "Sounds good to me. What do you want me to do?"

Kurt: "You get the big dishes."

Dad: "OK."

Kurt: "Daddy, I love you."

Dad: "I love you too, Son."

■ ■ ■

This is a conversation with twelve-year-old Sara, who is familiar with this apology expectation.

Dad: "Are you ready to cooperate?"

Sara: "Yes, Dad."

Dad: "Do you remember what started all this?"

Sara: "Yes, Dad. I got into an argument with Mom about the dishes."

Dad: "And then what happened?"

Sara: "I called her a name and walked out the door."

Dad: "Is it OK to talk like that and treat your mom like that?"

Sara: "No, Dad."

Dad: "What are you going to do next time?"

Sara: "I'll put away the dishes without arguing, and I'll say, 'OK, Mom' in a pleasant voice."

Dad: "And what if you don't feel like putting away the dishes?"

Sara: "Well, I guess I shouldn't call her a name?"

Dad: "Are you asking me?"

Sara: "No. I shouldn't call Mom any names."

Dad: "And why not?"

Sara: "Because that's not nice, and it's not true."

Dad: "What could you say if you don't feel like doing it?"

Sara: "I dunno."

Dad: "Well, you could say, 'I really get tired of putting away these stupid dishes. When I get my own place, I'm just gonna buy paper plates so I don't have to wash another dish for the rest of my life.' How does that sound?"

Sara: "Sounds good to me. Should I set the table with the paper plates tonight?"

Dad: "Very cute. Nice try."

Sara: (thinks about her dad's idea to verbalize how much she hates the dishes) "Yeah, I suppose I could say that. I am sick and tired of washing those dishes."

Dad: "Tell me about it. That's why we had you. We needed a dishwasher"

Sara: "Cute, Dad."

Dad: "So what about the walking away from Mom?"

Sara: "I guess that wasn't too cool."

Dad: "You're right. It wasn't cool. It was cold!"

Sara: "I know. I was just so mad."

Dad: "Yeah, but walking away made it worse with Mom."

Sara: "But I didn't want to talk about it then."

Dad: "OK, you don't have to talk about it. Just take care of the dishes like you were asked. But whatever you do, don't leave in a huff, especially after calling your mother names. I won't stand for that!"

Sara: "OK."

Dad: "Are you ready to talk to Mom?"

Sara: "I guess. I've got a lot to say to her, don't I?"

Dad: "I'll say. But I think you'll feel a lot better afterward."

Sara: "Yeah, I like the 'afterward' part. I just hate getting there."

Dad: "I hear you." (Dad waits and watches her face. He's looking for that deep sigh of trying to gather as much courage as possible. She finally looks up and sighs. Dad touches her shoulder for encouragement.) "Ready?"

Sara: "Yeah."

Dad: "Honey, could you come in here? Sara has a few things to say." (Mom enters the room and sits next to Dad. Sara only glances at her. She is embarrassed.)

Sara: "Mom, I should have put away the dishes even though I didn't want to." (She pauses as if she is losing her conviction.)

Dad: (firmly but encouragingly) "Keep going."

Sara: "And I shouldn't have called you that name, and I shouldn't have walked away from you. I'm sorry. Next time I'll do my job and just talk about how much I hate those dishes rather than taking it out on you." (Long pause. Sara is looking at the floor.)

Dad: "You're almost done."

Sara: "Will you forgive me?"

Mom: "Yes, honey. I forgive you." (Mom reaches over and gives Sara a hug. Sara just lets out a big sigh. They embrace for a few seconds while Dad watches. Finally Dad breaks the silence.)

Dad: "Good job, Sara. You showed a lot of maturity to take responsibility for what you did and to admit it was wrong."

Sara: "Thanks, Dad. I couldn't have done it without you."

Dad: (teasingly) "You mean you *wouldn't* have done it without me."

Sara: (smiling) "Whatever."

Dad: "Well, it's just nice to have things all patched up."

Sara: "Yeah. I like it like this."

Mom: "Me too. Sweetheart, do you remember that time Sara was so mad at you and she didn't know what to call you? All she could think of was, 'You bad man!'"

Dad: "Yeah, and I had to bite my lip from smiling because I knew she was so mad at me, and I didn't want to make her think I was laughing at her."

Sara: "Yeah, I still think you're a bad man."

Dad: "Yeah, but now I can smile and you know I still love you."

Sara: "I guess."

Dad: "Whoa. Wait a minute. Really, honey? You have to guess?" (Sara looks up at her dad with some sadness in her eyes. Her dad moves over next to her and puts his hand on her knee.) "Oh, honey. Now

I'm sorry. I love you very much. You are my favorite daughter."

Sara: "Dad, I'm your only daughter."

Dad: "There, see? That proves it. But seriously, I can't wait to see you when I get home. I smile while driving home thinking of all the life you explode with when I come through the door. You always make my coming home so exciting. I can't wait to hear about your day."

Sara: "Really?"

Dad: "Yes. Really. I love you very much." (He envelops her in his arms. Sara resists for a split second, but then melts in his embrace. They sit like that for about twenty minutes while Dad recounts his favorite memories of his life with Sara. Sara just drinks it all in while feeling her dad's tender strength all around her.)

CELEBRATION

It may sound strange to be discussing celebrating after what may have been a painful experience. But celebration puts the icing on the cake. This is the time to celebrate the return of your harmony. Find some way to commemorate this experience, especially the fact that it ended so well.

This is exactly what Scripture teaches us to do. God would often instruct his children to pile up stones to build an altar to mark the spot where something significant occurred (Gen. 12:7; Exod. 24:4; Judg. 6:24). When the people passed by the pile of stones at a later date, they would remember the significant event that had occurred there. The father of the prodigal son killed the fatted calf to celebrate the return his son, who "was dead and has now returned to life" (Luke

15:23). At the Communion table we celebrate the Lord's death, which brought us salvation.

This celebration with your children doesn't have to be something as extravagant as killing the fatted calf. Personally, I'm saving our fatted calf to celebrate the Cubs winning the World Series. The point is just to do something, no matter how minor. Find some way to signify that the air is clear and there is no trace of lingering pain or hostility. Manifest your restored relationship in some tangible way. Even a photo may suffice in a pinch.

Last year I had to discipline Dugan for lying. After it was all over, I wanted to commemorate the experience. He is getting a little too old for a hug, a dish of ice cream, or a bag of balloons to mean much to him. And the offense of lying seemed to warrant more than just playing catch in the backyard. It needed to be a little more special. Ever since we traveled to watch the Olympic games in Atlanta, Dugan has been an avid supporter of Coca-Cola. The gas station was selling a case of Coke for five dollars, so I sneaked over there to get one. I returned and presented him with a case of Coke to commemorate his commitment to honesty. Every time he drank one of those Cokes, he was reminded of how much he was loved. That was the best five-dollar investment I have ever made.

Special food or drink along with the anticipation while traveling to get it is one of the best ways to commemorate the end of something and the beginning of something else. Food is a physical symbol of love. The pleasure of eating food together is an intimate activity that can have a powerful effect on our memory. Celebrate!

Summary

Restoring your relationship with your children after helping them clean up a bad attitude is a deeply satisfying experience.

It usually involves seven stages: pain, brokenness, remorse and sorrow, repentance, forgiveness, reconnecting, and celebration. The attitude adjustment is never complete without the restoration of your children's hearts to yours. This relational harmony is one of the early mirrors your children will have of what it is like to be reconciled to God.

In the last chapter I promised to offer one more power tool to use in helping to adjust your children's bad attitudes. Let me pose the question you may have been wondering about but were too polite to ask aloud: So what happens if my children won't do the work I assign them to do? What can I do if they absolutely refuse to "work out" their bad attitude? What then, buster?

Well, I'm glad you asked. Read on.

Reflection Questions

Take a few minutes to think about these questions. If possible, discuss them with your spouse, another parent, or a group of parents. Write down your observations, feelings, and goals in a journal.

1. In what ways can you model brokenness and confession to your children?
2. In what ways will you help your children learn to apologize?
3. How do you communicate forgiveness?
4. How can you improve the reconnecting phase after you discipline your children?
5. How would you describe the afterglow you feel after reconnecting?
6. How can you make the afterglow experience stronger?

7. What words of love and affirmation can you use to restore your children's hearts to your own?
8. Study the story of the Prodigal Son in Luke 15:11-32.
9. What part of this process will be difficult for you?

*Physical punishment cleanses away evil; such
discipline purifies the heart.*

— P r o v e r b s   2 0 : 3 0

11

Assigning Exercises

Our house is right next to a school yard, and as I write these
words, I can hear the football coaches yelling instructions to
the players. "Come on! Let's go, let's go, let's *go!* Hurry up!
You can run faster than that!" I remember how hard those
practices were for me—wearing all that equipment, feeling
exhausted from the heat, doing the endless calisthenics, having to repeat boring drills, and ending up with wind sprints
until we almost collapsed on the ground. Then our coach
would tell us we were just *starting* to look like football players. "Gee, thanks, Coach."

When it came to game day, the physical agony we had sub-
jected our bodies to paid off. We had the stamina to finish the
game strong and sometimes pull out a win when the other
team would tire. Sure, we would still grumble about the physical "punishment" the coaches inflicted on our bodies, but now
I can better appreciate the price it takes to finish strong.

Discipline starts with our bodies. In *The Spirit of the Disciplines* Dallas Willard writes: *"Human personality is not separable
in our consciousness from the human body. . . .* [italics added]

This fact is what makes it necessary for us to make our bodies, through the disciplines for the spiritual life, our primary focus of effort in *our* part in the process of redemption."[1]

Our children may not appreciate the discipline we are teaching them. I did not particularly appreciate all the hard work I endured in football practice, but it paid off on game day. The hard work also helped me develop other good habits, which still bear fruit in my life.

I suggested earlier in this book that we must embrace conflict with our kids. I suggested that if conflict is handled well, it will enhance the relationship. *If you continue confronting the conflict, you will connect with your kids.* But what if you have used all of the tools described so far, and your kids still won't budge? What then? This is when our commitment to that principle is really tested.

Is this the time to yell at them? Is this the time to place them in the time-out chair for half an hour? Is this the time to send them to their rooms for an hour? Is this the time to take away television or phone privileges for a week? If our children insist on sticking their big toes across the line in the sand, what should we do—cut them off? Or do we quickly retreat, drawing another line and feebly insisting they don't cross the new one?

As you know, I don't suggest any of those tools because they are ineffective. If your children haven't changed their attitudes yet, they will shortly. Remember, you are the adult. You have more strength. You are the authority. Your children will eventually surrender the battle of wills. Keep at it.

THE FINAL TOOL: EXERCISE

The final tool in the progression of discipline is exercise. Yes, that's right—good old-fashioned physical exercises as in push-ups, sit-ups, jumping jacks, pull-ups, or running. The next step in attitude adjusting is just simple, basic exertion. "The only way human character is transformed with grace is by discipline and *activity.*" [italics added][2] When your children refuse to do the work, they will have to do some calisthenics. *If your children won't work out their attitudes by working, then you will give them a workout.*

At this moment I wish I could be a fly on the wall to watch your reaction. When I first present this information at seminars, some people just roll their eyes and think, *Oh, brother, this guy is really nuts.* Other people scrunch their foreheads and think, *Did he say what I think he said—exercises?* Others snicker and think, *Yeah, right. I can't get them to work, but now they will do push-ups for me.* Others laugh right out loud and think, *Are you kidding? That will never work with my children!* Some people even get mad and think, *That is the cruelest thing I have ever heard. That must be some kind of child abuse!* Let me suggest that it is more abusive to leave your children with their deadly attitudes than it is to try to help them get free from them.

When I first heard of the exercise tool, I had all those same reactions. Your kids may even have some of those same initial reactions (as well as a few others), but not for long. I've had parents tell me their kids liked the exercises at first. But after a few repetitions, the kids realized this wasn't some new game, and it wasn't fun anymore.

When children are stubborn, they have thrown out the challenge: "I don't want to have a good attitude, and there is nothing you can do about it." Parents' internal response to that remark is, "You know, you may be right, but I'm going to give it a good try. You may never change your attitude, but I am going to make you work harder to keep it than it would be to lose it."

If you can't get your children to exorcise their own bad attitudes, then you will exercise their bad attitudes out of them. If you get to this point, remember that it is because your children have *chosen* not to soften their attitudes. This is the point at which you *choose* to respond with another level of discipline.

CONDUCTING AN ATTITUDE-ADJUSTMENT SESSION

When kids are unwilling to soften their attitudes through the work tool, they will do the exercises for no other reason than that you tell them to. If work is too complicated for them to obey, then you will make it as simple as possible. They must submit themselves completely by doing the exercises.

When we get to this point on the Progression of Discipline chart, we are at a very primal level of power. Most experts advise parents to walk away from conflict, calm down, and talk about it later. The problem with that is the message it sends to children. Children think they are stronger and have more power than their parents. While that thought is intoxicating to them, it also frightens them. Deep down inside, children know they need their parents. When parents let children off the hook here, children feel abandoned at their crisis point. This is when children need their parents to get them on the right path, even if they don't want to go there. Children feel safe, secure, and loved by parents who make this happen.

Probably the best way to illustrate this tool is to give you the dialogue of an attitude session so you can hear and feel somewhat the intensity of how it runs.

Todd is twelve years old. His sister, Missy, is nine, and his pesky brother, Alex, is five. Todd has been having lots of problems lately. He was too rambunctious on the bus ride to school, so the school personnel assigned him a seat next to his sister. They were hoping he would cooperate so he could regain the privilege of sitting with his friends. Todd picked on Missy by poking at her, sliding into her when the bus turned corners, and pretending to spit in her hair.

Todd's parents had already explained how they expected Todd to treat others. They even had him write down very specific rules of respecting others ("No pretend spitting in other people's hair" and "Sit still and talk quietly when on the school bus"). He had been assigned most of Missy's chores in order to try to teach him the importance of serving her rather than undermining her peaceful life. Todd's parents had used the work tool, assigning Todd several work assignments that took him a whole day to complete. He did them all fairly well, resulting in a few brief periods of peace and harmony. But Todd's change of heart didn't last very long.

At recess, Todd didn't stop himself from "accidentally" running into a line of children waiting to go inside. At his soccer game he got a yellow warning card for yelling at the referee. All in all, Todd has not been having a very good month.

Todd's mom and dad haven't seen their son act like this before. They are baffled as to why he would do this. They have had several talks with him. He doesn't identify any reason for his slide in behavior. He just complains: "People are picking on me. I don't do anything to deserve all this hassle." Comments like those are indicators that Todd isn't taking responsibility for his behavior or attitude. He doesn't think anything is his fault and would rather blame others for his problems.

It is becoming more obvious that Todd really thinks he is something special and doesn't have to live by the same standards that everyone else does. Todd's parents wonder if this is just "normal adolescent behavior" beginning to kick in. But they decide that if being rude is normal, then everybody is in big trouble. Todd's rude, obstinate behavior is totally unacceptable. He is a time bomb waiting to explode. Finally he does.

It's Saturday afternoon. The family has returned from doing several errands together, and Ken, Todd's dad, asks him to carry in the bags of groceries. Todd complies but makes his displeasure obvious with a loud sigh. He accentuates his not-so-subtle frustration by carelessly dropping a bag on the countertop. Todd's attitude is not lost on his dad. Todd's mom gives her husband a what-do-we-do-now? look. Missy and Alex sense the tension in the air so they hurry to hang up their coats and get out of Todd's way. Todd goes to the phone to call someone. His dad decides to give Todd a simple test and says, "Todd, will you please put away the groceries before you call anyone?"

Todd unloads. "Why do I have to do everything around here? You don't make Missy do anything. I have to do it all."

It looks as if Todd wants to have it out now. Todd's dad is a little nervous, but he's ready. "Todd, I just asked you to put the groceries away."

"I'm just sick of all this!"

"Sick of what?"

"Just everything."

"Do you want to talk about it?"

"No. But I suppose you do."

Ken takes a deep breath and tries to explain things—again. "You did some of Missy's jobs—"

"I've been doing *all* her jobs!" Todd interrupts.

"That's just not true, Todd, and you know it. You did those jobs for Missy last week because you've been so rude to her on the bus. And after you did them, I thought your attitude was better, but apparently it isn't."

"Oh, here we go with 'my attitude' again. I'm tired of hearing about 'my attitude.'"

"And we're tired of your rudeness to everyone. We're going to put a stop to it today!" Todd's dad is getting steamed now.

"I'm not doing any work either! That's stupid. It doesn't change anything."

"Apparently not. We're going to try something else today. Since you don't think work is the answer, we're going right after the heart of your bad attitude. You need some practice respecting people. I will not stand your being rude and disrespectful to us anymore. We're going to see a new Todd around here. I'm not going to be getting any more reports from the school or watching you insult the soccer referee anymore. This may come as a big surprise to you, but you are not the center of the universe. There are other people on this planet and in this house. And believe it or not, we are not all here just to serve you or take your snotty attitude. Today, right now, you need some basic practice respecting people. You are going to start with me. This is what we are going to do. I'm going to tell you what to do, and you are going to do it. Do you understand?"

Todd adopts an I-don't-care-what-you-say-or-do-to-me attitude. He gives his dad a big sigh, crosses his arms, and stares out the window, trying to look bored.

"OK, here we go. We're going to start with doing some push-ups. Get down on the floor, and give me twenty push-ups."

By this time Missy and Alex are wide-eyed looking at their dad and Todd. Ken tells his wife to take the kids to McDonald's for lunch because this will probably take awhile and this is not a spectator event. (Ken does not want to humiliate his son in front of anyone. He wants to respect Todd's dignity.)

Todd is just standing there, not sure what to do. His dad waits for the rest of the family to leave. As soon as they are gone, Ken barks, "OK, break time is over. Get down and give me twenty push-ups!"

Todd just looks at his dad without moving. He is stunned. He's not sure his dad is serious or not. He's also trying to see how determined his dad is.

Ken doesn't give him time to mount any objections. He moves closer and sternly says, "*Now!* Get down, or I will help you get down."

Todd is so shocked that he gets down and starts doing the push-ups.

"All the way down and all the way back up. Bend your arms! Don't just move your hips up and down!" Ken is remembering how his coach sounded.

"This is how I do them in gym class."

"Well, this isn't gym class. This is an attitude-adjustment class, and so far you are flunking. Now start over, and count them aloud!"

"But I already did ten of them."

"Not what I saw. You were just moving your hips up and down. Now start over."

"But I'll get my good pants dirty. Mom won't like that." Todd is grasping at straws. He doesn't want to submit at all.

"I don't care about your pants. I care about your attitude. I care about how you treat people. I care about how you obey your mother and me when we ask you to do something. And I'm going to teach you to start caring about those things more than your pants. Now start doing the push-ups!"

"One . . . two . . . three . . ."

"That's better, keep it up. All the way down and all the way up." Todd is pretty strong. He can do the push-ups fairly quickly. He is starting to burn off some of his anger and resistance.

"Eighteen . . . nineteen . . . twenty."

"Good, now just stay in the push-up position." Todd holds the "up" position on his hands and toes.

"Now, what started all this?"

"I dunno."

"Wrong answer. Give me ten more push-ups."

"I dunno why!"

"OK, we'll be here for a while then won't we?"

"But I don't know."

"OK, maybe by doing more push-ups the answer will come to you. Now do ten more. *Go!*"

Todd starts to do them.

"Count them aloud." (Todd's dad wants him to submit in every way possible.)

"One . . . two . . . three . . ."

"Do you think your attitude has anything to do with this whole thing?"

"Nine . . . ten. I dunno."

"Wrong answer. Ten more push-ups."

"What? I can't do any more. My arms hurt."

"Then I suggest you not get any more wrong answers. I gave you the right answer. Now give me ten more."

"OK, because I had a bad attitude."

"Good answer. Let's keep going in this direction. Give me ten more."

"But I said what you wanted."

"Yes, you did. The ten more was to give you another

chance to say what I've told you to say and it wasn't 'but I said what you wanted.' I want your response to be 'OK, Dad' whenever I ask you to do something."

"Ah, c'mon. I'm not gonna say that."

"Then we're going to be here a long time today."

"But I'm too tired now."

"You aren't too tired to argue with me."

"That's different."

"Yeah, I know. Your arguing tires me out. We're going to stop it today. No more arguing. Now give me ten more push-ups."

"But I can't."

"Get started. *Now!*" The anger in Ken's voice gets Todd started, and he does a few, weakly.

"Five . . . six . . . I can't do any more." He falls to the floor.

"Get up and finish them, or you will have more to do."

"But my arms hurt! I can't stand it anymore." Todd is getting angry.

"And I can't stand your rotten attitude anymore! I can't stand the way you treat your mother, sister, and brother anymore! And it's gonna stop right now! Do you understand?"

"OK, OK, but I can't do any more push-ups."

"No, Todd. Wrong answer! You are practicing doing what I tell you to do. And so far it isn't going too well. You are still arguing with me. You're still trying get by with doing the minimum. Now get up in the push-up position!"

Todd struggles up.

"That's better. Now I want to see that same kind of effort when we tell you to be nice to Missy and Alex and to respect the teachers at school and to obey the bus driver and to obey the soccer referee!"

"But—"

"*No!* No buts. This is not negotiable! You will respect everyone you see, or you will have to answer to me. Do you understand?"

"OK." Todd is beginning to give in.

"Now do ten push-ups."

"But I only had four more to do." Todd is transitioning from arguing about *whether* to give in to *how much* he has to give in. But he is still arguing.

"That was before you stopped. Now you have to start over."

"That's not fair. You can't do that!"

"Todd, I'll tell you what's not fair. It's not fair that you have to complain every time we ask you to do something around here. It's not fair that you pick on Missy because she can't sing perfectly. It's not fair that you tease Alex until he gets mad and hits you and you complain about it. It's not fair that your mother has to put up with your lip when she asks you to do the dishes. It's not fair that I have to argue with you to do your homework. That's what isn't fair. Well, I've got news for you. That's not going to happen anymore. When we ask you to do something, your response will be 'OK, Dad, I'll do it right away.' That's what I expect from here on out. That is what is fair from now on! Let's get started on those ten push-ups."

"OK, I'll try."

"You'll do more than that. You *will* do them, or we'll be here even longer. And since you insist on arguing, I want you to say, "'OK, Dad, one. OK, Dad, two. OK, Dad, three' as you do the push-ups." Todd keeps dragging his feet, so his dad wants to make him work just a little harder. Ken is trying to eradicate as much of the bad attitude as he can get.

"OK, Dad, one. OK, Dad, two."

"That's much better." Todd is almost there. He is worn out and wants to stop the exercises. He is over halfway submissive at this point.

"OK, Dad, nine. OK, Dad, ten." Todd remains in the push-up position.

"Good. That's much better. Now stand up."

"OK, Dad." Todd slowly stands. He is tired. Todd's dad is getting a reading on him. He is definitely sore. He stands squarely on both legs. He crosses his arms in front of him.

"Put your arms down."

"Why?"

"Because I said so. And say, 'OK, Dad.'"

"OK, Dad." There is a hint of exasperation in his tone of voice.

"Watch yourself. We're not done yet."

"OK, Dad." He says it matter-of-factly.

"I want you to do twenty-five jumping jacks." Todd's eyes open wide, but he doesn't say anything. He's catching on. "And I want you to repeat, 'I'll respect Mom, one; I'll respect Missy, two; I'll respect Alex, three' in order like that."

He starts jumping. "I'll respect—"

"You forgot something." Todd's dad picks up on the fact that Todd's attitude got lazy when he stood up.

"What?"

"You forgot to say, 'OK, Dad.'"

"OK, Dad. I'll respect Mom, one. I'll respect Missy, two . . ."

"That's better. Keep it up. Good."

Todd's resistance is gradually ebbing. It is almost gone. His heart is getting softer as his body is getting more tired.

"I'll respect Mom, twenty-five." Todd is breathing pretty hard.

"Do you want a drink?"

Todd says, "Yes, please."

By accepting the gift of water, Todd is exhibiting a humble position. He is admitting his need for something. If he was still angry, he would not accept anything from his dad. His pride and anger would still be in control. Todd thinks saying please is the key, and it is nice, but it is just gravy. The real question was whether or not he would accept an offer of mercy from his dad. Pride is a stupid thing sometimes. It will prevent us from accepting what we desperately need, even a simple glass of water.

Todd gulps down the whole glass of water.

"Do you want some more?"

"No, thanks." Todd stands in front of his dad silently. Ken is again surveying Todd's body. The boy's arms are down at his sides, relaxed (and tired). His face is open. His eyes are more calm.

Ken begins the verbal portion of this exam. "So what was it that started this, Todd?"

"I wouldn't put the food away."

"That's right. What else?"

Todd thinks it's a fill-in-the-blank test. It's really an essay exam. "Well, I wasn't being very nice."

Todd's dad says nothing. He wants to see if he has to pull teeth or if Todd will pick up the slack. He just looks at Todd. Todd doesn't know what to do. "What do you mean you weren't very nice?"

"Well, I complained about helping carry in the groceries."

"Right." Ken gives Todd a little encouragement.

"And, uh, I haven't been nice to Missy."

"Good."

"And I've talked rude to Mom." Breakthrough! Todd isn't

just repeating what his dad has said to him! He's thinking on his own.

"What do you mean?"

"Well, the other day, she asked me to help Alex pick up his K'nex pieces, and I whined about it. And I was mean to Alex when I was helping him." His lip is quivering a little bit.

"What did you do?" Todd's dad asks softly.

"I pinched him."

Todd's dad is silent for a few moments. He wants the truth of Todd's rude misbehavior to sink in. "What do you think you need to do?"

"I suppose I should apologize to Alex." Todd smiles sheepishly.

"I think that's a good start, Son." Todd's dad moves toward his son and squeezes him in a bear hug. Todd grunts and then melts into his dad's arms. They stand there for several minutes in silence. Ken asks, "Well, what kind of attitude do you have now?"

"Well, I guess you could call it smashed."

Todd's dad chuckles. "Smashed, huh?"

"Yeah, like smashed to smithereens."

"Is that good?"

"Yeah, I'll say. It was a bad attitude . . . you know, 'Bad to the Bone' attitude."

"You won't miss it?"

"Why, will you?"

"Not for a minute."

"I won't either."

"So what do we need to do to wrap this up?"

Todd lowers his eyes. He pauses for a full minute, thinking. His dad waits quietly for Todd to gather his courage to speak humbly. "I'm sorry, Dad, for being so rude to you and the others. I know I should be nicer to you."

"Will you be more thoughtful of others?"

"Yeah, I'll try to not be so selfish." He pauses again for a few seconds. "Will you please forgive me for being so rude?"

Ken looks deep into his son's eyes. "I forgive you, Son." He gives him a big hug—not a playful hug but a strong, affectionate, holding kind of hug. Todd just soaks it all in. Ken holds him for as long as Todd stands still. Finally, Todd stirs, and his dad loosens his grip.

Ken asks, "Shall we go meet everybody at McDonald's? They're probably waiting for us."

"Naw. Let's cook some burgers. Just you and me. I'll start the grill."

"Oh, OK. Sounds good. I think we have some of your mom's great potato salad left over. Todd, you won't forget to apologize to your mom and Alex and Missy, will you?"

"No, Dad, I promise." He pauses and gives his dad an inquisitive look. "It's all right to say, 'No, Dad' isn't it?" he asks as he escapes his dad's grip and runs away.

"Hey, get back here. Give me fifty push-ups."

"You gotta catch me first."

"Don't worry, I know where you live. Hey, Todd, there is something I'd like you to do. Would you please take out the trash to the street?"

"Sure, Dad. Right after I put away the groceries. Anything else I can do?"

"Yeah. Let's make it a good day."

"Whatever you say, Dad. You're in charge."

"And don't you forget it either, buddy."

"Don't worry. My arms will remind me."

■ ■ ■

Todd is pretty clean now. He should enjoy at least a few days of closeness with his family, maybe more. Gradually the afterglow will fade, and things will return to normal. But Ken has redefined "normal." Todd knows that his parents expect him to be polite and to cooperate, and he knows what his parents are prepared to do if he is rude or stubborn.

In terms of success, I would rate this attitude adjustment an 8 or a 9. If Todd had cried, it would have signaled an even greater impact. Tears signify a deeper level of brokenness and hence a longer-lasting repentance. But tears are not necessary. Todd was able to change his attitude without crying, and that was good. It is painful to make your children cry when you are disciplining them. Todd learned some things by this encounter.

This attitude session was about a 6 in its level of intensity. Todd's dad had to push him several times. And if Todd had wanted to, he could have pushed back against his dad quite a bit harder. That would have required his dad to push back even more firmly. Todd may yet ratchet it up in future session. His dad will have to be ready.

Sometimes a warning is sufficient to stem the tide of a bad attitude. Todd responded very well. He identified his shortcomings without too much prompting. His earlier training in apologizing paid off in his knowing what he needed to do to repair the damage in his relationships.

I have personally participated in about forty to fifty attitude-adjustment sessions involving exercises (most of them with teenagers at the boarding school where I used to work). It is never easy. In the midst of it, it is scary. The stakes are high. It feels as if we are in a cave with very little light. It is intense. Real lives are at stake here. This is not a drill. Even after an adjustment session is over, I still have a lot of feelings to sort through. In the sessions that I have done with my own kids, I spend time debriefing with my wife about what happened. An attitude adjustment is not pleasurable but it is necessary. My son's or daughter's clean heart is the only thing that makes it worth it.

Before you even begin to think about attempting this kind of attitude adjustment with your children, consider several important issues.

1. A major attitude-adjustment session is an unusual occurrence. It should be rare. If your doctor's first choice is to do surgery, then you would get a second opinion. Like surgery, *prolonged exercises to adjust your children's bad attitudes should always be the last option.* Some children are exceptions if they are very strong willed. I have a strong-willed son, but once he learned the consequences of defiance, he quickly learned the pain of push-ups is greater than the pleasure of arguing.

Minor attitude adjustments may occur more often. After the exercise tool has been introduced, sometimes a swift set of exercises snaps children back to reality. And the reality is that the parent is the authority and the child is cooperative.

2. Give your children several chances to turn their attitudes around during the exercises. If your children complain about how hard the exercises are, you can remind them that (1) this whole thing started because of what they did wrong; (2) they can stop anytime if they decide to change their attitude; and (3) they can show a changed attitude by doing what you ask them to do. When I ask my children, "Are you ready to let go of this bad attitude?" I am saying inside, "Please, hurry up and give in so we can end this pain. This is killing me much more than it is you."

Todd displayed a fair amount of cooperation. He did not

drag out the adjustment. Dad didn't have to remind him that he could end his ordeal if he would simply admit his wrong, express his remorse, promise future cooperation, apologize, and do the work originally asked of him. If Todd had fought for a long time, his dad would have calmly reminded him, "Todd, this isn't all necessary. You could end this very quickly."

When children don't take the easy way out, they say volumes. They are saying that they *need* to do this. They need help getting rid of all their frustration, anger, hurt, or whatever is overwhelming them. They need help to contain what they are unable to contain by themselves. By "exploding" with their bad attitude, they are saying they need help getting themselves under control. I love my children enough to do that for them.

As you discipline your children, remind them that they can choose a good attitude at any time. They can go back to relational harmony as soon as they decide to. Remind them how the whole mess started and that as soon as they agree to cooperate, you will stop. They hold the keys to their attitude. Encourage them to use those keys so you can get back to harmony.

3. *Help your children do the exercises for as long as they refuse to obey.* Most of the time your children will not even question whether they have to do the exercises. They will just start to do them. They may try to argue with you or move at a snail's pace, but they were probably doing that in the first place. When I have been part of other attitude-adjustment sessions, I've had kids look at me as if I were kidding and even laugh as if the whole idea were a joke. But when I looked at them solemnly, lowered the pitch of my voice, and raised the volume a notch, they knew it wasn't a game. At least it wasn't a game they were going to win.

In those rare instances when the kids balk at doing the exercises, it can get dicey. If Todd had refused to do the push-ups, his dad would have helped him. It is easy to hold the back of a child's belt and lift the body up and down. No one likes to be manhandled, and kids are no exception. It is humiliating. We take away their last shred of independence when they leave us no choice. But that is exactly the point. They leave us no choice. If they demand that we let go of them (as they usually do), then we can demand that they do the exercises on their own. No one likes to be humiliated for very long. As long as they refuse the option of doing the exercises without any help, we should be able to live with ourselves for temporarily humiliating them in private. If kids take it this far, they will submit to doing the exercises on their own pretty quickly.

4. *Our goal should be to humble our children's hearts, not humiliate them.* Todd's dad had his wife take the other two children to McDonald's so Todd would not have to endure their gawking at him. Todd's being humbled is a private affair. It is not entertainment for his siblings. At times, it is not possible to send the rest of the family away. But try to find a relatively private place, like the basement or garage. Or you can tell the other kids to go outside until they are called to return. It's OK if they hear about what transpired, but just the headlines from you. Todd can say anything truthful about what happened. It will serve as a warning to the others, and they will also shape up for a while.

At no time should you call your children "stupid" or "bad" or any number of destructive names. Confront them with their bad attitudes and lack of obedience. Nothing more, nothing less. Name-calling is inflammatory, and you don't want to blow this up any more than necessary. You don't light a match when there is gasoline on the floor.

5. *Move to solidify your children's softened heart attitude.* This is facilitated in four ways: your words, your actions, their words, and their actions.

Your words will speak volumes in moments like these. Praise even the slightest move toward cooperation and repentance. When Todd showed signs of submitting, he was rewarded with a "good" from his dad. It wasn't much, but it helped to encourage him.

Your actions will relieve their anxiety about whether or not you still love them. As discussed in the last chapter, your actions of affection will reassure them how much you still love them.

Their words will help their external changes percolate internally. Take advantage of the shifting momentum. While they are heading in the right direction, shift from using the exercises to having them express their new attitude in words. Having them speak words from a clean heart helps them internalize their external posture. You want them to manifest their new attitudes to make them as real as possible. Their new attitudes are like wet cement. Help them "write" as many positive things on it as you can before it hardens into their new internal posture.

Their actions will solidify their change of heart too. Give them simple, easy, quick tasks to do. Ask them to put away the dishes, fold the laundry, or sweep the kitchen floor. This allows them to express their newfound joy and energy. Let them experience the fruit of all their labor. *Let them feel and express the sweetness of cooperation rather than the bitterness of rebellion.*

Let's look at how the tool of exercise fits on the Progression of Discipline chart:

Progression of Discipline

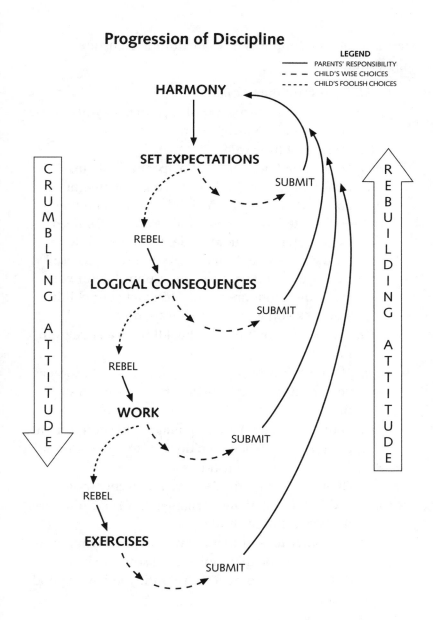

LEGEND
— PARENTS' RESPONSIBILITY
– – CHILD'S WISE CHOICES
····· CHILD'S FOOLISH CHOICES

HARMONY

SET EXPECTATIONS

SUBMIT

REBEL

LOGICAL CONSEQUENCES

SUBMIT

REBEL

WORK

SUBMIT

REBEL

EXERCISES

SUBMIT

CRUMBLING ATTITUDE

REBUILDING ATTITUDE

■ ■ ■

Here is another example of how an attitude adjustment might sound:

Child: "You want me to *what?*"

Adult: "I want you to do ten push-ups to help you change your attitude. Now get started."

Child: "Why do I have to?"

Adult: "Get started now or I will help you do them." (Child begins to do them.) "You kept arguing about what time you had to be home, and then you refused to put your clothes away. You need help to change your attitude. I will not allow an attitude like that. You have to do them because I told you to and because I'm responsible for you." (Why questions are a trap. Don't let your children sidetrack you with this irrelevant discussion.)

Child: "Well, you don't have to be. I'll be in charge from now on."

Adult: "Not if this is how you are going to act. As soon as you are able to make better choices, we can stop this."

Child: "But I am ready. You keep making me do these stupid push-ups. There, I'm done. Can I get up now?"

Adult: "We can stop the push-ups as soon as I see a change in your attitude. Give me twenty more."

Child: "Well, I'm not going to change it." (The child starts the next set of push-ups.)

Adult: "I'm sorry to hear that because it means your arms are going to be that much more sore when we are done. I'm not going to leave until you have a good attitude."

Child: "This is stupid. It won't make me change my attitude!"

Adult: "Well, we've already tried everything else. And you may be right. This may not change your attitude. But we're going to keep trying, so I suggest you change it before your muscles get too sore."

Child: "I'm going to tell my teachers [or the police or neighbor or relative] you were hurting me!" (This is an idle threat and a pitiful attempt to gang up on you. The child is beginning to weaken and is looking for reinforcements. This is also a good way to learn who the child thinks his or her allies are against you. It could even be the other parent.)

Adult: "That's a good idea. I think they should also know how to deal with your bad attitude. You could be doing push-ups for them too." (If you seem intimidated, you will only prolong the ordeal. This is not abuse. *Abuse is not offering them a chance to stop the discipline.* All they have to do to stop is change their attitude. Abuse is threatening to hit them, hitting them, locking them in a closet, or not letting them eat all day.)

Child: "I hate you!" (The child is getting desperate now.)

Adult: "That's OK. You don't have to like me. You just have to obey me now."

Child: "You don't love me." (The child is really softening now and needs to hear how much you love him or her.)

Adult: "If I didn't love you, I wouldn't invest this much time in disciplining you."

Child: "How many more do I have to do?" (The child's voice is getting softer by the second.)

Adult: "Give me five more good ones."

Child: (The child does five more very quickly.) "May I get up now, please?" (This is the beginning of what you were looking for all along.)

■ ■ ■

What are the messages we are sending to our children with this disciplinary strategy?

1. Children will be held responsible for their attitude and behavior. When they won't take care of bad attitudes or cooperate fully, then we will help them. They will eventually learn that it is easier for them to change their attitude rather than to let it get to the point where their parents need to become involved. They can choose the easy way or the hard way.

2. Parents have authority and will use it. Parents have more power than children do. God help us when children have equal power or more power than adults have. Children are entitled to equal respect, dignity, and fairness—but not equal decision-making power. Parents are responsible for training their children. Inflicting sufficient, necessary pain is always a part of discipline. The more the rebellion, the more pain necessary to turn children away from it.

3. Submission is a crucial capability to have. Our children's inability to submit to trustworthy people will condemn them to much strife, loneliness, and suffering. Learning how to submit is a requirement to trust. The ability to trust someone is a cornerstone of building a loving, intimate relationship. Loving, trusting, and submitting to parents are vital for children's health. Children may survive without learning to submit, but they will not thrive. Their spirits will thirst for intimacy. When that happens, they are either easy prey or they prey on others.

BE FLEXIBLE

Work and exercises can be interchangeable tools. They are analogous to a socket set and a set of wrenches. Sometimes the choice of tool depends on the job to be done. Or you may just develop a preference for one tool over another. Use whichever tool you think will work the best for your particular child, situation, or time schedule. If you have been using one successfully, then keep using that one. If you think switching tools might get them to change their attitudes more fully, then try the other tool.

For my daughter, exercise is a better choice than work. The reason is simple—she likes to work. She loves to clean. About the only chores she hates doing are the dishes and cleaning up the dog messes in the backyard. Those jobs are not enough to help her work on her attitude, so I usually have her do exercises. It usually doesn't take her long to change her attitude.

The reason I presented the exercise tool as the last one on the Progression of Discipline chart is that exercises are the most intense. Exercises are like concentrated power. It is the more confrontational of the last two assignments. Exercises are more likely to cause the greatest resistance, so I use them as a last resort. But it may be different with your children.

The only way to determine which tool works best for you and each of your children is to experiment. Try them both. When you debrief the episode with your spouse, debate the merits of work vs. exercise for that particular confrontation. Try to figure out which one works best in which situations for you.

I hope this section doesn't confuse you or sound inconsistent. Adjusting attitudes is not as easy as following a recipe. We can't simply follow steps *A-B-C* and produce obedient children. We need creativity and flexibility. These tools and the progression in which I recommend them have worked well for me, but it may be different for you. Take these tools and create your own style after experimenting with them.

OTHER TIMES TO USE EXERCISES

An attitude session is not the only time exercises can be used as a tool for discipline. Sometimes I use sit-ups for reminders. I might say, "You forgot to hang up your coat again. Do five sit-ups and say, 'I will hang up my coat when I come inside' with every sit-up." It is a quick reminder. It adds a little spice to the practicing tool. It can surprise them and make them think next time. It's also a little quicker and slightly more painful.

When Sharon or I find our children's things lying around, we pick them up and put them in a basket in our closet. Then once or twice a week, we bring out the basket and charge the children five push-ups per item. Even if they say they don't want the item anymore, they have to buy it back, and then they can dispose of it or give it to someone. In this way the exercises are a currency. When you think about it, that's exactly what money is—time and exertion in a tangible form. I would rather have my children *feel* the consequences of their bad attitudes than merely pay a fine by throwing nickels, dimes, or quarters into a "fine bucket."

Sometimes when our kids show a bad attitude by moving in slow motion, I send them outside to run to the end of the block and back. That usually gets their blood flowing again. I use this exercise often when our children have trouble getting their schoolwork done. I tell them that running will help them think a little more clearly because they will get more blood flowing all the way up into their brain.

Sometimes kids intentionally move slowly to aggravate

others. This is called being passive-aggressive. All that phrase means is that they are finding a passive way to express their bad attitude. It is very subtle. Besides moving slowly, other common passive-aggressive behaviors are forgetfulness, tardiness, carelessness, and clumsiness. A pattern of these behaviors may require some intense "practice sessions" to overcome these tendencies.

Another time to use the exercise tool is out in public. Sometimes our children are uncooperative when we are in a mall or store with them. If verbal warnings have failed, then we leave the mall and go stand next to our car. We have the kids do some jumping jacks or simply have them jump up and down until they are ready to control themselves in public. By going to the car, we avoid humiliating them by being in full public view. But they are still aware that people are moving around in the parking lot, and sometimes this pressure will get them to change their attitudes. By being next to the car, we are also in a position to leave if our children make a big scene.

All these suggestions are creative ways we found to utilize this tool. I hope you find them helpful. If you have misgivings about this tool, as I did in the beginning, keep reading. I think you will find some of your questions answered in chapter 13. If your children are very stubborn and try to distract you from your goal by throwing tantrums, see appendix A for some ideas of how to handle tantrums. If you want scriptural examples of how God used similar discipline tools, see appendix B. Don't just take my word for it.

Summary

If your children do not respond to the first few tools in the progression of discipline, try the exercise tool. It can help your children exercise (exorcise) away their bad attitudes. If your children respond to the exercise tool and make wise choices, they return to relational harmony.

Part 3 will discuss some precautions to take when using these tools, some answers to frequently asked questions about these tools, the effectiveness of adding spanking as an accessory to any of the tools, and how parents need to work together as a team when using these tools.

Reflection Questions

Take a few minutes to think about these questions. If possible, discuss them with your spouse, another parent, or a group of parents. Write down your observations, feelings, and goals in a journal.

1. What are your reactions to the attitude-adjustment tool of assigning exercises?
2. What are your misgivings?
3. What do you think you have to win by trying it?
4. What would keep you from using this type of discipline?
5. What types of discipline have you been using: spanking, time-outs, grounding, etc.?
6. Are you using these tools because they are effective or easy?
7. What do you gain and lose in using these tools?
8. What recent encounter with one of your children's bad attitudes could have been handled effectively with the exercise tool? Think through what that scenario might have looked like.
9. What value do you place on your children's attitudes? Are they worth fighting for?

Using the Tools Well

The Lord is like a father to his children,
tender and compassionate to those who fear him.
For he understands how weak we are;
he knows we are only dust.

— P s a l m   1 0 3 : 1 3 - 1 4

12
Taking Caution

As parents we have the awesome responsibility and authority to shape our children's characters and attitudes. So far this book has discussed the merits and guidelines of using several tools for discipline. Before we go any further, I would like to discuss some cautions in using the tools. Like any power tool, they can be used for great good or great harm.

There are two situations in which we should put on the brakes rather than push full-steam ahead into an attitude adjustment. The first situation is when the behavior that we see as a bad attitude is really something else. It may be that our children are dealing with physical limitations. It may be that they are merely trying to voice a different opinion. It may be that they are expressing their need for independence. The second situation in which we should use caution is when our children have suffered some kind of physical abuse of which we may not be aware.

Let's look at these two kinds of situations so that we can recognize them when we see them.

WHEN SOMETHING ELSE LOOKS LIKE A BAD ATTITUDE

Physical Limitations

We need to be careful not to interpret physical limitations as bad attitudes. When it comes to the three E's—eating, eliminating, and exhaustion—give your children the benefit of the doubt and don't turn these situations into major bad-attitude battles.

1. Eating. Battles with food usually concern three areas: when to eat, how to eat it, and what to eat. *When* food gets eaten varies greatly from family to family. It even varies from day to day. Those sorts of rules are pretty much up to parents' discretion. Just try to have some consistency. Not eating right before mealtimes is pretty standard, but other than that, there isn't much worth arguing over.

How to eat is just another social rule. Obviously the standard for how we eat in a restaurant or as guests at someone's home is different from the standard for how we behave at home. Attitude problems can manifest themselves in children who disregard normal family rules for eating. Handle them the way you would handle attitude problems for any other expectation. But use common sense. We don't use the same standards with toddlers that we use with teenagers.

As far as *what* foods to eat, many people will not agree with me, but that's OK. Food is primarily a health issue. I don't recommend making food selection an attitude issue.

I speak from plenty of experience with this. Family experts say that siblings have to be opposite so they can have their own identity. With our second child, that is true in the food area. Whereas Dugan has always eaten anything (and now everything), Breeze's diet consisted of cereal, pizza, peanut butter, french fries, macaroni and cheese, and an occasional hot dog. The first question she would ask when we told her we would be eating in someone else's home was "What are they serving?" followed by "What will I eat?"

We tried the sit-there-until-you-eat-it tactic, the we'll-save-it-for-your-next-meal method, the if-you-eat-it-you-can-have-some-ice-cream scheme, and even the there's-nothing-else-to-eat ruse. It didn't matter. Nothing worked, and it left a bad taste (pun intended) in everybody's mouth. We decided to try the this-is-what-we're-having-fix-something-for-yourself system. We are all much more relaxed now. And Breeze has grown into a healthy, energetic ten-year-old girl.

When we go to someone else's home now, we don't worry what Breeze will eat. We simply say, "I don't know what they will be serving for dinner. If you don't like it, then you can just eat the bread." If she complains, all we have to say is, "Honey, it is your choice not to eat this food." It used to be necessary to tell her to stop whining about it, but now she knows better.

Breeze makes her own decision about what she will or won't eat. If she is hungry, that is a natural consequence of her choice not to eat what is served. A home is not a restaurant; if your children don't like what you are serving, then they can make their own sandwich. I've never seen children starve to death when there was food in the home. Eventually, they will eat something. Breeze has gotten daring enough to add to her diet. Now she will eat salsa and chips, grapes, and even green beans.

We do set limits on junk food. We don't allow a meal of potato chips or cookies. But generally, we have decided that the battle over what foods to eat is not the place to use our energy. We don't want to win this battle over food if it means losing the war for our children's hearts.

2. *Elimination.* Potty training is one of the first major battles

parents have with children. It can set the stage for all future tests of wills. However, elimination should not be the testing grounds for a submissive attitude. This is one where you and your children should both win.

Potty training is a cornerstone of the building blocks for self-determination. It is children's first significant opportunity to assert themselves. Gaining mastery over their bodily functions can really set the stage for your children's future confidence. If we make those experiences a major hassle rather than a major celebration, our kids lose the satisfaction of managing their own body. We don't want to make our children feel ashamed because they do not learn something as quickly or competently as we would like them to.

Don't try to rush potty training. Remember one of the guiding principles for setting expectations: Children have to be physically capable of doing something before they should be expected to do it. And while they are mastering these complex social/body functions, expect them to make many mistakes. Mistakes are how they learn. Don't expect perfection in their bathroom abilities.

I suggest that you limit your training in the area of bathroom use to the tool of rewards. Reward each and every step toward gaining mastery of their body. Use whatever motivates your child. Don't make potty training a sore subject; make it a celebration.

3. *Exhaustion.* Exhaustion is another body issue. Tiredness in children can often appear to be a bad attitude. Rather than engage in an attitude adjustment with your tired children, make sure they get some rest. Going to bed is not a threat or punishment. Don't say, "That's it. I've had it! You just earned yourself an early bedtime for that." Say, "I know you're tired, so I'll let that go now, but I want you to come over here and

relax for a while." You don't even have to say anything about an early bedtime because they will just argue with you. Simply make sure to get them to bed at least an hour early.

Give your children grace when it is nearly bedtime or when they have missed sleep the night before. The day after an overnight party is never a pleasant one for the parents. Sharon and I decided to limit the number of their sleepovers in the summer to cut down on this unpleasant experience.

Exhaustion also results from a short-term physical illness. We all get a little whiny when we feel ill. Don't confuse pleading for some TLC as a selfish attitude. But even sick kids can still say please and thank you as you serve them. Being sick doesn't promote a child to a Greek god, which is my son's fantasy.

In general, I don't feel fair disciplining children for a bad attitude when the real problem is exhaustion. I can't expect them to control themselves when they don't have the energy or strength to do it.

Voicing Different Opinions

Another situation that may be mistaken for a bad attitude is when your children are trying to express their own opinions. As long as your children can express their opinions without an argument or rude tone of voice, they should be allowed to express their ideas, even if they disagree with yours.

We should encourage our children's opinions and preferences to emerge and reveal who they are or who they want to be. Our children's opinions are part of their growing, changing identity. Navigating these choppy relational waters can be a challenge.

Whenever you and your children disagree, there are two levels of communication. The first level is the topic of discussion, such as how to use money, whom to spend time with, what to wear, etc. The second level is how politely that information is exchanged. Debate teams may argue their opposing viewpoints quite passionately and then go out for coffee together. We wonder how they can be friends when earlier they seemed so angry with each other. They agree on the rules of engagement. They don't insult each other or sling mud. They challenge the other people's ideas, not their identity, character, or value as people.

Parents can teach children how to disagree in appropriate ways by modeling that behavior. Parents and children can be passionate without being nasty. But modeling isn't always enough. Setting explicit expectations becomes an important part of teaching children how to disagree appropriately. Use some of the tools suggested in chapter 7. Teach your children to choose less offensive words. Explain how to challenge people's ideas without attacking them as people. You could even role-play these situations.

To put it succinctly, your children may not agree with you on *what* to think or say, but you can agree on *how* to say it. Resolving disagreements often takes a tremendous investment of time. The relational harmony that results is the best dividend. Respectfully communicating ideas is a critical relational skill and will prevent the dialogue from getting derailed into a dead-end argument. We should endow our children with this conflict-resolution skill as early as possible.

I want to clarify a couple of things. Opinions are not responsibilities. Children may have an opinion about a responsibility, but they still have to fulfill that responsibility. For example, my daughter may not agree that rooms need to be clean, and she will be free to live up to that standard when she has a home of her own. In our house, however, she has a responsibility to help keep it clean. She lives here and dirties it, so she helps clean it. Pretty simple.

Submission doesn't mean that my children have to agree with my opinions. They don't have to have my taste in music, clothes, hairstyles, etc. My son may not like having to wear his nicer shirt to go out to eat, but he doesn't always have a choice. He may discuss his disagreement with me as long as he doesn't take a snotty attitude about it. In fact, the more submissive he is to my asking him to change his shirt, the more I am willing to compromise on which shirt he wears. Submission does mean my children accept my guidance on things that matter.

If you are frustrated because I don't tell you which opinions are worth fighting for and which aren't, I'm sorry. I can't do that. I suggest wrestling with God on those sorts of discussions. He may have something specific to say to you. Sometimes he simply says, "Do whatever you think best." It can be frustrating, but that's how he works sometimes. If an issue is really important, then God has probably already talked about it in the Bible somewhere. Parents need guidance too; go to God's Word for it. Seeking guidance from wise people is always helpful too.

Growing Independence

The third situation that is often mistaken for a bad attitude is our children's expression of their growing independence. We want our children to have confidence in themselves and to develop the ability to think on their own. How do we distinguish between children's budding, independent spirits and rebellious attitudes? The answer, once again, lies in *how* they express their independence. The key is respect.

We parents must develop the ability to discern when children are simply asking questions rather than challenging authority. There is a difference between "I don't understand why" and "Why do I have to?" The former is truly inquisitive; the latter is purely whining. The former is "Teach me" and the latter is "Make me." Once again, parents are in the position of teaching not only *what* to do but also *how* to do it.

When trying to discern between respectful questioning and disrespect, use the discernment tools we discussed in chapter 9. Look at the body language. The root of the word *respect* comes from the Latin word *specio*, meaning "to view." The word *respect* originally meant "the act of looking back." When your children are showing respect, they will look back at you. They will look you in the eyes. Respectful children will be more willing to engage you eye-to-eye. But don't forget to check other clues also, such as body posture, tone of voice, and willingness to talk.

I used to work in the emergency room at a local medical hospital. The doctor would call me in to perform a psychological evaluation to help determine the best course of treatment for a patient. Needless to say, I was pretty scared when I first started. It was intimidating to work in the hustle and bustle of an ER. My supervisor gave me some great advice: "When you aren't sure what is going on, just keep asking questions. Take your time."

The same advice applies when trying to discern respectful versus disrespectful questions from our children. Keep applying gentle pressure with your questions until their attitude becomes clear. Then you can proceed accordingly.

We need to remember that we are fallible parents. We are going to make errors in judgment. If you've done the best you can and just can't be sure, err on the side of grace and give them the benefit of the doubt.

If in giving your children grace, you learn later that they

really did have a bad attitude, don't worry. You will get another chance. The bad attitude will come around again. Catch it next time, and then help them adjust it. By doing it that way, you can remind them of the second chance afforded them this time. They will feel treated fairly, and the discipline will be more internalized.

WHEN YOUR CHILDREN HAVE SUFFERED ABUSE

If you feel that your children have suffered any form of physical, mental, verbal, or sexual abuse—from a neighbor, a sibling, a baby-sitter, your spouse, or school personnel—the attitude-adjustment process will need to be handled differently. Children who have been abused may panic when the firmest tools of discipline are used. Repeatedly abused children lose their trust in others. Some of them almost lose their *ability* to trust in others. It is very difficult to repair that damage. If you discover or even suspect that your children have been victimized in some manner, get help from experienced professionals.

If your children seem to have an excessive reaction to your reasonable use of power, they may have suffered some form of abuse. A look of terror in their eyes signals that something is wrong. Abused children are fearful. Most children respond with anger and some fight. Abused children may react to discipline by getting frantic or very withdrawn. Either extreme is worrisome and needs to be investigated further.

Specifically, exercises may be too intense for abused children. The previous tools all the way up to and including work should be appropriate, but exercises may not be. You don't have to totally reject exercises as a possible tool, but just administer exercises very carefully. If you use the progression of discipline like a ladder and descend it methodically, you have already done what an abusive person does not do. You will have kept your cool and not have crossed the line into harshness. That in itself will make a great impression on your children. They may realize that you will not mistreat them the way the abusive person did. Your self-control can help heal the wounds from their abuse.

The restoration phase of discipline will also make a huge impact on abused children. Abused children are accustomed to condemnation and constant ridicule of their mistakes. They are left to try to pick up the pieces of their self-worth by themselves. Abused children have never experienced genuine reconnection. They know brokenness; they don't know healing. Forgiveness is a foreign concept to them.

Genuine love can melt even the toughest hearts. Discipline and abuse are two very different phenomena.

Many parents have been abused as children. People with that background have an understandable hesitation about using strong tools for discipline. Work and exercises may seem extreme to people who shy away from such powerful tools. Please understand my intention. If gentler tools are sufficient, then keep using them. If a pair of pliers will loosen a bolt, don't use a pipe wrench or a blowtorch to loosen it.

Summary

You may still have lots of questions: What if I am too strict? Where do I draw the line with my child? What is rude and sassy? What is a legitimate expression of children's feelings or opinions? What if I draw the line in all the wrong places and that makes things worse? That's good. Those excellent questions indicate that you want to do the right thing. Questions like those suggest that your heart is tender. The difficulty in answering these questions is that there are so many variables involved. Each situation is unique because each person and family are unique.

Look to the examples of other parents whom know you well and who have blazed the trail and have raised respectful, well-adjusted children. Seek their guidance about whether or not you are too strict or too lenient or just right when it comes to disciplining your children. Be honest with them. Tell them specifically not only what your children did but also exactly what you said and did so they can give you wise counsel. "Get all the advice and instruction you can, and be wise the rest of your life" (Prov. 19:20).

Now turn to the next chapter, which tries to answer a lot of the questions parents have about the discipline tools discussed in this book.

Reflection Questions

Take a few minutes to think about these questions. If possible, discuss them with your spouse, another parent, or a group of parents. Write down your observations, feelings, and goals in a journal.

1. As you think of your children, in what areas or at what times do you think you might be demanding too much?
2. How has your childhood influenced your parenting and disciplining?
3. What different opinions do you allow your children to express?
4. What are the signs that your children are independent yet respectful?
5. From what other parents can you seek wise counsel?

It's like this: When I was a child, I spoke and thought and reasoned as a child does. But when I grew up, I put away childish things.

—1 Corinthians 13:11

13

Answering Some Questions

This chapter is for those of you who say, "Yes, but . . ." You agree in theory with the tools I've described so far, but you have some serious reservations. I did, too, when I first saw them put into practice. I'd like you to imagine this chapter as a fireside chat in which we can talk out some of those reservations. I may not know your specific questions, but as I have presented this material at seminars and used it with clients who are having a hard time disciplining their children, I have heard dozens of questions. Let's tackle some of them here.

Some of your questions may be about the biblical and theological underpinnings of these techniques. I try to answer some of those questions in this chapter by using the words of our heavenly Dad. I've also included an appendix that explores more fully God's view of discipline (see appendix B).

Each section includes a "Yes, But . . . " section and a "Consider This:" section. Perhaps you will find your questions answered here.

Yes, But . . .

Work and exercises are extreme. Making my children work until they break or making them do exercises until their bodies are worn out is cruel. These methods are abusive.

Consider This:

Most of you have "taken over" your children at one time or another. You have made them do something they didn't feel like doing. When your children were babies, you probably wrestled with them as you struggled to put on their coats, hats, and mittens before you took them out into the cold. They may have arched their backs in anger, pulling their arms away from you, kicking their tiny legs as hard as they could, and screaming as if you were sticking them with a needle. Sure, you would try talking calmly to soothe their cries, but sometimes it just didn't help. You couldn't take them outside in the cold without risking their health, and they were too young to learn from natural consequences.

Do you think your "suffering" children understood what you were doing or why you were causing them such distress? Of course not, but that didn't stop you from doing what was in their best interest. You were not only willing to allow their discomfort, you were causing it because there was a higher purpose to be served—protecting them from the harsh elements outside.

Yes, But . . .

I would have to take control of their bodies like that only for infants. I wouldn't have to do anything like that once they get older.

Consider This:

Have you ever forced your toddlers to wear diapers when they would rather run around naked? If not, then you must get your carpet cleaned every week. Or else you have very compliant children.

Have you ever had to brush your children's teeth when they didn't want you to brush them? What if your children arbitrarily decided they were not going to brush their teeth anymore? You could try the reward tactic. You could try to outlast them with the natural-consequences tool and hope they get grossed out by the buildup of food on their teeth. But after a month or so, you probably would find a way to force your children to brush their teeth, even if you had to hold them down and force their mouth open to do it.

What if your elementary-age children refused to bathe? What if they let their hair get greasy and grimy? What if you started seeing lice? What if they stopped all personal hygiene? Don't we have a responsibility to care for our children and teach them health and hygiene?

Isn't children's refusal to maintain personal hygiene a symptom of something far more serious, like a smelly attitude? Don't wait until you can literally smell your children before you smell their bad attitudes.

God can smell a bad attitude. "The incense you bring me is a stench in my nostrils! Your celebrations of the new moon and the Sabbath day, and your special days for fasting—even your most pious meetings—are all sinful and false. I want nothing more to do with them" (Isa. 1:13). God wants respectful attitudes and genuine, obedient hearts from us. We should want the same for our children.

Yes, But . . .

Force may be necessary for an infant or a young toddler, but I wouldn't feel comfortable using such a technique on an older child, especially a teenager.

Consider This:

What if you overheard your children planning to break into your neighbors' house to steal their money? Wouldn't you "restrain" them and keep them with you until you could make sense of this foolishness?

What if you found marijuana in your children's coat pockets? Wouldn't you severely restrict their freedom with whatever means necessary until you could be reasonably assured they would not use it? Isn't that "taking control over their bodies"?

What if you found a note that indicated your children were planning to run away? Wouldn't you keep them home until you could be assured they wouldn't leave? They want to leave, but you won't let them. I bet if they tried to get out the door, you would try to physically restrain them. That is confining them against their will. We would all do it.

Yes, But . . .

OK, maybe I would do something if my children's physical safety, well-being, or health was an issue, but my children aren't that bad off.

Consider This:

Since I don't know you, I have to take your word for it. However, if you really want to be sure, ask several other adults who regularly spend time with your children. Ask them what areas of your children's lives need improvement. Ask them to be bluntly honest. If everyone gives high praise, that's good. I'm glad you are not currently facing any critical issues.

However, what if your children decided they were going to become sexually active? Are they mature enough to cope with the consequences of their sexual behavior? No! Wouldn't you try just about anything to prevent this behavior? Some people would consider that to be intrusive. The other choice is to do what many other parents do: throw up their hands and say, "We can't stop them. I give up."

Yes, But . . .

Yes, I do have some moral standards I would enforce, but is a bad attitude all that important? It doesn't seem to warrant all this intensity. Your tools of changing their attitudes seem like a boot camp.

Consider This:

Childhood is a kind of boot camp; it is training for life. "Teach your children to choose the right path, and when they are older, they will remain upon it" (Prov. 22:6). Training doesn't have to be endless repetitions of push-ups and cleaning the shower with a toothbrush. Those are used sparingly and only when necessary. Remember that children have the choice of when to obey. Parents simply supply the motivation for quicker submission.

Yes, But . . .

Lighten up. It's just not as bad as all that. A little bad attitude doesn't seem like that big a deal.

Consider This:

God's perfection is offended by even the least imperfection. "Dead flies will cause even a bottle of perfume to stink! Yes, an ounce of foolishness can outweigh a pound of wisdom and honor" (Eccles. 10:1). How many drops of arsenic does it take to make a gallon of water deadly? A bad attitude can poison children's character as effectively as a few drops of arsenic poison a jug of water. Are we willing to let our children grow up with malnourished bodies? Of course not. Then let's not settle for malnourished character development either.

Yes, But . . .

Does a little foolishness or rebellion warrant such strong tools?

Consider This:

Apparently God thought it did. "Rebellion is as bad as the sin of witchcraft, and stubbornness is as bad as worshiping idols" (1 Sam. 15:23). God hates rebellion. He realizes a little foolishness can grow into fully developed arrogance and rebellion. Oh, it may not always be obvious. It takes an observant, involved parent to detect a whiff of rebellion. There is no such thing as a "little rebellion." It's like being a little pregnant—either you are or you aren't.

Yes, But . . .

That was only in the Old Testament; the key word being *old*. Didn't God end all that concern for the law when Jesus came? Didn't Jesus teach us about loving God and each other (Matt. 22:37-40)?

Consider This:

True, Jesus talked a lot about love. He said things like "I have loved you even as the Father has loved me. Remain in my love. *When you obey me*, you remain in my love, just as I obey my Father and remain in his love" (John 15:9-10, [italics added]). Jesus thinks that obedience is very important. In fact he says that love will manifest itself in how we behave.

Regarding the Old Testament law, Jesus said, "Don't misunderstand why I have come. I did not come to abolish the law of Moses or the writings of the prophets. No, I came to fulfill them. I assure you, until heaven and earth disappear, even the smallest detail of God's law will remain until its purpose is achieved" (Matt. 5:17-18).

Another time Jesus said, "Until John the Baptist began to preach, the laws of Moses and the messages of the prophets were your guides. But now the Good News of the Kingdom of God is preached, and eager multitudes are forcing their way in. But that doesn't mean that the law has lost its force in even the smallest point. It is stronger and more permanent than heaven and earth" (Luke 16:16-17).

Yes, But . . .
Even with attitude? Does Jesus think attitude is really that important?

Consider This:
We've already talked a lot about this, but this is an important point to grasp. As you read the following quotation, don't you get the feeling that Jesus was getting exasperated with his best friends? Apparently even the guys who were with him the most had trouble understanding this important point.

"Are you so dull?" [Jesus] asked. "Don't you see that nothing that enters a man from the outside can make him 'unclean'? For it doesn't go into his heart but into his stomach, and then out of his body. . . . What comes out of a man is what makes him 'unclean.' For from within, out of men's hearts, come evil thoughts, sexual immorality, theft, murder, adultery, greed, malice, deceit, lewdness, envy, slander, arrogance and folly. All these evils come from inside and make a man 'unclean'" (Mark 7:18-23, NIV).

Paul makes some definitive statements about attitude too. "Your attitude should be the same that Christ Jesus had. Though he was God, he did not demand and cling to his rights as God. He made himself nothing; he took the humble position of a slave and appeared in human form. . . . In everything you do, stay away from complaining and arguing, so that no one can speak a word of blame against you. You are to live clean, innocent lives as children of God in a dark world full of crooked and perverse people. Let your lives shine brightly before them" (Phil. 2:5-7, 14-15).

Both Jesus and Paul would say that a person's attitudes are very important.

Yes, But . . .

The Bible has some strong words about adults' attitudes, but it doesn't say much about children's attitudes. Should we be so concerned about their attitudes?

Consider This:

Listen to the catalog of sins listed in this passage: "But God shows his anger from heaven against all sinful, wicked people who push the truth away from themselves. . . . Their lives became full of every kind of wickedness, sin, greed, hate, envy, murder, fighting, deception, malicious behavior, and gossip. They are backstabbers, haters of God, insolent, proud, and boastful. They are forever inventing new ways of sinning and are disobedient to their parents" (Rom. 1:18, 29-30).

How did that "disobedient to their parents" get mixed in with all those other despicable behaviors? The Bible doesn't suggest that adults are to be obedient to their parents. Adults are to love and care for their parents but are not to remain under their parents' authority. Paul must be referring to children when he makes that statement. By including that phrase with all the descriptions of sinful behavior, Paul is implying that children's disobedience is absolutely unacceptable to God. Remember that obedience to parents is one of the Ten Commandments.

Yes, But . . .

Still, doing all that hard work or being forced to perform exercises seems so rough.

Consider This:

I couldn't agree more. It is very rough. God intends for discipline to be rough and painful.

> "'My child, don't ignore it when the Lord disciplines you, and don't be discouraged when he corrects you. For the Lord disciplines those he loves, and he punishes those he accepts as his children.' As you endure this divine discipline, remember that God is treating you as his own children. Whoever heard of a child who was never disciplined? If God doesn't discipline you as he does all of his children, it means that you are illegitimate and are not really his children after all. Since we respect our earthly fathers who disciplined us, should we not all the more cheerfully submit to the discipline of our heavenly Father and live forever? For our earthly fathers disciplined us for a few years, doing the best they knew how. But God's discipline is always right and good for us because it means we will share in his holiness. No discipline is enjoyable while it is happening—it is painful! But afterward there will be a quiet harvest of right living for those who are trained in this way." (Heb. 12:5-11)

Yes, But . . .

Come on, it just seems so extreme.

Consider This:

Believe it or not, these tools still don't take discipline as far as God does. And I'm not even talking about when God disciplines us. I'm talking about what he tells earthly parents to do with their rebellious children. I'm warning you, hold on to your hats. "Suppose a man has a stubborn, rebellious son who will not obey his father or mother, even though they discipline him. In such cases, the father and mother must take the son before the leaders of the town. They must declare: 'This son of ours is stubborn and rebellious and refuses to obey. He is a worthless drunkard.' Then all the men of the town must stone him to death. In this way, you will cleanse this evil from among you, and all Israel will hear about it and be afraid" (Deut. 21:18-21).

Did you realize that the punishment for repeatedly disobeying parents was capital punishment? Please don't misunderstand me. I am not saying we should use this tool to motivate our children's obedience! We should never even threaten to do so! I am using this passage to show you how seriously God takes rebellion in children.

Do you still think these tools are too extreme? Taking over children's bodies and making them do work or exercises may seem cruel and unusual to the casual observer. But if you didn't know what was going on, a cesarean-section operation would also look cruel and unusual, until you saw the newborn baby.

I grant you, it is very painful to watch an attitude-adjustment session. We can all feel the children's anguish. But wouldn't it be even more painful to see your children grow up and be crippled or even destroyed by their bad attitudes?

A bad attitude is a progressive disease that methodically kills its victims. The worst part of this disease is this: It convinces its victims that they have no disease so they are not even ashamed of their "disgusting" behavior (see Jer. 8:12). A bad attitude always blames someone else. "It's not my fault" is a key symptom. "I couldn't help it" is a telltale indication that your children have it. Don't let this lethal condition claim one of your children. You are the preventive medicine and the antidote.

May God give us the wisdom to see our children through his eyes as we work to help them overcome their rebellion.

Summary

When we study God's Word, we realize that he is serious about dealing with bad attitudes. His perspective can help us see our way when we confront our children's rebellious attitudes. For a more thorough discussion of how God disciplined his children, see appendix B.

The next chapter discusses an additional tool you may find helpful in training your children: spanking.

▪ ▪ Reflection Questions

Take a few minutes to think about these questions. If possible, discuss them with your spouse, another parent, or a group of parents. Write down your observations, feelings, and goals in a journal.

1. Write down your objections to these tools of discipline and either review what's been said from Scripture or search the Scriptures yourself to see what God says about discipline.
2. What new ideas and insights have you learned from this chapter?
3. Does anything hinder you from disciplining your children effectively? Time? Fear? Lack of knowledge or experience?
4. What can you do to improve your relationship with your children?

Fathers, don't aggravate your children. If you do,
they will become discouraged and quit trying.

— C o l o s s i a n s   3 : 2 1

14

Adding an Accessory: Spanking

Spanking is controversial. Some parents swear by it, while
others swear against it, and still others have sworn never to
use it. Kids just swear at it.

You may be wondering, *Why do you go to all the trouble with*
the extra work or exercises? Just give them a quick swat on the
behind, and they won't do that again. For some children it is
just that easy. If that works for you and you are comfortable
with it, then keep doing it. If you say your relationship is
repaired and harmonious after that really quick discipline, I
won't argue with you.

However, my experience is different. I've found that training children is like cooking from scratch. If we take the time
to do it right, the results are noticeably better. Internalization
of good attitudes needs time to simmer and grow. Repairing
any damage to the relationship also takes time.

The danger of spanking is that it can become the easiest
and quickest method of administering pain. It can become a
lazy person's way of gaining submission from children. As
with time-outs, spanking runs the risk of losing its effective-

ness by being overused. If the spanking is not working, what do you do? Spank some more? Yell louder? Spank harder? Some child experts do recommend that. Spanking is like the trump card of discipline. Once you use it, it's gone. There is nothing else to follow it up.

When spanking is overused, children eventually learn to stiffen their bodies against the swats. What begins as stiff bodies hardened against the swats soon gets internalized into stiff-necked, hard-hearted children. We have to be careful to use these disciplinary tools in a godly manner.

I'm not against spanking. I'm against the *careless, casual overuse* of spanking. Too often, the emphasis is on the pain and not on the restoration necessary after a spanking.

The advantages of the work and exercise tools are that they give you much more latitude in dealing with discipline problems. There is no such thing as a "soft spanking"; that would be an oxymoron. However, you can assign a soft work assignment commensurate with the offense committed. Spanking limits your options. And if there is anything parents need when disciplining, it is options. Work and exercises offer much more variety in terms of intensity and actual work being done. These tools give parents numerous things to do to match the strength required to break a bad attitude. Spanking is limited to hard, harder, and "uh-oh, now what?"

Some parents don't like spanking because it seems too close to abusive behavior. It can be if it is done too hard or too often or on an inappropriate place on the body. Some parents were abused as children and would rather not use spanking at all. I'm not saying you should or should not use spanking; it is a matter of personal preference. If you decide not to spank, be sure you have other power tools to help enforce your limits. If you do use spanking, then I suggest using it like any power tool—with respect.

A recent issue of the *Family Policy* magazine focused its entire issue on spanking. It cited much research that had been done.

> Surveys indicate that 70–90 percent of parents of pre-schoolers use spanking, yet the incidence of physical child abuse in America is only about 5 percent.[1]
>
> Teaching parents appropriate spanking may actually reduce child abuse, according to Larzelere in his 1994 review article on corporal punishment.[2] Parents who are ill equipped to control their child's behavior or who take a more permissive approach (refusing to use spanking) may be more prone to anger and explosive attacks on their child.
>
> The Swedish experiment to reduce child abuse by banning spanking seems to be failing. In 1980, one year after this ban was adopted, the rate of child beatings was twice that of the United States.[3] According to a 1995 report from the government organization Statistics Sweden, police reports of child abuse by family members rose four-fold from 1984–1994, while reports of teen violence increased nearly six-fold.[4]

The publication was able to draw this conclusion: "Appropriate disciplinary spanking can play an important role in optimal child development, and has been found in prospective studies to be a part of the parenting style associated with the best outcomes. There is no evidence that mild spanking is harmful. Indeed, spanking is supported by history, research, and a majority of primary care physicians."[5]

Research supports what the Bible has been teaching for

271

centuries: "A youngster's heart is filled with foolishness, but discipline will drive it away" (Prov. 22:15).

Spanking and physical abuse are two very distinct actions. Look at the important differences outlined in the chart:

	Spanking	**Physical Abuse**
The Act	Spanking: One or two spanks to the buttocks	Beating: To strike repeatedly (also kick, punch, choke)
The Intent	Training: To correct problem behavior	Violence: Physical force intended to injure or abuse
The Attitude	With love and concern	With anger and malice
The Effects	Behavioral correction	Emotional and physical injury[6]

WHAT WARRANTS A SPANKING?

Spanking can be a very effective tool when it is used properly. It has its place in the tool chest of discipline.

In our family we have spanked our children (after age two) for only one reason—lying. We consider lying to be the most damaging thing children can do to any person or relationship. We want our children to know the importance of respecting themselves and others by always telling the truth. If children aren't truthful, they will never be able to enjoy authentic relationships. Lying also destroys a person's character.

When our children were very young (after two years old), we would sometimes spank them for not cooperating, only after repeated warnings. At that age, they were too young to be able to work or exercise. They were too small to do anything or to understand what was going on. A couple of swats on the rear usually got them to behave (as long as their misbehavior wasn't due to fatigue or hunger).

The only other reason I would consider spanking my children is if they stole something (we haven't faced that situation yet). Stealing is another blatant offense to another person. Children understand stealing. They have no doubt experienced the insult of having another child grab away a toy or cookie.

Lying and stealing each break one of God's Ten Commandments. These two laws are probably the first ones children are able to comprehend. They come shortly after the "obey Mommy and Daddy" rule. Telling the truth and not stealing are rules I have to obey along with my kids. It is easier for my children to accept the severity knowing that I am bound by those rules also.

I believe disrespect is destructive as well, but I don't think rebellion can be spanked out of a child. In that situation, it's too easy for a spanking to turn into a beating. I consider work or exercises to be more humane and effective in dealing with general rebellion.

If you choose to use spanking to discipline your children, know what issues warrant your using it. Then make sure that your children know clearly beforehand what actions will get them a spanking. Just as with any other consequence, in order for it to feel fair to the children and for them to internalize the lesson, they need to know what awaits them if they choose to disobey the rule.

SPANKING AS A FORMAL PROCESS

Spanking should be done only as part of a ceremony. It is a formal process. The best way to describe the procedure is to compare it to the legal proceedings of a courtroom. In the family court there are two main characters: you and your children. You each have a different role to play.

PARENTS' ROLES

Police—As the police, you need to protect your family. Your first role is to make sure no one is going to commit any more offenses. Stop the damage.

Paramedic—In your role as the paramedic, stop any bleeding (literal or figurative). Make sure everyone is all right and not about to go into shock. Comfort those in pain if needed. Calm down others when necessary.

Investigator—Now comes the hard work. As an investigator you gather all the available evidence regarding a situation. Develop your own style, ranging from the approach of Sergeant Joe Friday, who wants "just the facts," to the approach of Lieutenant Columbo, who just scratches his head because he can't seem to make sense of all the minuscule discrepancies. Interview everyone who might know something about what happened. Follow up any and all leads to verify testimony of other witnesses.

District Attorney (Prosecutor)—The D.A. decides if a "crime" was committed and determines the seriousness of the crime. The D.A. then determines whether there is sufficient evidence to prosecute. Weigh the reliability of the evidence based on the veracity and character of the witnesses. Reinterview witnesses if there is any discrepancy in their testimony. Parents will want to work together to discuss the situation and assess the consequences. Then the D.A. presents the evidence in the court.

Judge—In your role as judge, you are in charge of the proceedings, making sure they run smoothly and fairly. This gives everyone a sense of security. Make sure everyone gets heard without interruption. The judge decides which information is relevant. "He did it first" may or may not be germane. "She didn't get in trouble for that" may be true but not pertinent to this case. You may have to make some legal judgments regarding family law. For example, did your children know it was stealing to take a cookie without permission? Did they know that not giving you the note from their teacher is the same as lying (withholding the truth, which propagates a lie)? Did they know that cheating on a test is stealing information? Parents may have to extend some grace to give warnings, mercy, and second chances. Be fair, but don't be played for a fool.

CHILDREN'S ROLES

As you present the case to the court, your children have a couple of roles to play.

Defense Attorney—Your children should have ample opportunity to ask anyone any relevant questions and test the fairness of the proceedings. This sense of fairness should help ensure that children will internalize whatever you are trying to teach them (for example, that it is important to tell the truth). The prosecutor (parent) also has the right to cross-examine any witness.

Defendant—Obviously, children are the defendants. Sometimes you may have more than one defendant, each pointing a finger at the other as the more accountable party. This is when it may be important to proceed slowly. Find out exactly who said or did what and in what order things happened. If there is a discrepancy in the facts, someone may be lying. Warn them about the penalty for "perjury," which would be an automatic spanking.

Jury—The "courtroom" process works best when the children play the role of the jury. The children have to convict themselves in order for them to feel that the punishment is fair, deserved, and reasonable. They may be the only ones who were actually there during the event. They heard not only the words but also the tone of voice of the participants. They witnessed the facial expressions during the "crime." They are the only ones who know the motive behind the actions. That information may play a vital part in determining the degree of offense.

The goal of these entire proceedings is to obtain a full confession from the guilty party. The defendants have to give a full disclosure of what they did wrong and say they knew it was wrong. You want to know the whole truth. Eventually this is what will strengthen your relationship with your children and build their character.

But let's suppose your children are lying and refuse to confess. The evidence against your children is overwhelming, but they won't admit it. The witnesses are all very credible, and the facts all point to the children's guilt, but they just won't give up their plea of innocence. What do you do?

We have faced this situation several times with our daughter. Sometimes she would rather lie than own up to what she said or did. This creates a tough situation when our son says one thing and our daughter says the opposite. What can parents do when faced with this predicament?

What we've done is use the exercise tool to get the truth out of whoever is lying. How do we know which one to assign the exercises to? We don't. They *both* do the exercises until one of them confesses the lie. We usually use the "holding the arms out to their sides" tool primarily so we can keep looking at their faces and eyes to try to get a clue as to which one is lying. The eye-to-eye contact wears down the resistance. Usually the innocent one looks more sad, and the guilty one looks more scared and angry, but sometimes it is hard to tell.

Yes, this is very unfair to the innocent party. However, I still use this tool for a couple of reasons. Sometimes even the one telling the truth did have some responsibility for creating the problem with the sibling, so the exercises have a way of extracting the entire story. But even if one child is entirely innocent, both are reminded of the importance of always telling the truth. The exercises serve as a painful reminder to our children of how much Sharon and I value telling the truth.

Some parents are concerned that their children will resent them for not believing them and/or their sibling. It's never happened to us because we make sure the children know how bad we feel for having to put them through the ordeal. We don't ask for their forgiveness, but we do tell them how sorry we are that they had to endure the pain. They have always understood the importance of truth telling.

When the guilty party eventually confesses, the child is not only punished for the lie but expected to apologize to the sibling. Talk about humbling! I think they would rather eat nails, but they have to do it.

What is interesting is that the innocent child usually doesn't resent the sibling. Maybe it is because the innocent child gets a *big* apology from the guilty child. I think the real reason the innocent person isn't resentful is that he or she is just relieved to have it over with and would rather just forget the whole thing and be friends again. When we've asked our kids if they wanted to be served in any way for all the pain of enduring the unnecessary discipline, they have always said no.

Let's take another scenario. Suppose you know with absolute certainty that one of your children is lying, but the child refuses to confess. What do you do then?

This is a tough situation, which requires a lot of discernment. You may want to call a recess of the proceedings and talk it over with your spouse or another trusted person. If after due deliberation you—the judge—decide that the "jury" has reached a wrong verdict, you have the power to override the jury's decision. In a situation like this, you are dealing with a hard-hearted, unrepentant, stiff-necked sinner who needs to be cleansed. You would be negligent if you allowed the child to continue with a guilty heart.

Most of these courtroom scenes develop over seemingly insignificant things. It will be an argument over who left the milk out after breakfast or how the calculator got broken or who said what to whom. But it is those "insignificant" things that reveal some attempt to conceal something ugly. That ugly thing could be selfishness, rudeness, or a bad attitude.

This level of scrutiny mirrors the depth of concern you have for your children. You care enough to examine every part of their lives with the bright light of truth. Light is warm and comforting to those who are honest, but it's blinding and painful to those who have something to hide.

A small piece of duct tape stuck on the Watergate Hotel door during a burglary eventually led to Richard Nixon's losing his presidency. Adam and Eve missed their regular evening stroll through the garden with God. When God asked where they were, their explanations resulted in their banishment from their home (Gen. 3:8-24). These "insignificant" incidents changed history.

Your children's mistakes will probably not have such broad-reaching effects as these examples. But seemingly trivial events may be very significant in your children's moral development. Diligently exposing the truth can be very painful for everyone, but that cleansing is the only way for God to work in their lives.

PARENTS ADMINISTER THE SENTENCE

If a spanking is deemed the appropriate sentence, then the parent carries it out. This is about the toughest part of being a parent. Administering the discipline is painful for everyone involved.

Sharon or I administer the spanking only after we have gone through the process I have just described. These procedures help ensure that we have calmed down enough so we are not out of control. Our children know exactly what is going to happen and why it has to occur. They fully cooperate with the administering of the spanking. I didn't say they like it, but they submit to it.

We use a spoon (wooden or plastic) on their rear end only. We use a spoon so they will associate the pain with the spoon and not our hands. When our children were very young, we used to carry a spoon in their diaper bag. You should have seen the look on their faces when they saw that the spoon was portable.

Right before we swat them, we ask them why they are getting spanked. We want them to understand clearly that this is the result of their lying or stealing (in our family's case), not our desire to be mean. This helps them verbally submit one last time. It is also a test to make sure they accurately understand why they are being spanked. We swat them only twice, hard. The goal is to make it sting. We want to leave a lasting impression on their character but only a temporary impression on their skin.

Make sure no other children witness the spanking. Your spouse is the only other person who is allowed to be present. This is *not* because you have anything to hide. This is so children don't feel humiliated in front of their siblings.

I have described the process leading up to a spanking in some detail. Each detail may not always be applicable in your family situation. Sometimes the investigation or prosecution is over very quickly. I have been describing what some situations will require, and others will not require as much time and energy as I have described. But if it does, then stay with it. Remember, this is also a test of your love for and commitment to your children.

Immediately after I administer the swats, I hold the children close while they cry. I tell them I hope they will remember how important it is to always tell the truth. They ask for my forgiveness, which I immediately give them.

Then I get to do the healing part. I tell them that I will never talk to them again about this incident. As far as I am concerned, it is over. It's as if it never happened. I tell them how much I love them. The restoration of the relationship is the key to making the spanking worth it. There should be plenty of love and tenderness after a spanking. I literally hold them for as long as they want to stay there. Sometimes it feels as if my son or daughter is just soaking up my affection as I hold him or her.

Then we celebrate the restoration of the relationship with a bowl of ice cream or cookies, or we go out and jump on the trampoline until I'm out of breath. However you choose to celebrate, be sure to follow up the spanking with some warm, friendly time.

WHAT ABOUT SPANKING TEENAGERS?

Most people think spanking teenagers is not an option. I agree that spanking teens should be one of the last options considered, but it is still an option.

I recently attended the twenty-five year anniversary celebration at the private boarding school where I used to work. I enjoyed speaking to a few of the former students. One young woman approached me with her two children and asked me if I remembered her. We had the pleasure of catching up on each other's lives as well as reminiscing about our school memories in 1980. She remembered my spanking her when she was a fifteen-year-old student. She joked that I spanked much harder than the administrator did. She also freely admitted that she deserved her spankings and that she learned some valuable lessons as a result.

I realize that many parents really balk at the idea of spanking teenagers. Parents think it would be too demeaning for their teenagers. If that is the case for you, give your teens a choice. Let them decide between a spanking and another alternative. The spanking is short and sweet (and stinging), but the alternative is not a piece of cake either. In my experience, the teenager often chooses the spanking.

The last time our son, Dugan, was faced with a spanking was right before he turned thirteen. Sharon and I were meeting with some friends at church, and Dugan was off with his friends playing outside. The entire group of kids was brought into our meeting room by one of the workers at the church. The kids had been distracting a meeting by playing outside the windows. We thought that was all and talked with Dugan about appropriate behavior, reminding him of our expectations. We didn't think any stronger discipline was called for.

The next day our daughter told us that Dugan had been hanging over a retention wall that was at least twenty feet high. We were shocked that he would do such a dangerous, foolish stunt. It turns out it was a kind of daredevil situation, and Dugan "had to" show off his bravery and strength by hanging over the edge of the wall.

The stupidity of that act warranted a stern lecture, which he got. However, withholding the information from us was another matter—that was lying. Dugan agreed that he had deliberately not told us for fear of getting into trouble. This told us he knew it was wrong. It didn't take much to show him that not telling the whole truth was just as bad as telling an untruth. He fully understood the concept of deception and agreed that was what he was knowingly guilty of. He knew that he deserved a spanking.

We decided to introduce another option at this point for a couple of reasons. First of all, this was the first time in a long, long time that Dugan had lied about anything. Second, when Breeze told us the whole story, Dugan did not deny it. He cooperated fully with our investigation. And finally, Dugan was almost thirteen years old, and we wanted to give him a choice in his discipline. We asked him what would help him remember the importance of telling the truth. We gave him a choice between a spanking or doing several work projects, which we outlined specifically.

By giving him a choice, we hoped his choosing would help him internalize the lesson. Either choice was good to help him remember. The act of choosing helps build children's character. Their own will is involved in the choice, so they own it more.

Dugan chose the work projects, which included sweeping the garage of summer dirt and leaves, straightening the garage, picking all the pumpkins off the vines and washing them, digging a hole 5 feet wide by 8 feet long by 18 inches deep in the garden, and putting all the pumpkin vines in the hole to use for fertilizer for the garden; mowing down the tall grass that had grown near the pumpkin vines, and cleaning up the entire area. This took him several hours.

I had to leave for work before he finished, so I could not inspect his completed tasks right away. I came home for lunch so he could show me all he had done. There were a few things that were not done well enough, so I had him go back to do a better job. I even helped him a little because he had such a good attitude. When we came in for lunch, we had this brief conversation:

"What did you learn?" I asked.

"Not to get caught."

"Cute."

"Just kidding."

"I know. What did you learn?"

"To always tell you the truth . . . to tell you everything that happens."

"By Jove, I think he's got it. Let's eat."

"Yes, I'm starving."

We did have the conversation about apology and forgiveness. While the conversation was not very emotional, it served to let Dugan know that he had a clean slate once again. Life could go on.

Summary

Spanking is a powerful tool that enforces parents' most important expectations (in our family those expectations are telling the truth and respecting other people's property). The process leading up to the spanking involves due process. Through it the children will learn the value of character (why they are spanked) and fairness (how they are spanked). Parents must act with the confidence of a paramedic, the perseverance of a detective, the craftiness of a prosecutor, and the discernment of a judge. Parents must educate the defendant about the seriousness of the crime as well as seek the truthful verdict from the jury. Punishment must be dealt out with reasonableness and swiftness. After the sentence has been served, the children must be restored to their rightful position as fully privileged family members, without a rap sheet tattooed to their foreheads.

▪ ▪ ▪ Reflection Questions

Take a few minutes to think about these questions. If possible, discuss them with your spouse, another parent, or a group of parents. Write down your observations, feelings, and goals in a journal.

1. For what offenses do you use spanking? Are the results satisfactory?
2. At your house is spanking a thought-through process or an impulsive event?
3. If you spank, what process do you go through?
4. What memories do you have as a result of being spanked as a child? How is the strategy proposed in this chapter different from what you experienced?

*[The father] must manage his own family well and
see that his children obey him with proper respect.*

— 1 Timothy 3:4, NIV

15
Working as a Team

Sean came to the first counseling session with his parents.
They wanted some guidance about how to handle his rowdy
behavior and uncooperative attitude. After some preliminary
questions about Sean, I wanted to explore the dynamics of
the parents' style of discipline. I asked them which one of
them was the tougher disciplinarian. Before either one of
them could answer, Sean said, "Dad is!"

Sean's mom was flabbergasted because she felt she administered most of the discipline. Before I could say anything,
Sean's mom asked him, "Why do you say that?"

Sean didn't hesitate. "Because Dad is bigger and stronger."
Sean knows that his dad is the tougher disciplinarian. Even
though his mom has had to handle 80 percent of the discipline, he knows his dad is the stronger one. Sean seemed to
have that innate "fear" of his dad's strength.

Is that good? Should Sean see his dad as the one with
strength? Doesn't his mom have any strength? What does that
mean for how his parents handle Sean?

PARENTS PLAY DIFFERENT ROLES
Fathers and mothers play different roles with their children.
Sean sensed that. Although fathers and mothers play different

roles, they are teammates. They are on the same side, fighting the same battles, working toward the same goals, cheering each other's successes, mourning each other's mistakes. Parents should be united. If they aren't, everyone loses, especially the children.

Fathers and mothers usually express their love for their children differently. Observe them with young children. Typically, this is what you see:

Mothers	Fathers
"Coo" at babies to relax them	"Boo" at babies to excite them
cuddle	tickle
snuggle	wrestle
suckle babies on breast	bounce babies on knee
pull babies toward them	toss babies up in the air
tell kids to be careful	tell kids to go for it
fear child's risk taking	cheer child's risk taking

I realize this is a broad generalization. Many mothers tell kids to go for it, for example, and many fathers cuddle with their babies. But generally speaking, this is how many parents behave.

"We do not need fathers to be mothers or vice versa. A child needs a mother doing the mothering job and a father doing the fathering job. There is enough latitude in each role to guarantee job satisfaction if each accepts himself and the other for what he or she is. . . . Even though mothers and fathers have different roles, both are essential to their child's healthy development. Luckily for everyone, each role has its special gratifications."[1]

Parents are not interchangeable. We don't all have to act, think, or feel the same. God wants us to live in unity, not uniformity. He wants us to work and live in harmony, not be clones of each other.

In chapter 1 we looked at a chart that illustrates the spectrum of love. Let's look at it again.

Spectrum of Parental Love

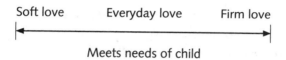

As we discussed in that chapter, the goal of love is *not* to find a balance somewhere in the middle but to embrace both ends of the spectrum of love. Many parents get locked into a battle as to which is the best way to handle their children. This is a mistake. Both parents bring experience and expertise into parenting. Parents have to learn to trust each other and tap into each other's strengths without trying to convince the other that his or her way is the best way. That ends up turning into a tug-of-war with the children being pulled like the rope.

I suggest that a mother's love is on the soft end of the spectrum and that a father's love is on the firm end of the spectrum. Generally speaking, mothers give the accepting, nurturing love, while fathers supply the backbone of love. That is not to say that a father's love can't be soft or a mother's love can't be firm. It is merely to suggest that both parents express their love in distinct ways. Love without expectations is indulgent; love without tenderness is oppressive. Both kinds of love are necessary for healthy childhood development. Children will survive without one or the other, but they will not *thrive*.

There is a lot of overlap in the middle of the spectrum. Both parents are involved in the everyday love, the practical expressions of love. Most expressions of love are gender neutral. Metaphorically speaking, both parents can grasp each other's arms and cradle their children together. They form a kind of safety net in which to catch their children so they don't fall through the cracks of life.

When it comes to disciplining children in everyday matters of training and guidance, both parents are involved. Which parent becomes involved in a particular situation is usually determined by who happens to be around the children at that time. But for major attitude-adjusting discipline, I suggest that fathers and mothers take on different roles. Both parents' roles are critical. One is not more important or better than the other. But they are different.

DADS TAKE THE LEAD WITH DISCIPLINE

When it comes to enforcing attitude-adjustment discipline, it usually works better if fathers are in charge. Fathers need to take the lead. Young Sean hit the nail on the head. He sensed that his dad's discipline had more strength.

Think of how God designed men. Dads have all the physical tools. Dads are bigger—the better to command respect. Dads are more muscular—the better to handle even the worst threat to parental authority. Dads have the deeper voice—the better to sound ominous and powerful when necessary. These are helpful in the discipline process.

First of all, the issues of size, strength, and prowess become increasingly significant for the growing child. The father is idealized as the ultimate power. This idealization makes the child feel protected from the dangers of the world.

Perhaps more important, it serves to protect the child from his own impulses. Limits are very important to a child's sense of security. Parents who provide a well-delineated structure are perceived as caring. Children give parents credit for providing such structure, even if they protest that it is more than they want.[2]

Fathers should use their strength to protect children from themselves. Setting and enforcing limits are things fathers seem ideally suited to do. When your children want to rough-house, whom do they seek out? Mom? Usually not. Fathers are usually built to withstand more physical punishment. Dads love a challenge. In fact it is usually a challenge for most men to *not* accept a challenge.

Most dads also have a competitive sense. They can tell when their children are trying to gain an upper hand, and they are usually more willing to subdue children's bad attitudes. Dads are willing to use their physical advantage to keep the relationship in line. Since dads already have the natural inclination to wrestle, whether physically or relationally, they can put that tendency to good use in the discipline process.

Some fathers also seem to have another advantage when it comes to discipline. They seem better equipped emotionally to discipline children. That is because some men do not seem to take it as personally when children are rebellious. They can better withstand the emotional barrage that children can fire at parents. Mothers generally have the stronger social and emotional attachments with children. Men seem better suited to provide the backbone around which to build the emotions.[3]

Proverbs 6:20 even suggests a difference between fathers and mothers. "My son, obey your father's commands, and don't neglect your mother's teaching." Fathers command, and mothers teach. This suggests that men have more strength, which commands respect. The mother's strength is in her patient training.

Do these masculine physical characteristics automatically prove that God wants fathers to discipline their children more than mothers do? Of course not. It is not a commandment. It just makes sense. Women's bodies are designed to nurture, while men's bodies are more suited to enforce and protect. Fathers should use their strength and leadership abilities to guide their children. Sadly, many fathers have abdicated this responsibility. Today's society does not encourage fathers to take that leadership role. Work has drafted men away from the family. Too many families have wrongly adopted the view that it is the woman's responsibility to run the family.

If you are a dad and if you have not been taking the lead in matters of formal discipline, I challenge you to consider redefining your participation in the family. Even if you have always left the discipline to your wife, make a change. Your wife will thank you. Your children may too.

Whenever you hear your wife raising her voice with the children, ask if she would like you to help. When you hear your kids arguing with her or each other, don't ignore it or say, "Honey, will you get those kids to be quiet?" Get up, and handle it yourself. Be firm but fair. Do it, and you will see a difference in how the family relates together. Your kids will respect their mother more and argue with her less if you assume your position as disciplinary leader in the family.

This doesn't mean that women should never discipline children. Mothers are with the children most of the time, and children don't wait until their dad is around to need discipline. The mother may still administer most of the discipline, but the dad should be the driving force behind it. But when the dad is there and the children need discipline, he should get up and do it! Being home is not "downtime" for fathers; it's when they should be most *on*.

MOTHERING ROLE

Mothers also have a vital role to play in the attitude-adjustment process. While mothers will obviously be involved in a lot of hands-on discipline, one of their primary roles is to be encouragers—of both the dads and the children.

Mothers encourage their children to obey. They encourage their children to cooperate and to stop arguing. Most children cannot withstand this two-against-one position for very long. Children don't have the stamina to fight both of their parents successfully. They will submit much sooner to parents who are united.

When mothers encourage their children to obey, the dads are also strengthened. Fathers need to know they have an ally. Otherwise it is tempting to give up the exhausting battle. By voicing encouragement to her husband, a wife declares her loyalty. She assures her husband that she will not be part of any tug-of-war between the children and him. The father is then free to concentrate on the attitude of the children. When children sense the unity in their parents' relationship, they feel much more secure.

I must confess that when Sharon and I first heard of this approach with the division of roles, we were not very receptive. We couldn't understand why this is necessary. It seemed so antiquated. What convinced us was how well it worked in practice. We found that our kids responded favorably to the roles we took on when disciplining them.

When I share this approach with my clients, I'm never sure what their responses will be. Most of the mothers look at me as if I had just released them from prison. They love the idea of dads taking the major role of disciplinarian. My biggest challenge is to get dads to take on this role. The work invested pays big dividends in the children as well as the marriage. Dads eventually experience that fact and enjoy the more harmonious family after the adjustment period.

Let's look at what these roles look like on the Spectrum of Parental Love chart.

Spectrum of Parental Love

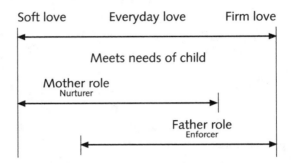

HOW CHILDREN FEEL ABOUT THE ROLE DIFFERENCES

Children feel more secure when they know what their parents' roles are. Children like the world to be predictable. They get uncomfortable when things change too often or too quickly. Predictable parents become a touchstone for children of all ages to test reality. Children need a stable relationship to ground them as they learn to understand and cope with the world's uncertainties. Having parents who provide predictable role models, especially the roles of nurturer and disciplinarian, helps kids feel secure and venture out into the world more confidently.

Children also think in absolutes. The world is either good or bad to them. Ever notice that when children are younger, they often ask about characters on television programs: "Is that a bad guy or a good guy?" Children have trouble tolerating a mixture of good and bad qualities in people. They don't know how to feel about those people, and they become confused. They wonder whether or not they should trust them. The disciplining parent temporarily becomes a bad parent to children. When dads take the role of the "bad guy," the children can still feel connected to their moms as the "good guy."

When children grow old enough to tolerate the uncertainty of the world and the complexity of human nature, they still need their dads to keep the role of enforcer. Children often grow to be bigger than their mothers, and their dads have to provide the line of strength and power. Of course, by the time children are teenagers, the influence lies more in the relationship than the power and strength. But don't underestimate the importance of fathers' size and strength when it comes to telling a sixteen-year-old to be home at midnight. A big, deep voice comes in handy at times.

WHAT HAPPENS WHEN THE FATHER ISN'T HOME?

The premise of this approach is that the strength, power, and authority to discipline come primarily from the father. God authorizes fathers to discipline their children: "And now a word to you fathers . . . bring [your children] up with the discipline and instruction approved by the Lord (Eph. 6:4). This authorization is also taught in Proverbs 1:8; 3:11-12; 4:1-5; 6:20-21; and 1 Timothy 3:4.

But how does a mother handle a bad attitude when her husband isn't around? When fathers are absent, mothers take over the authority to discipline the children.

A father delegates this disciplinary authority to his spouse. He explains to the whole family that when he is gone, the mother has the authority to discipline on his behalf. He tells his children that they are to respect their mother as much as they do him. If he is to insist on respect when he is gone, then he must ensure that his children respect their mother when she is home as well. When it comes to discipline, the mother's authority comes from her husband.

A father can hand over the responsibility to his spouse in several ways. First, he passes it verbally to his wife by saying to his children, "When I'm gone today, I expect you to do what your mom tells you to do without arguing or whining. What did I just say, Son?" Dad sets the expectation. If he needs to say it a little stronger, then he says, "Mary, look at me. When I get home tonight, I'm going to ask your mom how you did on your chores. If she tells me that you did a poor job or if your attitude was complaining, then you will have to deal with me when I get back. Do you understand? Now have a good day at school. And Mary, honey. I love you. Let me give you a hug."

If a mother needs backup help during the day, she can call her husband for advice. The father may choose to talk with the stubborn child on the phone: "What's this I hear about your giving your mom a hard time? I don't want you treating your mom like that. You do what she tells you to do. If you don't shape up right now, then it will be a long evening for you when I get home."

If the dad is out of reach during the day and hears about the terrible day when he gets home, he can say something like this to his child: "Apparently you had a hard time doing what your mom asked you to do. When your mom says something to you, it is the same as if I were saying it to you. You know what we expect from you. Don't argue when your mom says no. Since it seems so hard for you to submit to your mom's authority, I will help you practice submitting to my authority. Go get the rag and cleanser, and I want you to get started on cleaning the toilet. I am going to help you clean up this bad attitude."

Dads, when your wives report an attitude problem, don't take time for discussion. You want your children to know that you back their mom 100 percent. You are not there as an investigator. Your wife does a good job of that. You are there to support her by lending her your strength and power. After the children's attitude is repentant, then they will have to seek their mom's forgiveness.

Here are a few more conversations to illustrate how dads fill the role of disciplinarian:

Sally has been testing the limits. Her dad decides to talk with her. In a sober tone of voice, he says, "Sweetheart, you haven't been cooperating with your mom very well lately. I want that to change today. Will you obey Mommy all day today?"

"Yes, Daddy."

"When she tells you to pick up your toys, you will do it right away, won't you?"

"Yes, Daddy."

"And when she asks you to put your dishes in the sink, what will you say?"

"I'll say, 'OK, Mommy.'"

"Good. I'm going to call your mom on the phone today, and she will tell me how well you are doing. I want to hear a good report about you. Do you know what will happen if I hear you were arguing with Mommy?"

"No."

"You will have to do some extra work when I get home."

"OK, Daddy."

"Now, what did I say?"

"Umm, you said if I fight with Mommy, I'll get a bad 'port

and you will be angry and I'll have to do work. I don't like doing work."

"Good. So be sure to obey Mommy."

"OK, Daddy."

"Good. And one more thing. Have fun too!"

"OK, Daddy."

If the child is older, then the warning is a little more threatening. It comes with a reminder of your expectations.

"Jon, you are going to have a good day, right?"

"I dunno."

"Wrong answer."

"OK," he says reluctantly.

"Do we need to work on the attitude right now?"

"No, Dad."

"Good. I'd like you to pick up the newspapers and put them in the recycle bin for me now." (Jon's dad gives him a little test.)

"But, Dad . . ." Jon starts protesting.

"And then you can put away the dishes. And I suggest you change your answer unless you want to take this further."

"OK, Dad. I'll have a good day today."

"Good. When are we going out for breakfast again? Friday?"

"Yes, OK. I'll see you tonight."

"So what are you going to do?"

"I know. I'll pick up the papers and put the dishes away, and I'll have a good day."

"And one more thing."

"What now?"

"I love you." Jon's dad gives him a poke on the arm and catches his eye to make him smile.

Jon's attitude may not be 100 percent clean, but his dad is giving him a chance to improve on it himself.

Before moving on to the next section, I thought you might like to hear from my wife about this issue. Sharon will add her valuable perspective on this issue of a mother's authority.

"Let me begin by saying that I am not a 'softie.' I've always held my own pretty well with our kids. I'm definitely a softer touch than Steve, but at the same time, I set expectations and expect them to be met. In other words, I don't just sit back and let Steve do all the disciplining. I do more than my share, believe me!

"When our son was younger, he responded to my discipline most of the time. However, at times Dugan's attitude was bad, and he was not about to let go of it. I made him do push-ups or other forms of exercise, but he still would not let go of his attitude. Rather than letting him upset me, I would simply look at him and tell him that since he wasn't responding to my discipline, I was going to call his dad. If I was able to reach Steve, I knew he would give me suggestions about what to do. Then he would talk to Dugan, and Dugan would cooperate much better.

"If I couldn't reach Steve, I would tell Dugan that his dad would deal with him when he got home. I then let it go. Dugan would worry a little and tell me his attitude was better, but I told him that it was too late. I went and did something else. Dugan would not be able to play very happily from that point on. He would be restless as he awaited his dad's return.

"Now that Dugan is fourteen, I know I could not discipline effectively if he required any firm limit setting. He's taller than I am, and his voice is going lower than mine. As tough as I try to sound, I feel as if I'm talking to a wall. I don't yell. I don't demand. I look at him and say, 'Obviously, you're not listening to me. You'll listen to your dad when he calls or when he gets home.' I then let it drop.

"And this is wonderful. The weight of discipline is off my shoulders. I throw the ball into Steve's court, knowing that he will take care of things. My energy level remains pretty high because I'm not exhausted from a losing battle. I'm completely confident that when Steve comes home, there will be a small or large storm, depending on Dugan. But soon the delightful calm will follow."

Let me comment further. I do not resent Sharon's passing the job to me primarily because I know I can trust her to back me up. I know she is not just setting me up to do the dirty work and get stuck with the bad-guy role. She knows her limits, and she does not allow our children to turn her into an out-of-control, screaming mother. She knows she can count on me to defend her when our children challenge her. She does the same for me.

AVOID DAMAGING YOUR KIDS

As you can see from the Spectrum of Parental Love chart, children's needs are met when both parents are working together for their good. However, if either parent pushes beyond the bounds of the spectrum, the children and parents will suffer. If soft love is taken to the extreme, the love turns mushy and ineffective. If firm love is taken to the extreme, the love turns harsh and brittle. Let's look at these two dangers more closely.

The Dangers of Firm Love

If firm love crosses over into harshness, the love no longer meets the children's needs. Parents who are harsh are meeting their own need for control. Scripture says it this way: "Fathers, don't aggravate your children. If you do, they will become discouraged and quit trying" (Col. 3:21). This verse is a warning for parents not to frustrate their kids so they lose hope.

Harsh treatment of children could involve:

- ignoring them to teach them what it feels like
- belittling their friends because you think they are bad influences
- relentlessly teasing them when they make a minor mistake
- insulting their ideas as foolish
- criticizing their interests as a waste of time
- laughing at their opinions because they might be immature
- slapping them across the face to teach them a lesson

Harshness fits in the Spectrum of Parental Love chart like this:

Spectrum of Parental Love

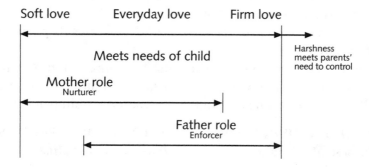

AUTHORITY VS. AUTHORITARIANISM

Bringing your children through an attitude adjustment will require you to exercise your parental authority. How you use your authority is important.

Some parents are afraid of authority because they have been victims of some abuses of power. I mentioned earlier that whenever I talk to parents about these tools of discipline, many mothers are relieved to hear that their husbands should be shouldering most of this responsibility. However some mothers have that look of terror in their eyes as I talk. These women have usually experienced the trauma of authoritarianism either at the hands of their father (or stepfather) or a husband. If the trauma was with their father, I do some work with the mother. If the trauma was with the current husband, then I teach the father how to use his authority in ways that are fair and safe. It still may not be easy for the mom, but she begins to see the difference with her husband and in the behavior/attitude of their children. The mistake is to conclude that power is bad.

God gives parents authority—the power and responsibility to correct and influence their children. God expects parents to be their children's authority (Prov. 3:11-12; 4:1-6). Authoritarianism perverts that authority; it crosses over the line and abuses power. Power is a neutral force, neither good nor evil. *How the power is used* determines its positive or negative value.

Firm love that crosses the line into harshness is authority that moves into authoritarianism. The chart illustrates some of the differences between authoritative and authoritarian parents.

AUTHORITATIVE PARENTS	AUTHORITARIAN PARENTS
Purpose of Discipline	*Purpose of Discipline*
heals relationship	to hurt relationship
confronts behavior/attitude	attacks identity or worth
breaks children's will	breaks children's spirit
lifts children with power	lords power over children
uses strength for guidance	uses strength for control

forgives and forgets
acts like a shepherd on the watch
focuses on children's need to dominate

Parents' Attitudes
exerts leadership
says, "I'm the servant; you learn from me."
uses power as scalpel
asks spouse for feedback
exerts emotional discipline
says, "You need help so I'll step in."
says, "Come closer to me because I love you."

Parents' Feelings
feels sad when children disobey
feels connected to children
feels sobered by responsibility
anger evaporates when children obey
feelings have focus
recognizes own weaknesses
says, "Let me help."

Parents' Style
allows respectful discussion
apologizes to children when wrong
stops own offensive behavior

reminds children of mistakes
acts like a lion on the prowl

focus on own need to dominate

Parents' Attitudes
is bossy
says, "I'm the king; you worship me."
uses power as butcher knife
knows all the answers
leaps to anger
says, "You hurt me so I'll get even."
says, "Get out of here because I can't stand you."

Parents' Feelings
feels powerless when children disobey
feels at odds with children
feels intoxicated by power
anger remains even after children have obeyed
feelings expressed carelessly
fears own weaknesses
says, "I'll show you!"

Parents' Style
never allows disagreement
never admits mistakes; apologizes insincerely
doesn't stop own outbursts

displays stable character	displays unpredictable personality
mood changes for good reason	mood changes without warning for no apparent reason
anger is under control	displays uncontrolled rage
raises voice when needs to	shouts continuously

Parents' Expectations are	*Parents' Expectations are*
understood	unspoken
clear	hazy
predictable	inconsistent
fair	unrealistic
consistently enforced	enforced when feels like it
enforced graciously	enforced harshly
modeled by parents	for children only

Children Feel	*Children Feel*
bruised	scarred
pliable as clay	shattered to pieces
molded	crushed
relaxed as babies	stiff as a corpse
comforted by hugs	destroyed by tongue-lashing
helped by friend	harassed by foe
filled with nourishment	drained of hope
flavored by salt	poisoned by salt
purified by fire	scorched by fire
playfully sweet	hopelessly bitter
gratefully cleaned	resentfully stained

Although the authoritarian person often is the father, mothers can also easily cross the line. When one spouse crosses the line, the other spouse should lovingly help the offending parent understand the serious damage that can be done to the children.

Handle harshness on the adult level. Get into the habit of debriefing with each other after a major attitude-adjustment session. Discuss even the minor confrontations you have with your children. This gives you practice in using the evaluation skills necessary to debrief the major attitude-adjustment sessions when they occur.

Later that day and even later in the week, ask each other questions such as:

- How did that go?
- What are some ways we could have done that better?
- How has Johnny been doing since the attitude adjustment?
- Do you think Johnny knew he was loved after we were done?
- Do you think our relationship with him is better now? Why?
- Did you feel I supported you?
- Could I have supported you any better?

If you feel that your spouse did not do a good job, never make that judgment in front of your children. That is the worst thing you could do. I've seen too many parents belittle the other parent. (This applies to divorced parents even more so because children are going to be ultrasensitive to it.) If a mother bad-mouths a dad to the children, she undermines both her and their father's authority. Children cannot and should not have to choose loyalty between parents. If pressured to, they will eventually reject both parents. If the offending parent wants to discuss the issue, that is another story. This will hopefully lead to the harsh parent's apologizing to the children. Modeling repentance is a powerful, relationship-building experience. If we have been harsh with our children, then an apology is necessary to repair the relationship.

The Dangers of Soft Love

The other danger on the spectrum of love is crossing the line from soft love into "mushy love." Mushy love is when one of the parents is in love with "loving feelings" rather than with the children. Those loving feelings are just as intoxicating and dangerous as power is for an authoritarian parent.

Mushy love may feel warm and cozy, but it is like quicksand. It can suck you under so slowly, you may not even be aware of it. The technical name for this issue is *boundaries.* When parents cross the boundary beyond healthy parental love into mushy love, it is called *enmeshment.* When this happens, the children's needs are no longer the priority. The parents' need for connection has overpowered them. These parents have an uncontrollable need to be loved, so they turn to someone who loves them—their children.

This is how mushy love looks on the Spectrum of Parental Love chart.

Spectrum of Parental Love

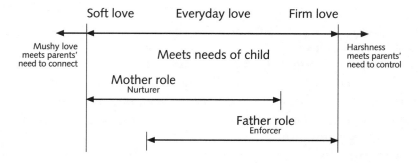

Parents who try to meet their own needs using their children do a lot of damage to the children. I'm not talking about sexual abuse. I'm talking about emotional, relational abuse. Children are not equipped to meet their parents' need for intimacy. Children will try their hardest and will sometimes manage to do a pretty good job, but they will lose their childhood. Children seduced into focusing on the neediness of their parents will grow up needy and will inflict the same curse on their own children. Children need to be *filled* with love, not drained of what they have. Parents should be focused on meeting all the needs of their children rather than expecting their children to help meet their needs.

This issue requires some close scrutiny. Carefully evaluate whether you may be expecting your children to meet your own needs. Ask yourself, "Am I trying to be friends with my children?" Children are not designed to relate to their parents as friends until the children are adults themselves. Children need parents, not more friends. Parents are not part of their children's peer group.

A parent is

- friendly but not a friend
- a role model but not a constant playmate
- approachable but not solicitous
- tender but not mushy
- understanding but not indulgent
- intimate but not emotionally incestuous

If you aren't sure what crossing the line into a peer relationship or friendship with your child involves, think about these descriptions. You cross the line into a peer relationship with your children when you

- ask them to hold you accountable (with your diet, exercise, work project, etc.)

- regularly ask them to remind you of things
- ask them what the other parent is doing when you aren't around
- regularly kiss them before you kiss your spouse after work
- are more enthusiastic about greeting them than about greeting your spouse
- ask them to keep secrets from the other parent
- let them sleep in your bed while your spouse sleeps somewhere else in the house
- confide in them how angry you may feel toward the other parent
- always expect them to care for their younger siblings
- discipline them and then apologize later for disciplining them because you fear they won't like you
- continually tell them you love them more than anyone else in the world
- tell them that they are more important, capable, or special than they really are

Another telling sign that parents would rather be a friend is when parents don't set or enforce limits with their children. These parents treat their children as if they were already adults. Let me quote part of a letter from a thirty-seven-year-old client, whom I will call Karen. She writes:

> My parents gave me lots of freedom. Their basic attitude toward me was: We love you. We will stand behind whatever you decide to do. But do the right thing. But they never told me what the right thing was. Lots of people told me I was ugly, geeky, and didn't fit in. I look at pictures of me at that age, and it's true. My parents told me it didn't matter. But it did. They didn't tell me about

deodorant or absolute truth or which fork to use or whether God was real. So I became absorbed in books. I read so many books, each one with its own view of truth. When I was ten, I escaped into fairy tales, and I just kept escaping as much as I could.

I began to do outrageous things to see if anyone would stop me. No one did. When I was thirteen, I remember wearing this skimpy dress to a party. When I showed my dad, all he said was, "You look nice." I felt embarrassed. I wanted him to tell me that I couldn't wear it so I could blame him. When I was fourteen, I escaped into drugs. Then I went on to do a lot of other outrageous things, but I'm too ashamed to tell you now. Mostly I didn't know any better. Maybe that's an excuse. I just didn't have the backbone to say no to temptation. All my friends thought my parents were cool. So then why did I feel so all alone? I still feel all alone. As I think about it today, I realize my parents were trying to be my friends. *But I didn't need any more friends; I needed parents!* All I wanted was to believe someone loved me! I still don't have a sense that I can count on anyone loving me. I have been searching for love all my life. What's wrong with me?

Karen readily admits that she tried to get her parents to stop her. She even realized it at the time. She agrees she would have fought against those limits, but now she understands that limits would have made her feel safe, protected, and cared for. Today Karen has a really tough time believing that she is a valuable person, partially due to her parents' permissiveness. How ironic that her parents' desire to have their daughter be their friend has left her feeling empty and distant from them.

Karen's parents haven't changed. Karen is trying to decide whether she should divorce her abusive husband. When she asks her father's advice, all he says is, "Whatever you decide, honey, we will support you." That sounds wonderfully supportive, but to Karen it feels like abandonment. Her parents still don't care enough to be involved! They should have an opinion! They should show that they care enough to help their daughter make this gut-wrenching decision.

Although the parent who is most often guilty of this mushy love is the mother, fathers can easily cross the line too. For example, fathers who want to be Santa Claus all the time have stepped over the line into mushy love. A father-child relationship can be incestuous without being sexual. Parents have to be careful not to cross over that emotional boundary.

After our children reach adulthood, we can begin to relate to them as friends. I look forward to the time when they are old enough for Sharon and me to open up to them about our struggles, fears, and failures. We are able to do that now to some extent, but it is mostly as an illustration to teach them something. We are not looking to our children for regular, emotional support.

Children will try to meet our needs. They love to play adult. When children grow up too fast, they give the appearance of having it all together, but they are only empty shells. They look confident, but that is only because they are terrified of revealing their secret fears and pain.

God the Father didn't refer to his children as his friends.[4] God didn't create Adam and Eve to meet his need for friendship. In fact, God knew the limitations of his relationship with Adam and created Eve so that Adam would not be alone. Scripture teaches how holy and different from us God is. God the Father doesn't invite us to refer to him as our friend; he invites us to call him Father. I think we're pretty fortunate to be invited to refer to him as our Father.

Jesus never referred to his disciples as friends until the very end of his life here on earth. In John 15:14-15 Jesus referred to his disciples as his friends because he confided in them everything his Father had told him. Jesus had no secrets from his disciples. However, Jesus did have an interesting expectation of his friends. He warned his disciples that their friendship was contingent on their "obeying his commands." Jesus offered them friendship with the condition that they love one another. Certainly that is a reasonable expectation for friendship. I think Jesus' offer is another example of his outrageous grace. It is an offer we would be foolish to refuse. Just remember that the offer comes only after God has firmly established his authority and holiness. For us to make a similar offer to our children before they are adults would not be healthy for anyone.

Friendship should be an option *after* our children are grown. Don't rush it. Our kids can always find more friends, but they will have a much more difficult time finding someone who will parent and love them better than you can.

WORK TOGETHER

Parents are teammates. They are like tag-team wrestlers. Each parent takes a turn working on the children's attitudes. The mom is the encourager while the dad is the enforcer. The dad roughs them up when necessary, while the mom builds them up. It is an unbeatable combination.

Each role supports the other. Fathers sometimes need their wives' help to keep from becoming harsh. Mothers sometimes need their husbands' help to keep from becoming mushy. Fathers and mothers need to complement each other rather than complain about and compete with each other.

Fathers have a tough job. They have to be firm enough to adjust their children's attitudes but soft enough to listen to criticism when they cross over the line into harshness. Dads can't afford the luxury of sitting comfortably on the firm-love end of the spectrum, waiting to handle just the big problems when they develop. Dads also have to soften up enough to be warm with their children. A good dad is like a lion: he needs to be strong, brave and fearsome yet tender, playful, and approachable. It's not easy being the king of the beasts. Good dads have a lioness so they don't get too beastly.

Moms have a tough job too. They have to be soft enough to nurture their children but firm enough to stand up against their children's inevitable attempts to take advantage of them. Mothers can't afford the luxury of sitting comfortably on the soft-love end of the spectrum. They must be firm enough to command respect.

Children need parents big enough to help them contain their wildly volatile emotions. Children need parents who are mature enough to lead them wisely. Children need parents who can be adults.

Twenty years ago I probably would have disagreed with about 90 percent of the information in this chapter. But twenty years ago I naively thought that parenting would be a piece of cake. When Sharon and I were first exposed to these ideas, we both thought they were outdated. We were not sold on the idea of fathers and mothers playing different roles. We have come to learn the wisdom of capitalizing on our differences and strengths. When it comes to discipline, we have learned it is good to play complementary roles and not competitive ones. Our marriage and our roles as parents will honor God by fulfilling our different functions in the family.

You may disagree with me on the fathering-mothering roles. I simply offer them to you as methods that have worked effectively when disciplining children. They may not fit with your personality or child. I leave that decision up to you.

Whatever roles you play, work hard at supporting each other's parenting skills. Defer to each other's strengths. Capitalize on your differences but work together. Christ calls us to live in unity, not uniformity. Learn to trust each other's judgment. Get into the habit of debriefing what happens when you discipline your children. Spend some time with your spouse and discuss how things went and how they might go better next time. There will always be a next time, so be ready. You are on the same team.

Reflection Questions

Take a few minutes to think about these questions. If possible, discuss them with your spouse, another parent, or a group of parents. Write down your observations, feelings, and goals in a journal.

1. How would you describe the father's role in discipline?
2. Where are you and your spouse in the spectrum of parental love?
3. Who does most of the disciplining? Why?
4. How can you support each other?
5. Does your style of discipline need to change?
6. With whom will that change start: you, your spouse, or both of you?

7. How well do you and your spouse work as a discipline team?
8. How can you and your spouse improve working as a team?
9. What would you like from your spouse so you could improve in your role with discipline?

part four

Special Applications

Father to the fatherless, defender of widows—this is
God, whose dwelling is holy.

— P s a l m   6 8 : 5

16

Using the Tools as a Single Parent

"Josh, please stop arguing and take out the trash," pleads
Linda, his mother.

"I'm in a hurry. I gotta go now . . . *without* the trash!"

"No you don't. You aren't doing anything until you take
out the trash!"

"Watch me."

Linda knows she can't stop Josh. It's humiliating even to
try. When her husband first left them, she and Josh had their
moments, but they always got through them somehow. Josh
seems to be over the shock and able to accept the changes. It's
been three years. He shouldn't still be angry. It doesn't seem
like anger. Josh seems to have decided that he doesn't want to
listen to his mother anymore. Linda feels powerless. Josh
seems to sense her helplessness and takes advantage of it.
What can she do?

I confess that I don't have a lot of personal experience as a
single parent. My biggest challenge is when my wife travels
out of town for a week or two. In no way does that qualify
me as a "single-parent club member." I could barely get a
visitor's pass to that club. I can barely begin to appreciate

what single parents have to cope with every day. And single parents have to do it day in and day out without much help or hope for relief.

Single parents deserve a special place in heaven—or at least a couple of weeks in Hawaii every other month. If you are a single parent and feel as if you can't do this alone anymore, you are right. Parenting is too much work to be done alone. Unfortunately, sometimes you have no choice. So what can be done to make the best of a less-than-ideal situation?

Discipline is different for single parents. The differences are more subtle than obvious. Let's look at the Spectrum of Parental Love chart to see where single parents fit on the range.

Spectrum of Parental Love

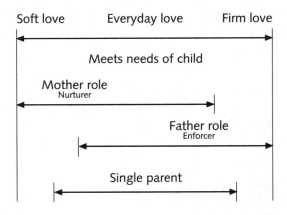

A single parent's range is much narrower. Working alone, a single parent does not have the latitude or degree of influence that two parents have as a team. There is no division of labor. One person has to do it all. It is very difficult for one person to play the "bad guy" *and* the "good guy." Both roles get watered down when one person tries to switch back and forth.

The problem of which role to emphasize is sometimes a matter of logistics. Single parents do not have as much time or energy to cover the range of disciplinary needs their children have. Single parents would love to have a forty-hour day so they could get everything done and still get enough sleep. With a hectic schedule, discipline often gets addressed only when it reaches the crucial stage. By then, it has grown into a major event. Since single parents don't have the luxury of extra time or energy that effective discipline requires, discipline gets shoved aside. Inconsistency becomes the norm. That's why time-outs, taking away privileges, or groundings are used too often. It doesn't take as much out of a person to sentence children to those punishments.

Every person tends to favor one end of the Love Spectrum or the other. Our personalities and upbringings predispose us to gravitate naturally toward soft love or firm love. It's very tempting for single parents to think, *I shouldn't make Susie work so hard around the house. She's had it rough since her father is gone. We will have a more relaxed home.* Other parents can't wait to "teach Scott a few lessons about respect, now that he can't hide behind his mother's apron strings."

As a single parent, it is easy to get stuck in a rut with discipline tools. A valuable and often necessary resource for effective parenting is input from other people. Ask a wise, respected friend for feedback about your parenting. You may be challenged to consider things you have never thought of before. You may be encouraged to know you are doing the right thing and not to give up. In the process, you may gain some of the companionship that was lost with the loss of your spouse.

As I've discussed before, crossing the line into either harsh love or mushy love is not good for children. Children can turn into pawns for meeting the parents' own needs. All parents have needs. When a spouse isn't there to meet them, it is tempting to turn toward children. Unfortunately, children are all too eager to try to meet those needs for single parents. Children are sensitive and vulnerable, wanting to please their parents. When children meet those needs, they learn to love that powerful, intoxicating feeling associated with pseudo-adult status. Single parents need to be especially careful to stay within the boundaries of meeting their children's needs and not their own.

How can you make the best of your situation as a single parent when it comes to discipline? Let's look at the ideal situation for a divorced couple. The ideal scenario would be to work with your former spouse as a disciplinary team. I know this would be unusual, but it would be great if it could be worked out for the children. Dads can still be the main disciplinarian and support the mother. Moms can remind the children how much their father loves them and that he is disciplining them because he loves them.

Children are not assets that can be divided. Divorced parents will always have a business relationship with each other because of the children. The better the parents can work together, the smoother the family business runs.

FOR SINGLE MOMS
Most single, divorced moms will not find it a good idea to enlist their former husband as a partner to help them with the discipline. In that case, you may try to recruit some other men to help you. You could probably use several actively supportive people for both you and your children. This is where your children's uncles can take a more active role in

rearing their nieces and nephews. Grandparents or cousins may be able and willing to contribute. Identify respectable coaches, scout leaders, or Sunday school teachers who would be willing to step into the father role.

If you sense some mutual affinity between your children and a mature, trustworthy man, ask him if he would be willing to take on some responsibility with your children. Explain what is missing in your children's disciplinary life. Ask the man if he would be willing to help out as a "godparent" for your children. Tell him that you would like him to be an "on-call dad," who could come over on short notice when you need some help with your children. If the man couldn't come over, maybe he would be willing at least to talk to your children over the phone.

It will take an unusually committed man to be this kind of godparent for your children. He would have to be willing to step into an intense situation and be comfortable with that. You would have to talk with him extensively about what you were looking for from him. You would also want to make sure that the way he has disciplined his own children has been effective and biblical. Churches can help single moms by identifying men who can help with this need (James 1:27).

Throughout history, the extended family has helped in the child-rearing responsibilities. Mary and Joseph depended on the extended family to help them parent Jesus. That's maybe why they didn't miss him for a couple of days after they left Jerusalem (Luke 2:44). They were accustomed to other friends and relatives helping with the parenting. Asking for parenting help may feel awkward, but allow a godly father to use his gifts to serve you and your children.

Am I suggesting that mothers in general and single mothers in particular cannot discipline their children? No, I am not.

Mothers do the bulk of disciplining children in today's society. They have the time and heart to do an excellent job of it. A mother's skills are invaluable to her children. I am in no way trying to diminish her contribution to the well-being of her children. What I am suggesting is that mothers can benefit immensely from the contributions and support of men in a father role.

If you are a single mom, remember that your children need more than just soft love. Do the best you can to fulfill the role of enforcer. Try to have the flexibility to meet the full range of your children's needs, even though it may not feel comfortable for you.

If you are struggling under the awesome responsibility of being a single mother, don't forget to make your requests known to God. Sometimes we don't have what we need because we don't ask God (James 4:2). If God doesn't answer right away, keep asking because God has a very special place in his heart for single parents.

FOR SINGLE DADS

Single dads don't have it quite as rough as single moms do when it comes to discipline. They still have to deal with the time and energy factor. But most dads have that strength advantage when it comes to discipline. Single dads may have to deal with the fear of "losing" their children if they are too harsh. Let me reassure you, if discipline is done well, the children will end up feeling closer to you after you have set expectations and firmly yet lovingly enforced them.

Some dads may need help with not crossing over that line into harshness. For your own benefit as well as for your children's, here is a suggestion. Tell friends (or a small group of fathers) you call regularly what is happening between you and your children, and ask for their feedback. Be honest with them. It will give you some of the needed support and confidence. Let them be honest with you. Listen to them if they tell you to lighten up or tighten up your discipline. As always, be aware of the overall goal of discipline—to enhance the relationship between you and your children.

Probably the most important advice I can offer is that you spend as much time with your children as possible—just hang out with them. You don't have to pack a special activity into every hour you are together. Children love simply being with you. The most important thing you have to give your children is you. You may not feel as if you are giving them much, but you are. Your time with them makes them feel very important and loved.

You can influence your children in one of two ways: by force or by your relationship. The love, trust, and intimacy of the relationship make up the preferred way to influence your children. The power of force is quicker and simpler, but use that only when necessary. Spending large quantities of time with children will pay off in huge dividends of influence with them. Be sure to make those regular deposits of time. Your payoff will be your children's interest in you, and that will be the most rewarding investment you ever made.

Reflection Questions

Take a few minutes to think about these questions. If possible, discuss them with another parent. Write down your observations, feelings, and goals in a journal.

    1. What are the biggest challenges you face with discipline?

2. Whom could you ask for assistance with disciplining your children?
3. What do you need to do before you are ready to ask that person to be a godparent?
4. Do you tend to lean toward soft or firm love?
5. Are there ways to work with your children's other parent to keep discipline consistent?

His unchanging plan has always been to adopt
us into his own family. . . . And this gave
him great pleasure.

—E p h e s i a n s   1 : 5

17

Using the Tools in Blended Families

"I don't have to listen to you!"

"Oh, yes you do, young man! Come back here! Don't walk away from me!"

"Who's gonna make me? You aren't my real dad anyway. My real dad wouldn't be as mean as you are. Things were just fine before you came along. I'm sick of living here. I'm calling up my dad."

If you are parents in a blended family—whether it is the result of a divorce and remarriage or an adoption or a foster-parent arrangement—you face unique challenges when it comes to discipline. You have the responsibility of rearing children to whom you did not give birth. You may wonder at first what right you have to discipline "someone else's" children. Sometimes when those children come into your family, they have been under the care of parents whose disciplinary goals may have been quite different from yours. You may wonder if the different expectations are confusing to the children. If your expectations are higher than what your children are used to, you may wonder what your expectations may do to your relationship with the children, especially if they bristle and start to attack you, as the boy in the opening illustration did.

Parenting someone else's children is an area in which I do have some professional experience. I worked as a houseparent for troubled teenagers. I didn't feel like their parent. Many times I didn't even want to be with them (and I know the feelings were mutual because they would tell me so). The teenagers my wife and I "parented" had problems serious enough for them to be sent to us for a year or so. Our job was to help them change their attitudes and behavior so they could return home to their parents. I was able to learn some lessons from these experiences as a foster parent.

BLENDED, ADOPTIVE, AND FOSTER FAMILIES

Remember when you had a substitute teacher in school? It felt like a vacation day. Your regular teacher might have left a few busywork assignments, but it was more or less a free day. You may remember a few substitute teachers who didn't let you get away with anything, but they were in the minority. You may have felt that most substitute teachers you had were just baby-sitting the class.

Disciplining children to whom you did not give birth is similar to being a substitute teacher in some respects. You are not immediately afforded the same level of authority. The new parent, like the substitute teacher, has to gain the children's respect. Most respect can be obtained by being fair and reasonable.

Be fair when expecting the children to learn the new family rules. Be reasonable in allowing the children some time to adjust to the new system and style of doing things. Be gracious and patient according to their age and maturity level. Give them plenty of warning about the new rules and your willingness to enforce them.

Parents in blended families must gain the respect of their children, but until the respect is gained, parents can insist that their children show them common courtesy. This basic level of respect should be expected from all children in all circumstances. Your stepchildren, adopted children, or foster children do not have to love or even like you, but they do have to obey you. You should expect them to honor and respect you.

Gaining respect requires an adjustment period, which also gives you time to get to know each other. Try to spend as much time as possible with them. Let them get to know you. Gradually build a relationship with them. It will take them some time to understand that liking you doesn't mean that they have to reject their noncustodial or biological parent. Loyalty becomes a tough issue for them to resolve. Be patient.

How do the disciplinary tools described earlier in this book fit the needs of these families? Attitudes are still just as important. Some children will try to use their unfortunate life circumstances as an excuse for bad attitudes. Loving parents will not lower their standards for their children. Attitude remains a key for success in life.

Parents still have to teach and train children, regardless of the changes in personnel. Children still have to learn submission and respect for others. The fifth commandment—honor your father and mother—doesn't have an exception clause for children in blended families. It doesn't say to honor only your biological parents.

Parenting nonbiological children carries with it some extra challenges. They may say things such as, "I don't have to listen to you. You aren't my real parent anyway!" Sometimes these messages are simply communicated with a sneering look that says, "I won't even give you the time of day." The insolent tone of voice may betray their contempt more clearly than the actual words. What do you do with these messages? Should you just ignore them? What are your children really saying? Let's examine some of the deeper messages these kids send and explore ways of dealing with them.

1. "I feel hurt and abandoned by my biological parent." This is true—all too true. Children feel terribly hurt by the loss. Divorce or death leaves a big wound on their hearts. They feel a huge loss of the family. Sure, they may still see each parent. But they will never have that family feeling again. Children always lose. Even adopted children may feel a vague sense of abandonment by their biological parents. To whom do they express those feelings? They express them to you, the parents closest to them.

What makes it so difficult is that they may express their hurt feelings as anger. Hurt is too vulnerable a feeling to reveal. Anger is the protective shield around the hurt. Anger is the armor that attacks rather than risks more hurt by exposing how hurt they are inside. Often the sneering, sarcastic statements are just cover-ups for the hurt underneath. So how do you respond?

Listen to your children talk about their feelings. Let them vent a little. Letting off some steam may be all they need to do. Empathize with their loss. Understanding their pain should help them feel some relief from it and offers them a chance for some healing. And don't just understand them; make sure they *feel* understood. After you have heard them spout off and they have calmed down, tell them about a time you felt a painful loss. Tell them how deeply you were hurt. Let them know how sorry you are for the way things turned out. (Remember that saying you are sorry is not the same as saying you are responsible. It simply means you feel bad also.)

However, their hurt or feelings of abandonment do not grant them a license to treat others in a rude manner. Society does not owe them a debt. Being mistreated or hurt by parents, whether real or imagined, is not a sufficient reason for prolonged misbehavior. Indulgence will not help them in the long run. After a reasonable time to express their hurt or disappointment, let them know they will be held responsible for expression of those feelings. Teach them appropriate ways to express their feelings. Unrestrained anger is not acceptable in a healthy family and society.

Listening to them should resolve most of their pent-up feelings. If words are insufficient for them to cleanse their body of their feelings, they may need some of those power tools previously discussed in this book. Some children prefer to "wrestle" to get those feelings out of their system. Proceed with your responsibility as a parent, and discipline them as you would any other children.

2. *"Cut me some slack. I've had it rough. If you discipline me, you are just another mean person like everyone else. Leave me alone!"* These words are pretty forceful. Some children have tragic pasts. Their story may be entirely true; their life history may make you cry. How should you respond to that message?

Go ahead and cry. Mourn their loss with them. Let them know how sorry you are for their pain. As I said before, make sure they feel understood. But don't ignore the rest of their message. They are accusing you of being mean. They want to be left alone with their pain. They won't say this, but they are afraid you will hurt them more. They desperately need their wounds tended to, but they won't let anyone near them. They are like a wounded dog that won't even let its master near without growling or snapping at him. These children are living in a constant state of shock.

Children who talk like this need immediate attention, in spite of their fear of being hurt more. They are already feeling abandoned by their loss. They feel as if life is useless. If you back off from these children, then you are confirming to them how hopeless they are. Don't let their fear and anger intimidate you. They are just testing you to see how much you care about them. If you leave them alone, you are abandoning them to a living torment. Their persistent pout is their own little hell. When you move toward them and their pain, then you show that you really love them.

What should you do? Confront them about their rude, insolent attitude and behavior. Remind them that they are not entitled to special treatment. They are not entitled to abuse others just because they may have been abused. Insist that they apologize to whomever they offend. You are not doing them any favors by allowing them mercy at this point. They can be shown grace and mercy after they repent. They have to take responsibility for themselves.

3. *"You don't really love me either. No one loves me. If I can't get love, then maybe I can get pity. You should feel sorry for me."* This message is similar to the last one. It is filled with self-pity. It packs a different kind of wallop. It is a challenge to prove your love by not enforcing the consequences. It's an attempt to manipulate you into thinking that the only way to prove your love is to let them off the hook.

These children are trying to get all the soft love they can from you. The implication is that after you fill them up with love, they won't misbehave. They are trying to make you think that if you can just keep their bucket of love filled, they will have a good attitude. And if you can't keep them filled with love, it becomes your fault that they have a bad attitude. Smooth, don't you think? All parents fall for this one at some point. That's all right. It's a problem only if you make it a habit.

These children have thrown you a curveball. Their self-pity looks like pain and suffering, but it is really hidden anger. In fact, their anger is so deep that it has developed into a rage that even they are afraid of. They are scared it will overpower even their parents, so they disguise it as sorrow. Granted, they are in deep pain, but they won't let anyone near it. Most likely these children will be very subtly rebellious. They will "forget" a lot or move slowly. They will have a million and one excuses why they couldn't get something done on time. Whatever they do get done will be late or of such poor quality that they might as well have not done it.

In technical terms, these children are passive-aggressive. They do not express their anger directly. They express their rage in sneaky, passive ways such as forgetfulness, moving slowly, being late, carelessness, and always having an excuse. Their offenses never seem sufficient to warrant severe discipline. Most people outside the family just feel sorry for them or annoyed with them, but no one knows what to do for them. The children just seem to want someone to take care of them, and they can usually get someone to do that.

Living with them can be infuriating because you can never seem to justify to yourself the frustration you feel inside. If you tried to explain what they did to people, they would look at you and ask, "Is that all? And you're that upset with that poor child?" Passive-aggressive children can make you think there is something wrong with you for getting so angry at such small infractions.

These children are in danger of being lost. If someone doesn't reach them soon, it may be too late. What does *not* work with these children is more gentle love. They claim to want it, but it never helps. You could be the most loving, patient, kind, gentle parent in the world, and it wouldn't matter. They don't trust it. They are so hurt, angry, and mistrusting that they will not truly accept your love. These children are masters at playing hide-and-seek. Chances are you will never find these children by just being patient and loving. They don't want to be found. They just want you to leave care packages at their post-office box, and then after you leave, they will come and pick them up.

So how do you reach these children? This is going to sound rough, but you need to confront these children continuously with every little mistake. These children should not be allowed to look at you cross-eyed without having to pay for it. They will feel as if you are the meanest parents in the world. And when they finally explode and tell you how much they hate you, they will show their true colors. All the garbage will come pouring out. When they manifest their true feelings toward you, then you will have found them. They will no longer be lost in their lukewarmness. You will have forced them out of hiding. You will have pushed them to face their rage.

Once you have done that, they will know that you are big enough to handle their fury. They will accept your help in facing their pain and relax in your gracious love. They will finally be connected to you. Your determined pursuit will have reaped the reward of their presence. By encouraging their rage at you, you will have shown them that they don't have to try to hold on to it any longer. You became the container for their rage, their abandonment, their hurt. That's what it means to be a mature, loving parent. That's exactly what Jesus did for us. He took our rage and absorbed it into himself.

After taking your children through this intense experience, I hope you can see how critical and enriching the reconnecting part of discipline truly is for the relationship. You are the crucial piece necessary for healing in your child. Without your relentlessly pursuing and confronting them, they would still be all alone in their pain.

4. *"I don't want to obey you."* This is what all the messages boil down to. "I don't want to!" is their real intent. Their various allegations may hold some merit considering their rough past. But when the accusations are used too often, they become a smoke screen for the children's true motives. They may try to throw you off track with some emotionally entrapping accusations such as "You are not my real parent." The overall mission is to escape their responsibility. They don't want to obey you. They are just like all other children in that regard. They just have another weapon to throw at you. Don't let their weapon be a secret one anymore. Don't let their accusations dissuade you from expecting respect and obedience.

Before I move on to the next section, let me state something that is obvious. Parenting is much more than contributing some sperm or an egg. Any physically mature person can do that. But only truly mature adults can be parents. Parenting is sacrificing your time, energy, attention, affection, and self for our needy, foolish, selfish children who desperately need our loving guidance. Comfort them when they are in pain. But don't let their manipulative cries for pity dissuade you from giving them what they really need.

Children in these situations will be terrified of being hurt again by adults who claim to love them. Don't let them confirm their worst fear by driving you away from them with their rebellious behavior. Don't let them become a self-fulfilling prophecy of failure. Show them that your love is stronger than their fear and anger.

DISCIPLINE CONCERNS FOR NONBIRTH PARENTS

Although I have never been a stepfather, I hope that my experience as a foster father for teenagers and my work as a counselor qualifies me to suggest some things. Stepparents, adoptive parents, and foster parents sometimes confess to me, "I don't feel as if I have a right to be my children's authority. I don't feel like their parent."

My flippant response is, "I don't always feel like being a parent either, and that is with my own biological children." Parenting is a decision more than a feeling. It is simply hard work at times. My polite response is, "If you are the parent, then you automatically have the God-given right and responsibility to guide them. Your feelings as to whether or not you feel like being a parent are irrelevant."

When I worked as a houseparent for teenagers, I did not "feel like a parent." I was only twenty-five years old. Most of the time I didn't even feel like an adult, let alone a parent. Yet I was a role model for those teenagers. I wanted to quit that job more times than I can count. But after many long hours of playing with them, talking and listening to them, enforcing the expectations for them, and living with them, I began to develop some very tender, caring feelings for those kids. We began to feel like a family. I had a lot of mixed emotions when the kids were ready to leave the boarding school and return to their homes. I was proud of their progress, yet I was sad to see them leave.

In the midst of a tough discipline session, some of the students would accuse me of not really caring about them. I would respond, "You can think whatever you want about how much I care. That isn't the problem here. Your attitude is the problem. You may not think I care, but I promise you this: I do care about your treating your teacher, your house-mother, your roommate, or me with respect."

A surprising thing would happen. I would actually start to care about those students. After I disciplined some of them for the tenth or twentieth time, I really started to care about their growth and development. I had invested a lot of time and energy into them. I wanted them to do well. I began to love them.

When I had my own children, it worked the same way. As I would change their diapers, burp them, rock them, and sing to them, those strong feelings of attachment grew. They continue to grow today, as I continue to care for them. My commitment to care for them generates my feelings of love for them. My children know they are loved. A lot of it is because I put so much of myself into them.

As a stepparent, adoptive parent, or foster parent, you may not have all the initial warm feelings that children's birth parents may have, but that is irrelevant. You didn't promise that you would always feel loving feelings. You have made a commitment to help parent them.

Discipline is one way for children to feel that you care for them. You may not always feel caring, but if you respond to their needs in a caring manner, tender feelings will sprout in you. Even more important, your stepchild, adopted child, or foster child will begin to feel loved. Children will eventually pick up on your feelings for them.

You may feel pressure to try to be like the parent you are replacing. Forget it. Even if you could imitate the children's biological parents exactly, the children wouldn't love you the same. They already have those parents. They don't have a parent like you. You bring to your children things that no one else can. You bring yourself.

THE BIOLOGICAL PARENT AND THE STEPPARENT

Let me make a few general comments specifically directed to blended families. These are families in which one of the biological parents is married to a person who becomes a stepfather or stepmother. This presents many issues for these families, but I will focus on discipline.

Biological parents play a crucial role in the successful administration of discipline in the new family. They have to alter their thinking. They have to move from "I am the parent" to "We are the parents." Biological parents have to learn how to share the parenting responsibilities with the new spouse. Biological parents still have the majority of the influence with their children, but they must be willing to bestow equal authority on their new spouse. Biological parents will have to surrender some of their power. They cannot "protect" their children from the new parent. The goal is to work as partners—equal partners.

As for the parental roles for discipline in blended families, they can still be identical to the ones described in chapter 15. There is no reason to have to change the roles just because one parent is the stepparent.

If the new stepparent is the mother, then the biological father has to support her with enthusiasm. He has to communicate clearly to the children that she has authority that is equal to his to set expectations and enforce them. If the children argue with the stepmom, the dad has to back her up. He has to step in and enforce the expectations or consequences the stepmom was trying to set. He may even overdo it a little bit, just to make it very clear that he supports his new wife 110 percent.

If the new stepparent is the father, the biological mother should give her support to him. She has to verbally convey his right (and responsibility) to set and enforce rules for the children. This dynamic is usually the harder of the two possibilities. Typically, the mom protects her children from harm. For her to let her new husband inflict even the slightest pain to the children requires that she have great faith in him. She may feel as if she is betraying her children to let her new husband enforce discipline.

Honest communication is a must between parents. A thorough debriefing helps solidify the disciplining of the children.

The question of loyalty becomes very important in everyone's mind. The children and the new spouse may feel some competition for the affection and attention of the biological parent. The children may feel as if a stranger has invaded their territory. They may secretly wish the intruder would leave. Since that most likely won't happen, they may try to at least keep the new person from gaining the top spot in the heart of the biological parent. These desires may manifest themselves in many ways. Younger children are more blunt with their feelings in wishing the new parent would leave now. Some children will argue more with the stepparent. Older children may be more subtle and simply not respond politely to the new parent.

The new stepparent may feel as if his or her spouse is more committed and supportive of the children. The stepparent may feel jealous of the children. If this feeling manipulates the truth, it will hinder the adjustments necessary to build a harmonious family.

Biological parents may feel as if they are being torn

between the people they love most. Biological parents need to end the tug-of-war by declaring that their spouse is the winner. This does not mean the children are not loved as much as ever. It means that when it comes to loyalty, the parent comes before the children. If this isn't clear, you will never be able to discipline your children effectively. A marriage is supposed to be a covenant. Rearing children is a job we work ourselves out of doing. If your primary family commitment isn't to your spouse, chances are you will eventually lose both relationships.

Biological parents need to welcome the stepparent to the parenting team. The challenge is to not force this relationship on the children. They should be allowed a reasonable time to adjust to the new parent. This is much easier said than done. The stepparent is different. Different is not bad; different is new. The unfamiliar takes time to become familiar. The amount of time the adjustment will take depends on numerous variables. Use your judgment as to when your children should be expected to have adjusted to the new situation. If you cannot agree on this transition, ask a trusted friend, church elder, or a trained professional for his or her opinion. Don't let the children drive a wedge between you and your spouse. Children need to get the message that this new parent is an authority figure. The children should listen to, respect, and obey the stepparent in the same way they do the biological parent. This message should be conveyed clearly and as soon as possible whenever the children try to undermine the authority of the new parent.

Sometimes the biological parent loses some of his or her uniqueness with the children. At times the children may prefer to relate to the new stepparent. As long as this is a genuine connection between them and not a manipulative ploy to drive a wedge between the parents or an attempt to avoid whatever they were asked to do, just enjoy the growing harmony in the family. This situation is not so much a problem as it is a welcoming of the new parent into the family.

NONCUSTODIAL PARENTS AND DISCIPLINE

If your children are living primarily with your former spouse, how is discipline affected?

A concern for noncustodial parents in the area of discipline is the fear that if you are too strict, you could lose visitation. This threat could arise from either the child or the other parent. This is unfortunate. Children may try to use any tool at their disposal to decrease their work and responsibilities. Threatening to tell the other parent how "mean" you are could have its desired effect and result in less work and/or very lax discipline. Parents can be blackmailed by their own children. This is a disaster. Children are no longer children; they become prizes awarded to the highest bidder. And the highest bidder is the one with the lowest expectations.

If your children are making threats to "tell on you," don't be intimidated by them. They are simply testing your resolve. They want to know how strong you are inside. Don't let them down. After the discipline is over and you are reconnected with them, they will forget their threats. When you successfully finish an attitude adjustment, you will feel close to each other. In hindsight, children will recognize their bad attitudes and how they deserved the discipline they received. Your children really don't want to lose contact with you. They simply don't want to obey you with a positive attitude.

If the custodial parent is threatening to stop the children's visits because he or she thinks you are too strict, what you say to the custodial parent is up to you. It all depends on the nature of your relationship. Some parents will understand, while others don't really want to. You will have to use your best judgment.

But if you are concerned, keep a detailed journal of everything that happened before, during, and after the attitude adjustment. Record who said what, when it was said, and your own observations of the children. Especially record what they said to you after everything was resolved. If anyone understands reasonable discipline and fair punishment, it is a judge. As long as you document everything, you will impress a judge or child-welfare person as a very conscientious parent who wants to raise children to know wrong from right. Judges would probably like to see more parents who are willing to enforce expectations. It may keep your children out of the courtroom in twenty years.

SPIRITUAL THOUGHTS

Have you ever thought about the fact that Jesus grew up with a stepfather? Joseph was not his "real" dad. By the time Jesus was twelve years old, he knew who his "real" father was (Luke 2:49). How did he know? Did his parents tell him? Did Jesus figure it out on his own? Did he have an intuitive sense that he was somehow different? Did he look different from his siblings? Did Jesus ever feel left out of that special family love between his brothers and sisters and mom and dad because he was different? Do you think Jesus ever felt ashamed that Joseph wasn't his real dad? Was Jesus ever tempted not to obey Joseph because Joseph asked him to do something he didn't feel like doing? Do you think Jesus ever thought Joseph didn't really understand him?

And how about Joseph? Do you think he felt intimidated by Jesus' "real" father? Was Joseph ever tempted to tell God to take his son back because it was just too hard to raise Jesus?

We don't really know the answers to these questions about Jesus' family. Knowing Jesus, we could probably make some pretty educated guesses, but Scripture is silent on these matters, but perhaps we can glean a couple of insights from it. Luke 2:50 says that Mary and Joseph didn't understand what Jesus meant when he referred to his Father, so chances are they didn't fully understand who they were rearing. However, verse 51 suggests that Mary knew that her son was special.

We do know that Jesus was perfectly obedient to his parents (Luke 2:51). God waited for the perfect moment to send his Son to earth. He was equally precise to handpick his only Son's earthly parents. Joseph and Mary had the awesome task of teaching Jesus all the earthly wisdom that they had learned. Like all good Jewish sons, Jesus listened to his earthly father's instructions. Joseph did not have perfect wisdom, but Jesus' perfect obedience to his father's training served Jesus well in his adult life.

If you have adopted children, foster children, or stepchildren and they lament the pain of rejection by their natural parents, you can tell them that you are adopted also. You can share some of your pain of feeling rejected, teased, and unloved growing up in your imperfect biological family. But now we have been adopted into God's family. Our heavenly Father has promised to make us his own precious children (Eph. 1:4-5; Heb. 2:11).

Reflection Questions

Take a few minutes to think about these questions. If possible, discuss them with your spouse, another parent, or a group of parents. Write down your observations, feelings, and goals in a journal.

1. Where are you in the spectrum of love (see chapters 1, 15, and 16)?
2. What do you need to do to be more balanced?
3. What obstacles are you facing in making discipline run smoother?
4. How are you contributing to those obstacles?
5. What do you need to do to remove those obstacles?

*If you ignore criticism, you will end in poverty
and disgrace; if you accept criticism,
you will be honored.*

— P r o v e r b s   1 3 : 1 8

18

Using the Tools with Teenagers

Any athlete understands the principle of "no pain, no gain." Successful athletes know that training is essential to their ability to perform. But they also know that training is hard work. It is often tedious and boring. They would much prefer to play and compete, but they endure intense training in order to succeed in their sport.

Good athletes also credit their coach or trainer for helping them succeed. What do coaches do? They teach, guide, motivate, and challenge athletes. Coaches push athletes to their physical and emotional limits in order to stretch and hone their skills. While that is occurring, some athletes bemoan the necessary output of time and energy. Only when they compete do they appreciate the necessary work to achieve the abilities they have developed.

Athletes will bond closely with the people involved in their training and will often credit them for their success. Very seldom do we hear athletes say, "I won this race because I ran until I thought I was going to die. And then I ran some more." They remember who helped and inspired them and the close relationships that were developed during that tough time.

Teenagers think they don't need training. They think they are ready to play the game of life. I don't know any teenagers who are ready for that challenge. As a teen, I used to think I was ready. We all probably did. But whether or not our teenagers realize it, they still need coaching, direction, and sometimes a push before they are ready to fly solo.

After giving seminars on how to use these tools, I respond to parents' questions. The most frequently asked question is, "What about teenagers?" At first, I was surprised by the question. The private school where I initially learned these tools was composed of all teenagers. My wife and I were the houseparents for ten teenage boys and later for ten teenage girls. The approach described in this book includes the tools we used with "our kids" in the private school. I knew these tools worked with teenagers. Until we tried them with our own kids, I wasn't sure they would work with younger kids.

Yes, these tools work effectively with teenagers. Everything I've said about these tools applies to teens. Teenagers need to respect parents. Just because your teenagers are physically as big as or bigger than you are doesn't mean they have the same authority. You are still their parents and are still responsible for them. You should not be afraid of them or of their threats if they don't get their way. What you should be afraid of is losing your relationship with them. Teenagers need role models. Teenagers need leaders to give them direction in life. Teenagers need parents.

Teenagers don't want people telling them what they should think or what they should like. They are trying to figure out who they are and where they want to go. And that is a good thing. The teenage years should be a time for parents to let go of the reins. Just don't do it all at once. Do it gradually. Older teenagers should be making most of their choices anyway. I'm talking about things like styles of clothes, hairstyle, how to spend their money and time, and what career to pursue. But parents should not abandon their teens to making decisions alone. Wise adults still seek out counsel. Teens still need guidance with their lives. Teens should explore various roads to discover new and exciting things about the world and themselves, but parents still need to guide them to stay on the important roads.

The level of respect that teenagers have for their parents should not be different from the level of respect seven-year-olds should have for their parents. The expectations for teenagers should not be as high as they are for younger children; they should be higher. Your teenagers are getting ready to leave the safety of home. They will have to rely on their own physical, emotional, mental, and social skills in order to survive. If they can't even get along with you without having a flare-up, no boss is going to keep them around for very long. People like Scottie Pippen who have tantrums and still keep their job are exceptions.[1] Only because of his superior basketball skills was he able to continue his career. The majority of us are not that indispensable at work. Our children's vocational future begins now. It is vital that we teach them respect.

Attitude makes an indelible first impression. Attitude is one of the things that employers look at when they consider an employee. Steve Stone was an all-star major league pitcher. He worked as an announcer for the Chicago Cubs. During one of the Cubs' broadcasts, Stone said, "Any scout can look at batting average, speed, and on-base percentage. Good scouting has to look at the head and heart. That is the secret of drafting a good baseball player." He's right. People evaluate us according to what's inside. A good attitude gets people ahead in life.

WHAT TO EXPECT FROM TEENAGERS

Teenagers expect to have more freedom, and they should have more. We have to make sure they understand the connection between freedom and responsibility. When they want more independence and freedom, we can celebrate with them their growing desire for more self-determination. Freedoms and privileges are the rewards of responsibility. Demonstrating a pattern of responsible behavior earns teenagers those privileges. Don't make the mistake of assuming they will pick all this up when they leave home. If they don't learn now, you may join a growing number of parents who have twenty-five-year-old or thirty-year-old teenagers who never leave home. Expect your teenagers to grow up and move on. Don't cripple them with poor work habits, leaving them with the expectation that someone will bail them out.

Let me make a few suggestions:

1. *Set expectations higher for teenagers.* Teens are on the verge of becoming contributing members of society. They should be able to take care of all their own needs in a few short years. Are your teenagers ready to do that?

Put them on a budget. Tell them, "This is how much money we have to spend each month for your needs. Instead of having us decide what to spend the money on, we will give you the money and let you buy the things you need. It may seem like a lot all at once, but just remember that this covers

- clothes (winter jacket, shoes, jewelry, etc.)
- entertainment (movies, CDs, outings to amusement parks, etc.)
- school lunches (and after-school stops)

- presents (for friends' parties, family birthdays)
- personal pets (including vet visits)
- car expenses (your insurance portion, 10 cents per mile)

Gradually wean them off depending on you for money. Negotiate a schedule for them to be financially self-sufficient by the time they are ready to leave home. Obviously this means they have some marketable service or skill they have been developing.

If they are going to college, ask them why and how much they are willing to contribute to their education. Unless they have a reasonable plan, they may not be ready to spend thousands of your dollars. Help them appreciate the value of time and important choices to be made. You are not a bottomless pit of resources.

Expect your teenagers to get up on time. If they oversleep, then let them (or make them) walk to work or school. Let them experience the real pain of logical consequences of being late.

Expect them to be kind and generous toward their siblings, friends, and community. They can decide where to volunteer their time, but expect them to learn the value and joy of helping others.

Expect them to choose positive friends. They may spend time with people you wouldn't, but get to know their friends. Ask your children what they like about them. Talk to them about the advantages of not getting serious with a member of the opposite sex while in high school. Encourage group activities.

2. Give your teenagers tougher work assignments. Whether it be for regular jobs or attitude-adjusting work, make their assignments harder. Instead of having them just sweep the garage, they could clean and organize the entire garage.

Instead of having them just mow or rake the yard, have them be responsible for all the landscaping—mowing, raking, weeding, edging the sidewalk, trimming bushes, rototilling, planting the garden, etc.

Increase the level of quality that you expect from their work. Teenagers should be able to do nearly everything you as an adult can do. If they can't, either teach them how or give them practice. Your payoff will come when they get their first job review from their employer. If the work is for attitude-adjusting purposes, inspect it with the white-glove approach. Make sure they are doing the best job they possibly can.

3. Give your teenagers options. I recently saw a newspaper photo of a young man from Eau Claire, Wisconsin, wearing a big sandwich-board sign on which was printed in bold letters: "I'm a thief." He was convicted of stealing $470 from the car shop where he worked. By wearing the sign around his neck for eight hours in front of the car shop, he reduced his sentence. Apparently this young man wanted to get his punishment over with quickly. Or maybe he wanted to save some money on the fine. Whatever the reason, he made his choice.

While I would never subject my children to public ridicule like that, this story illustrates a point. Teenagers like options. One way to give them options is to offer them choices as to how they want to be disciplined. You might offer a choice of immaculately cleaning the car or doing fifty push-ups while repeating the phrase "I will talk politely to you." Tell them they can rake the entire yard or be their sister's personal butler for the rest of the day in order to teach them the importance of being kind to their siblings.

If they don't like the choices, ask them what their choice

would be for a fair discipline. If they come up with something reasonable, let them do that. That encourages their negotiating skills and rewards their creative thinking. If they argue that they don't want to do *anything,* tell them you will make the choice for them if they won't do it themselves. Just be sure to follow it up with an attitude check. Keep in mind that the goal is a good attitude and respectful relationships.

ATTITUDE ADJUSTMENTS WITH TEENAGERS

If your teenagers try to ignore, walk away, or yell at you when you try to talk to them, they are sending warning signs that your relationship needs intensive-care treatment. Don't wait. Like any injury or illness, it only gets worse if it's left untreated. Your teenagers may need an attitude adjustment.

An attitude adjustment for teenagers is basically the same as one for children of any age. I am not suggesting that an attitude adjustment with a teenager is identical. Teenagers will take a bigger investment of time and energy—in other words, work. It is much more work to change the attitudes of teenagers than the attitudes of younger children. That's why it is so important to start early with children. Don't let them grow up with a bad attitude and expect them to grow out of it. It doesn't work that way.

About the only other difference is the intensity of the session. Since teenagers have more strength and energy, you will have to use all you have to confront them. This is especially true if you are just starting to work on their attitudes.

I suggest that you start slowly. Explain your expectations thoroughly and patiently. Admit that you should have started with them earlier but that you are still learning also. Give them some grace in getting used to the idea of being expected to have a good attitude or working more around the house. But when the time comes to enforce the expectations, jump in with both feet. Don't apologize for your standards. God set standards for us, and we should set them for our children.

If you have a teenager who is particularly difficult, you may benefit from the suggestions outlined in appendix C, "Dealing with Difficult Teenagers."

I want to end this chapter with a column written by the late humorist Erma Bombeck. She titled it "Measure of Discipline Also Measure of Love."

> "You don't love me!"
>
> How many times have your kids laid that one on you? And how many times have you, as a parent, resisted the urge to tell them how much?
>
> Someday, when my children are old enough to understand the logic that motivates a mother, I'll tell them.
>
> I loved you enough to bug you about where you were going, with whom, and what time you would get home. I loved you enough to insist you buy a bike with your own money that you could afford. I loved you enough to be silent and let you discover your friend was a creep. I loved you enough to make you return a Milky Way with a bite out of it to a drugstore and confess, "I stole this." I loved you enough to stand over you for two hours while you cleaned your bedroom, a job that would have taken me 15 minutes. I loved you enough to say, "Yes, you can go to Disney World on Mother's Day."
>
> I loved you enough to let you see anger, disappointment, disgust and tears in my eyes. I loved you enough

not to make excuses for your lack of respect or your bad manners. I loved you enough to admit that I was wrong and ask for your forgiveness. I loved you enough to ignore what every other mother did or said. I loved you enough to let you stumble, fall, hurt and fail. I loved you enough to let you assume the responsibility for your own actions at age 6, 10, or 16. I loved you enough to figure you would lie about the party being chaperoned, but I forgave you for it—after discovering I was right. I loved you enough to accept you for what you are, not what I wanted you to be. But most of all, I loved you enough to say no when you hated me for it. That was the hardest part of all.[2]

Reflection Questions

Take a few minutes to think about these questions. If possible, discuss them with your spouse, another parent, or a group of parents. Write down your observations, feelings, and goals in a journal.

1. Who was the person who pushed you to work harder than you thought you could?
2. What positive things developed as a result of that person's pushing?
3. In what ways do your teenagers express rebellious attitudes?
4. What steps can you take to start dealing with the negative attitudes?
5. Whom will you enlist to help you if your teenagers need an intense attitude adjustment?
6. In what areas of your teenagers' lives are you not parenting enough?

7. How would you rate your teenagers' responsibility and maturity in:
   - respect to family? friends?
   - time management?
   - money management?
   - home chores?
   - service to others?

Guide my steps by your word.

PSALM 119:133

19

Putting It All Together

Disciplining our children is only a means to an end. The goal is a vibrant, loving relationship with our children. The tools discussed in this book always have that goal in mind. In fact, these tools will not work unless they are used in the context of a loving relationship.

As I said in the first chapter, because many other books have already been written about the soft side of love, I felt it was important to concentrate here on the firm side of love. I hope that it has been helpful to read about, evaluate, and try some of the tools. You may not agree with everything I've said. That's all right. If this book has caused you to think about what you do and why you are doing it, then perhaps it has helped you become a better parent.

We must remember that we are our children's authority just as God is our authority. God is our role model and mentor in everything, including how to discipline children. There is none better.

Start tenderly, as God did with Adam and Eve. He provided the perfect garden, made sure all their needs were taken care of, provided food, beautiful surroundings, meaningful activity, and companionship with himself and with each other. God also warned them of the danger in their new world: "'You may freely eat any fruit in the garden except fruit from the tree of the knowledge of good and evil. If you eat of its fruit, you will surely die'" (Gen. 2:16-17). God wants to provide for his children's needs. He also wants them to be safe and to trust him. These should be our parental goals as well.

Start disciplining your children early. The younger they are, the more teachable they are. Whatever expectations you start out with will just seem normal to them. If your children are age two or younger, start at the beginning. Provide for their needs and sometimes their wants. Give them a safe environment and set a warm tone in the home. Begin to teach them your expectations. Enforce the logical consequences. Give them little jobs to do as soon as possible. If they are physically able to do something, teach them how to do it. The more skills they can master, the more self-confidence they will build.

Encourage your children to express their feelings even when they are young. Help them find the words to describe what they are feeling so they can begin to have some understanding and mastery over them. Your challenge is also to teach them how to express their feelings appropriately. This is the beginning of teaching them that hitting, pushing, name-calling, threats, or any physical violence is not acceptable. They will eventually learn that when they express their feelings appropriately, they are more likely to get what they want.

Teach your children that their attitudes are just as important as their behavior and that you want them to have positive attitudes. Tell them what logical consequences they will have to face if they persist in negative attitudes or if they disobey you. Back up your words with verbal and/or practice repetitions of how to say or do something.

If logical consequences don't help their attitudes, then move on to work. If they settle into a disrespectful, argumentative, rude internal posture, help them "work it out" of their system. And if they refuse to change, move on to the exercises. If they balk at the exercises, then manually help them until they are willing to do them on their own.

Start off slowly and build the intensity of the discipline to match your children's challenge. By building slowly, you are giving them several chances to change their internal posture on their own.

If your children already have negative attitudes, that is another story. Whatever age your children are, you might want to start off the new system with a bang. State your expectations clearly. Tell them what the rewards are and warn them of the consequences. Then enforce the consequences. Warn them that you will not accept their bad attitudes; surprise them with your determination to adjust them.

Their rebellious energy will dictate how much disciplining power is needed. But while rebellious children will dictate the *duration* of the attitude adjustment, you decide the *direction*. You are not starting the problem, but you will finish it. You are not looking for a confrontation, but you will not shy away from it anymore either.

After their attitudes have been adjusted and they have apologized for their insolence, be sure to reconnect and replenish their love tank. Do not leave them vulnerable to feelings of bitterness or resentment after having their attitude adjusted. If they feel loved, they will find it easier to submit to you. If they don't feel loved, they will fight you even harder the next time. They won't want to go through the humbling experience without knowing there will be a payoff for all the work. The payoff for children is feeling loved and having freedom. The payoff for parents is relational harmony.

Children need you when they are having problems with their attitudes. You wouldn't desert them if they fell off a bike; don't desert them when they fall from grace. Restore them to your heart. Using God's example of fatherhood and lots of prayer, you will be giving them a good opportunity to live long and fruitful lives.

You are realistic enough to know that not every attitude adjustment you attempt will be successful. Disciplining children is a skill. Like any skill, it will take practice to learn it. Sharon and I were fortunate in that we got to practice parenting before we had our own children. Other people have tried these tools and have found them to be effective; still others are working to make them successful with their children.

Our relationship with our children will grow and go through phases. When God first related to his children, as recorded in the Old Testament, he referred to himself simply as God. He was very approachable in the beginning, but at the same time he reminded his children that he was the "authority in their lives." Later God revealed to us that he is like a father—another step toward intimacy. After Jesus came to earth, God revealed more of his own character through his Son. Jesus modeled how to be a child; he was respectful and obedient. Our children should be expected to follow in his footsteps, but we must help them. Just before Jesus left earth to return to his Father in heaven, he invited us to become his friends, but only if we are willing to obey him (John 15:14).

Our relational development with our children will follow a similar path. Our roles as parents will grow from the nurturing authority to the teaching enforcer to a kind of mentor and finally to somewhat of a peer and friend when our children leave home. These roles are not rigid, and there is a great deal of overlap.

As you parent your children, you may run into problems you can't solve. If this happens, remember two things: First, talk out a difficult situation with your spouse, a close friend, or other people who have parented their own children effectively. Describe in detail the troubling situation and ask for direction. Second, just keep at it. Even if things don't go perfectly, the effort is worth it. Children are not machines. They don't always respond the way we expect or would prefer them to. Remind yourself that you are learning a skill and that it takes practice.

My prayer is that you will be encouraged to love your children, especially when they reveal their sinful natures. God knows, that's when we all need love the most. But my other prayer is that you will hear God speaking to you. His Word is what really counts. The psalmist said: "How sweet are your words to my taste; they are sweeter than honey. . . . Your word is my only source of hope. . . . As your words are taught, they give light. . . . Guide my steps by your word" (Ps. 119:103, 114, 130-133).

May God guide you in your parenting. He's good at that. He loves to help his children. He likes it even more when we *let* him help us.

*[Christ] personally carried away our sins
in his own body on the cross so we can be dead
to sin and live for what is right. You have been
healed by his wounds!*

— 1 P e t e r 2 : 2 4

Appendix A: Handling Tantrums

If you find that your children go out of control when you try to
discipline them with the tools described in this book, then I
offer you an auxiliary tool: holding or restraining your children.

This tool is helpful for the times your children have tantrums. Sometimes children just lose it and become violent.
They try to kick, hit, bite, or scratch you. Toddlers are most
famous for this kind of behavior, but I've seen much older
kids have tantrums too. If your children flail around on the
floor or attack you, then they are literally out of control. They
have lost their ability to maintain their personal equilibrium
and have degenerated into a mass of unrestrained energy.

There is no worse feeling than feeling out of control. Imagine driving down a steep hill and trying to apply the brakes,
only to discover that you have none. That is how panic feels.
Most people's worst fear is to lose control of their own bodies, whether through falling, an assault, or some illness such
as epilepsy, cancer, or insanity.

When your children lose control of their bodies, they, in

effect, have no brakes. If you simply ignore them or leave them alone, they not only feel terrifyingly out of control but they also feel abandoned, hurt, and angry. When you ignore a tantrum, you basically say to your children that they are on their own. I don't recommend sending them that message. This is definitely the time to move *toward* the conflict. So what do you do?

You have the option of using your body to hold them, to restrain them. You use all the strength necessary to wrap up their arms and legs and hold them perfectly still. You become a living, loving container for them. When you hold your children this way, you prevent them from misbehaving. You save them from the humiliation of losing control. Your own body becomes their governing body. You hold them together until they can demonstrate they are back in control of their bodies. This is definitely the most loving thing you can do for them at this point.

Rewards, punishments, work, and exercises are all attempts to teach self-discipline. These are external tools to help rebellious children learn internal discipline. Holding accomplishes the same thing in a physical way. Holding is a loving tool to subdue out-of-control children. Holding imparts self-control, peace, and—best of all—connection with parents.

Tantrums become a test children use to see what their parents will do. Tantrums become another way for parents to show their love. What better response to a tantrum than for parents to absorb and contain this "explosion" without anyone getting hurt or humiliated.

Holding your children imparts your strength to them so they can eventually internalize that ability themselves. It's as if we become the Jell-O mold in which our kids will shape and harden themselves. If we don't hold them, the "Jell-O" will harden into shapeless blobs. Before they harden into bitter, grotesque shapes, let's help mold them into lovely, loving people.

POSITIONS TO HOLD CHILDREN

The goal of holding is to contain children's exploding energy. In order to do this, you have to stop their ability to flail their arms or kick their legs. Eventually they will wear themselves out by struggling against you. The dynamic is similar to what happens with the exercises, except with the holding you get just as much of a workout as they do.

Many parents ask, "How should I hold my children? What is the best way?" Before I answer, let me say that the position is much less important than the fact that you hold them. At times, you may be doing well just to be holding on to them at all. Don't worry so much about how it looks or how you got there. The important fact is that you are holding them. You are in contact with them. They will be fighting you, and they definitely won't like it at first, but they won't feel alone or rejected by you. They will end up knowing how much you love them.

If you have a choice and can maneuver your children the way you would like to, this is what I suggest. I have listed these suggestions in order of preference, from most preferred to least desirable. I also recommend that you use these techniques only with children whom you know you can contain. These techniques are not effective with teenagers unless you have backup help. I'll say a bit more about that later.

1. *On your lap, child facing you.* This hold is probably only for very young, small children. It is almost like a hug except the children's legs will be bent and pressed against your stomach or chest. Their arms should be squeezed against

their chest. Your arms will probably just be wrapped around their back, holding them tightly against your chest.

2. On your lap, child sitting sideways. This hold is identical to the last one except the children face sideways. Their body is curled up like a ball with their knees pressed against their chest. Your arms are wrapped around them to contain their arms and legs. You can squeeze them to your chest as tightly as necessary. This is a nice way to hold them because it is similar to cradling them when they were infants. When the children eventually wear themselves out, you are already in a comfortable position to comfort them.

3. On your lap, child facing away from you. As children get older, bigger, and stronger, you may have to use your legs to stop their legs from kicking. In this position, imagine you and your child are squeezed onto a toboggan with the child's back against your chest. Your arms are wrapped around them, holding their arms to their chest while your legs are wrapped over their legs.

Holding as described in the first three suggestions may not be enough for some children. At that point you may need to move toward positions that are more like restraining than holding. The next two suggestions are ones that I recommend fathers do, although some of the illustrations given later in this appendix show that moms can do them successfully. I learned these positions from my training and experience as a child-care worker and counselor. They are similar to positions a careful law officer would use to restrain an out-of-control person. These positions are physical, but they are not cruel, demeaning, or harmful. They are more humane than hitting, slapping, or punching (which is what many parents resort to at this point). Again, remember your goal: to contain the children until they can contain themselves. You are not trying to punish them, even if they have hit you or kicked you. This is not a place to "pay them back" or "let them know what it feels like." If you have those feelings, then you may be out of control too and may need help from other adults.

4. Lying underneath you, child faceup. Sometimes you settle for whatever position you can maintain. This one is like a wrestling position with your children's shoulder blades pinned to the floor. You can use your body weight to help hold them down. Some children get pretty strong, and you may need to use your weight advantage. I do not suggest that you sit on them like a king. That position would be unnecessarily demeaning. You can either spread their arms apart or pin them to their chest.

5. Lying underneath you, child facedown. This is the least preferred position because the children are facing away from you. At times this is the only way to subdue them. You have to stop them from attacking and flailing, and sometimes you have to take what you can get. Hold their arms out to their sides or pinned underneath them. Do not hold their arms behind their back. Use your legs to hold theirs down. As they calm down, you can maneuver them next to you or onto your lap for the restoring phase of this ordeal.

DEALING WITH YELLING

This may be the time when you hear your children explode verbally. Let your children blow off a little steam, but not for very long. If they are getting carried away (calling you names, threatening you, screaming wildly, or trying to bite you), warn them to stop the verbal assaults. If they refuse, cup their mouth with your hands (so they can't bite you). Hold firmly. If necessary, squeeze hard to prevent bite attempts or head twisting.

Sometimes you even have to stop them from trying to head-butt you. This is done by pulling their head toward you and holding it against your chest. The other option is to firmly hold their head to the floor. This protects both of you from harm. The forehead is the thickest bone in the body. If you get hit with this weapon, it will definitely hurt you more than it hurts them, especially if you get hit in the nose.

Maintain this position until they promise to stop. They may spit and lick your hand, but that's OK. Tell them that as soon as they promise to control their mouth, you will let go. That will be the first step in their getting themselves entirely back under control. If they break this promise, it is easy to reapply your cupped hand.

They may say some pretty mean or scary things. Here are some of the most common threats with some suggested responses:

- "I'll just kill myself!"—"Not as long as I'm holding you."
- "Then I'll kill myself later!"—"Then you will just have to stay by my side all the time. Is that what you want?"
- "No!"—"Then don't make that threat."
- "I hate you!"—"That's OK. You just have to obey me."
- "I'll never obey you!"—"Then we'll be here for a long time."
- "I'm gonna run away!"—"Not until your work is done."
- "You're hurting me!"—"Then stop fighting me."
- "I can't breathe!"—"Then stop yelling." (Be sure they can breathe.)
- "Let go of me!"—"I will as soon as you can control your body."

Just be sure you are not purposefully inflicting unnecessary pain. You are restraining them, not brutalizing them. You will have to use quite a bit of strength, but be sure to use only what is necessary.

These threats are tests to see how you will react. If the children find one that gets a reaction from you, expect them to use it often. The threats are just their anger coming out in words. Whatever you do, don't stop trying to restrain them. Most likely, they are trying to get you sidetracked from what you are doing. If you let them do that, you will have given away your power to change their attitude. They will feel as if they have found your Achilles' heel, and they won't let go of it. Keep the focus on their ability to control themselves and their attitude and to cooperate with you, not on their threats. You can't totally ignore the threat, but certainly downplay them until later.

After your children have calmed down and you have gone through repairing the relationship, you can ask them if they still feel like carrying out their threat. Most likely they won't feel that way anymore. But if they still say they feel like doing any of those things, have a long talk with them and find out why. Chances are, they simply don't like the discipline or just feel very discouraged about something.

Tell them you don't like the tougher discipline either. Tell them that if they agree to obey you with a good attitude, you won't have to use those tools of discipline. Remind them that you bring out those power tools only when they force you to. Say that you would rather have them obey you the first time you ask them to do something. Remind them that you still love them and won't ever stop loving them.

DEALING WITH OTHER ASPECTS OF TANTRUMS

We've discussed how to handle your children when they are physically or verbally out of control. Let's look at a few more ways you can move your children back to control.

1. Let your children cry. Dealing with a tantrum is as intense as it gets. Emotions will be running full force. Tears are welcome as an outlet for all the intensity.

2. Talk to your children. Use soothing tones to help them relax. Let them hear the self-control in your own voice. As calmly as possible, tell them you will be happy to let go of them as soon as they demonstrate that they are ready. Over time they will draw the necessary strength from your body and tone of voice to relax and regain control.

3. The first way your children can demonstrate their regained self-control is with their words. They should say anything you ask them to say with an appropriate tone of voice. This is a good time to have them practice verbally submitting to you.

4. Release your children. Take it slow. You don't have to let them go all at once. You can release parts of them by stages. I suggest starting with their legs. You could say things like "As soon as you stop trying to kick for a minute, then I will move my legs off of yours" or "As soon as your arms relax for two minutes, then I will let go. I want you to turn around and face me so we can talk. Agreed?" You can release them all at once if you want. They should be calm and cooperative. Their breathing is the barometer. When it has been slow and steady for a while, they are ready to talk about what happened.

5. Decide whether your children should finish the work or exercises originally assigned to them before they exploded. You may make some alterations in light of what happened. Use your own judgment. You may want to give them a minor test, or it may just be a time to offer some grace to them.

6. Restore the relationship to harmony as always. Remember, you did not cause the tantrum; you only discovered it on your journey into your children's hearts. You did not supply the fuel or ignite the explosion. Like a bloodhound, you simply followed the smoke until you found a raging fire. Then you stayed to calm and extinguish it. Your feelings may be raging also. That's OK. Take your time to calm down with your children.

One final point to make regarding this holding tool is an important one. The only limitation of this tool is the relative size and strength of the adult. In other words, this tool can be used for children of any age. If you can hold them when they act out of control, then do it. It is effective from toddlers through teens. I've seen it used with all ages.

But you may want to think twice before using it with teenagers or other children you may not be able to subdue. If you try to subdue them but can't, you weaken your position and run the risk of their thinking they don't have to listen to you at all. That is not a good position to be in. By the time they are that big, I would hope that you won't have to resort to brute strength to influence them. The strength of your relationship should have been fully developed by now. Older children should listen to you because they are in the habit of cooperating and you have a meaningful, trusting relationship.

It's time for an illustration of how this looks in real life. Rather than giving you another example from my own family, I asked Emma, a friend of mine, to write about her own experience. I've been talking to her about trying this tool with her son, and she has had occasion to use it a few times.

▓ ▓ ▓

It's 2:35 P.M. Any minute now, my eight-year-old whirlwind will come bounding in the door. It's been a long, busy week for both of us. I'm glad to be done with commitments and schedules. The door swings open and sixty-five pounds of energy bursts in, tossing his backpack randomly on the floor.

"Hey, pal, whatcha got for me?" He's not much of a conversationalist when he first gets home, so this has become my shorthand greeting for "Hi, how are you? How was your day? What did you bring home from school to show me?"

To this, I get an irritated response of "Have you seen my red book?"

"What red book?"

"You know, the one from school," he says, spitting the words at me.

I sigh, starting to see that a monster is presently inhabiting my child's body. I'm not liking his tone or manner, but I figure I'll deal with it after we locate the "red book." I find a book he brought home weeks ago. I show it to him to see if this is what the fuss is about. It is. I know this not because my son's heart pours forth gratitude but because the monster releases an onslaught of rudeness.

"I needed that today! Why didn't you send it back with me?"

"That's not my job. This is your responsibility."

He stomps off to the kitchen.

"Max, come here, please." No response. I try the request again, this time a little more firmly. "Max, come here." Still, nothing. Ignoring me is not acceptable. I get up, walk into the kitchen, grab Max by the arms, and help him to "come here." He is less than cooperative, clutching at things along the way.

We reach the designated spot, and I let go. Scowling, he walks about three feet away.

"No, Max, I said to come here." I grab him and pull him toward the spot. He now becomes deadweight, a pile of belligerence congealing on the floor. I reach down to pull him up.

"Ow! You're hurting me!"

"Then get up. If you stop fighting me, it won't hurt."

He manages to get upright. I look at him. "I don't like your attitude, and I do not like your tone. Twenty-five jumping jacks. Now."

He walks off to his room and turns to face me. I know he is considering slamming his door. "If I don't see them, they don't count," I remind him. He does them. Barely, halfheartedly. He stomps into his room, still dripping with attitude. The monster is still very much present.

"Max, lose the attitude."

He doesn't even consider it. "It's not my fault!"

It's time to up the ante. "OK, that's enough. I want you to get the floor picked up and then vacuumed."

Just to show me he still thinks he is boss, he very dramatically arches his back in protest (accompanied by various moans and groans) and falls to the floor, where he begins to flail his arms and kick his feet. I sit on the couch, stifling a laugh at this ridiculous behavior.

He begins to scream, "Mom!"

I refuse to answer to this.

"*Mom!*" he tries again.

I say nothing. I will not do verbal battle with him.

"*Mo-o-om!*" he hollers. He moves to within inches of my face. He screeches one more time, "*Mo-o-om!*"

I know it's time for the ultimate weapon, the weapon known for its power to banish monsters and release little boys from captivity. Seems we're going to have a bit of wrestling here today. Having been through a few of these, I do a quick mental assessment. I better get ready to get down and dirty; things could get a little sweaty. I leave to put my hair up and take some layers of clothes off. When I come back, I find he has wandered back out into the kitchen. I approach him from behind, wrapping my arms around his body and upper arms. I pull him out into the front room where there is carpeting. And so the battle begins.

I maneuver to get us both sitting on the floor, my arms still wrapped around his arms and body, with my legs wrapped around his. I struggle to contain him. He's nearly as tall as I am, and he's strong. His strength combined with his extreme stubbornness require all my strength and energy. And I quickly sense that this time around he is determined to fight me with all that he's got.

He screams. I cup his mouth. He throws his body weight to knock me off balance. I lose my grip off and on. Each time I do, he tries to hit or kick or bite me. I pin him, belly down, holding his arms out away from his body, using my head to hold his head down, wrapping my legs around his to control the kicking. Throughout this struggling, he alternates screaming, "I can't breathe! You're hurting me! You're killing me!" I'm very aware of how I am holding him, and I know I'm not hurting him. I'm careful to not have my full body weight on him. I use just enough weight to hold him down. I know he's fine, and I wait for the tantrum to work its way out.

"Get off of me!" he demands.

"I'll be happy to as soon as you can control yourself."

I relax for a second, thinking he might be ready to do that. Big mistake. He was waiting for the opportunity. He manages to partially break loose and get up to his knees. He then gives me a head-butt with the back of his head. I am not pleased. I had been frustrated with my inability to contain this child for very long. Now with this final insult from him, I am reenergized, reminding myself that I can still outmuscle this kid. So I wrestle him back down to the floor without worrying about being too gentle. I push his head down with my free hand, pinning it to the floor. "You will *not* do that," I tell him sternly. "You will *not* hurt your mom!"

He struggles against me for another five or ten minutes. We have ended up in the sitting position we first started in. The struggling has stopped. His resistance lessens. The angry tears are gone. He turns to me to be held. I hold him, rock him, caress him.

I start to relax, thinking it's over; we made it. Just as I am feeling relieved, Max notices the time. He looks at me in panic. "Can I watch *Spiderman?*" he pleads.

"No," I tell him, bracing for a new onslaught. "You still have to do the vacuuming."

He breaks into sad tears, then looks up at me. "Can you tape it?" Always the negotiator, this one.

I laugh and tell him, "Yes, I can put in a tape for you."

He begins to clean up things from the floor and gets out the vacuum. I hear him muttering something and come closer to hear. Fearing I might hear him complaining, instead I hear, "This is my fault, isn't it?"

"Yes, it is," I tell him sadly.

"I'm stupid."

I put my arm around him and look at him. "No, you're not stupid."

"Yes, I am. I'm stupid."

"No, honey, you're not stupid. You made a bad choice, that's all. That doesn't mean you're stupid. We all make bad choices." I give him a hug and a kiss, and he goes about his vacuuming. As soon as he's done, he announces to me that he will wrap up the cord and put the vacuum away as soon as *Spiderman* is over.

"No," I tell him. "You need to do that now, and then we have some things to take care of."

I see a few sad tears as he wraps the cord up and puts away the vacuum. I have him come sit next to me on the couch. It's time to talk about what happened and tie up any loose ends. When I ask him to tell me how he acted when he came home, he suddenly has a case of amnesia. So we run through it together. We talk about his rudeness about the book and his disobedience. The amnesia seems to be fading. I remind him that those are not acceptable ways to act. We do not treat each other like that in this house.

Snuggling up next to me, he looks up, a tear running down his cheek. "I'm sorry for disobeying you and . . . what's that other thing?"

"Being rude?"

"Oh yeah. I'm sorry for being rude." He pauses for a second here. I just wait for him.

"Anything else?"

"Yes. Will you forgive me?"

"I forgive you. I love you, Buddy." I hold him close and kiss him. After a few seconds I look him in the eyes. "Do you know I love you?"

"Yes."

"Do you feel loved?"

"Yes."

"Do you feel sad anymore?"

"No."

"Do you have any questions for me or anything you need to tell me?"

He shakes his head no. So we snuggle some more, and I talk to him about how moms and dads are in charge of kids and how God is in charge of moms and dads. I can see the wheels turning in his head. He looks up at me with a smile and says, "And the kids are in charge of the toys."

I chuckle and tell him, "Yes, they are."

It just feels so good. I am content to sit and enjoy the moment. But one eight-year-old little boy has other thoughts. "Can I watch *Spiderman* now?"

I laugh and say, "Sure, just give me one more big ol' hug."

We hug tightly. I let go, expecting him to scamper off to the TV. Instead, he sits next to me and jabbers about his day. I sit listening and looking at him, grinning like a fool because I got my kid back!

■　■　■

That is a real-life illustration of reconciliation. Emma and Max were reunited as mother and son. I asked Emma what would have happened if she had not used the holding tool with Max. She was very embarrassed to tell me, but she finally did. She even wrote it down for me. This is what she said:

■　■　■

"How would I have handled this sort of behavior in the past?" Now there's a question I'd just as soon not answer.

Things would initially start with verbal warfare. I would yell; he would yell back. I would yell louder. He still wouldn't listen, so I would continue to get louder and angrier. We would both become emotionally out of control. I would reduce

371

myself to his emotional equal. My frustration level would be extremely high. I would feel that I had no control over the situation, no control over Max, and no control over myself.

Out of frustration, I would resort to intimidation, shaming, belittling, name-calling, threatening, whatever. When all else failed, I would stomp off very dramatically to the kitchen to get a spanking spoon (hands are for loving, you know). This would strike terror into Max's heart—he knew what was coming. He would start screaming, "Wait! Wait! I'll do it! Give me another chance! Please!" But that only seemed to fuel my anger. So I would spank him—hard—in a complete fit of rage.

He would be so terrorized, and I would still be full of anger. It was so horribly ugly—the way I acted, the way I felt. I hated it. I hated myself for being like that. And nothing was resolved. There was no brokenness or repentance or understanding on Max's part.

Later, when I was calmer, I would find myself apologizing to Max and asking for his forgiveness for my behavior when the focus really should have been on his disobedience. But how could it be? We would still talk about that, but it's rather pointless to try and stress his disobedience when his mom has been a raving maniac. There was no real reconciliation between us. It was very self-defeating. I always felt like a complete failure as a parent.

■ ■ ■

Holding is a very effective tool to use when battling bad attitudes. It engages children. It is lovingly confrontive. It is strong. It reconnects children and parents and re-creates a loving relationship.

Children like it too. In fact one mother told me that when she was holding her child, he said to her right in the middle of the encounter, "No, Mom. Hold me like this." He let her get hold of him, and then he resumed his struggling. He knew he needed his mom's strength to struggle with himself. He needed the comfort and security of her arms.

One mother of a twelve-year-old son had to grab onto him to stop him from pushing her away from him. He fought back, and his mom just held on to him. She told me she was quite scared until she realized he was not using all his strength. They were almost the same size, yet he restrained himself so he wouldn't hurt his mom or break the connection. He acted as if he was fighting her, but he was actually relieved she was holding him. Her added strength helped him to fight his own internal attitude. He didn't want to be overwhelmed so he let his mom help him.

You may have noticed that in every example a mother was doing the discipline. I did that to show that mothers can use this tool also. But just like work and exercises, dads are better equipped to use this holding tool. Most moms would rather have their husband use these power tools anyway. Moms seem to bruise more easily both physically and emotionally. It's not that women can't use a chain saw, splitting ax, or post-hole digger, but men can usually use them more easily and more effectively. It is the same with these tools to discipline children. Dads, step up and learn how these tools work so you can use them skillfully.

As you can well imagine, using this tool with teenagers should be done with extreme caution. Teenagers may not always let themselves be held. And you may not be able to restrain them by yourself. Teens want to discover their own strength, but they also wrestle with wanting to feel that security. Teenagers still feel loved when their parents set reasonable limits. When you enforce your expectations, you tell them that you care enough about them to make them do what they should be doing. Rude teenagers feel out of control. Inside they are begging someone to stop them. They are testing you to see just how much you really care about them. If you feel confident that you can hold and subdue them, then use this tool. Just be careful not to start something you can't finish. Stopping in the middle is worse than not starting at all (see appendix C: Dealing with Difficult Teenagers).

WHAT DOES GOD THINK ABOUT EXERCISES AND HOLDING?

Would God go to extremes like physical holding or restraining to obtain a heart? God not only sanctioned these tools of attitude adjustments, but he also used them. God used extreme physical endurance challenges as a way to bring about deep attitude changes. He had his children wander around in a desert for forty years until they were ready to go "home." Wouldn't you call forced "camping" in the desert a long-lasting attitude adjustment? What is an afternoon of pain for our children compared to forty years of tribulation or even an eternity of torture?

Paul assumes the same principle when he writes to Timothy and advises him to "exercise . . . unto godliness" as training to lead his church (1 Tim. 4:7, KJV). In this verse Paul uses the word *gumnaze,* from which we derive our English word *gymnasium.* "Train *(gumnaze)* yourself in godliness; for while bodily training *(gumnasia)* is of some value, godliness is of value in every way, as it holds promise for the present life and also for the life to come" (1 Tim. 4:7-8, RSV).

Dallas Willard has a keen historical perspective of how God changes lives through spiritual/bodily disciplines.

It is almost impossible in the thought climate of today's Western world to appreciate just *how* utterly unnecessary it was for Paul to say explicitly, in the world in which *he* lived, that Christians should fast, be alone, study, give, and so forth as regular disciplines for the spiritual life. We of course tend to think of ascetic practices as oddities of human history, prominent only in "pagan India," perhaps, or in the spiritually degraded "Dark Ages" of Western Europe. But such thinking is far from the truth. It's an illusion created in part by our own conviction that our unrestrained natural impulse is in itself a good thing and that we have an unquestionable right to fulfill our natural impulses so long as "no one gets hurt."

But thoughtful and religiously devout people of the classical and Hellenistic world . . . knew that the mind and body of the human being had to be rigorously disciplined to achieve a decent individual and social existence. This is not something St. Paul had to prove or even explicitly state to his readers. . . . It is, rather, a wisdom gleaned from millennia of collective human experience. There is nothing especially religious about it, though every religion of historical significance has accepted and inculcated it in one way or another. It has a special importance in religion, but it also is just good sense about human nature.[1]

Simply put, changes in our spiritual selves begin by disciplining our bodies. The ancient world knew this. Our modern culture has been seduced into thinking that we should feel good all the time. This thinking has infected our spiritual beliefs. Real growth always involves death (John 12:24;

1 Cor. 15:36). God gave us the gift of physical disciplines to help us get our spiritual lives into shape. Let's use these effective, godly, loving tools for our children's ultimate benefit.

The discipline of holding your children sometimes ends up being a wrestling match. God wrestles with his children. God was serious about doing battle for Jacob's heart, and he wrestled with Jacob all night long. Not only was Jacob sore when he was finished, but he also ended up with a dislocated hip and a changed name—Israel—as a result of that battle. The very name *Israel* means "he struggles with God." Israel, the man, walked with a limp for the rest of his life as a reminder of that encounter. God did not seriously damage Jacob, but he did leave a lasting impression. Your children may not walk with a limp and you may not change their name, but you will feel differently about each other after a long-lasting wrestling match.

God is not above wrestling with his children. Are you? Are your children worthy of engaging them in a battle of the wills? God will go to whatever lengths are necessary to soften his children's hearts. We should be willing to make the same commitment to our children. God is looking for submissive hearts in all of us. When our children's hearts become that tender, then the relationship is as loving as it can get. That is the goal.

If you want further examples of God's discipline from Scripture, see appendix B. I pray that as you read, God's Spirit will speak clearly to you regarding these tools.

When Israel was a child,
I loved him as a son.

Hosea 11:1

Appendix B: Looking More Closely at God's Discipline

"You make me so angry! Why did I ever want kids in the first place?" What kind of parent would ever say something so harsh? Maybe you have overheard someone say those words. Maybe you heard that from your own parents. Maybe you have even said that to your children. If so, you are in good company.

God said that about his children. Yes, God said that. He regretted ever making mankind. In fact he was so disgusted, he said he regretted making all his creatures: "Now the Lord observed the extent of the people's wickedness, and he saw that all their thoughts were consistently and totally evil. So the Lord was sorry he had ever made them. It broke his heart. And the Lord said, 'I will completely wipe out this human race that I have created. Yes, and I will destroy all the animals and birds, too. I am sorry I ever made them'" (Gen. 6:5-7).

Did God really mean that? God never says anything he doesn't mean. In fact, he even repeated it. He got so exasper-

ated with Israel that he told Moses, "I have seen these people
. . . and they are a stiff-necked people. Now leave me alone so
that my anger may burn against them and that I may destroy
them. Then I will make you into a great nation" (Exod.
32:9-10, NIV).

God was on the verge of wiping out the entire nation of
Israel. These were the people he had just finished leading out
of slavery in Egypt. Maybe God really does understand some
of the frustrations of being a parent.

GOD SETS EXPECTATIONS

The books of Leviticus and Deuteronomy are full of detailed
instructions about how God wants his children to worship, to
treat each other, to use money, and to prepare and eat their
food. He leaves no room for doubt.

God is concerned with every aspect of our lives. We should
also be as involved with our own children. We should not
only guide them and teach them but also know what their
preferences are. They are God's gift to us. They challenge us to
grow, and they sometimes give us great joy. More examples of
God's commands are found in Deuteronomy 6:6-9; 27:14-26;
and Joshua 8:34.

GOD USES TESTS

God often used tests to prove whether or not his people were
truly submitted to him. "I did this to test Israel—to see
whether or not they would obey the Lord as their ancestors
did" (Judg. 2:22).

God's tests began in the Garden of Eden when he told
Adam and Eve not to eat from a certain tree. His children
flunked the test. Abraham passed some tests and flunked others. Abraham flunked the test to wait on the Lord for his

promised son. He slept with his wife's servant and had a son, Ishmael. Ishmael is the forefather of the Arab nations that torment Israel to this day.

Abraham passed the most amazing test of all. God eventually gave one-hundred-year-old Abraham his promised son, Isaac. Years later God told Abraham to kill his son as a sacrifice to God. Abraham did not argue, although he must have been heartbroken. He tied up his son, laid him on the altar, and set the wood ready for the fire. Abraham had the knife in his hand ready to slay his son when an angel of the Lord called out from heaven, "Abraham! Abraham! . . . Do not lay a hand on the boy. . . . Do not do anything to him. Now I know that you fear God, because you have not withheld from me your son, your only son" (Gen. 22:11-12, NIV). Could any of us have passed that test?

When Joshua was clearing out the Promised Land, God let a few nations survive. "They were left to test the Israelites to see whether they would obey the Lord's commands, which he had given their forefathers through Moses" (Judg. 3:4, NIV).

Perhaps the most famous test of all was given to Job, who was tested beyond the limits of most people. The most amazing aspect is that he had not done one thing wrong. Job was a righteous man with a submitted heart. Yet God allowed even Job to be tested.

So when your children tell you in their most whiny, angry tone of voice, "This isn't fair," remember that God uses and allows tests, even with obedient children, to see whether they have a truly submissive attitude.

GOD'S OWN PROGRESSION OF DISCIPLINE

God used a progression of discipline in his dealings with the pharaoh who had made the nation of Israel into his slaves.

Each time Moses asked Pharaoh to let the people go, the sequence of events was the same. Pharaoh would refuse, so God would send a plague. When Pharaoh suffered the effects of the consequences, he would relent and agree to let the people go. But after the plague stopped, Pharaoh would change his mind—harden his heart—and once again refuse to free the slaves. The progression of discipline would intensify each time Pharaoh refused to obey God.

Pharaoh's Attitude Adjustment

God demonstrated his use of a progression of discipline in the well-known story of Moses and Pharaoh. When God decided to free Israel from slavery and give them the Promised Land, Pharaoh resisted. That was a bad idea. But God was very patient with Pharaoh. He kept asking him to cooperate, but Pharaoh refused every request. Each time Pharaoh refused to obey, the progression of discipline intensified.

Plague one: All the water in Egypt turned into blood. But "Pharaoh's heart remained hard and stubborn" (Exod. 7:22).

Plague two: An invasion of frogs. Pharaoh promised to let Israel go out into the desert to make sacrifices, but he reneged after all the frogs were cleaned up. When the pressure was off, he hardened his heart again (Exod. 8:8-15).

Plague three: An infestation of gnats. Pharaoh's heart remained hard, and he would not listen. By now, even his magicians (who had been able to duplicate the first two plagues) were telling Pharaoh that "this is the finger of God!" (Exod. 8:16-19).

Plague four: A plague of flies. This plague had a twist—the flies were *only* in Egyptian houses! Pharaoh tried to compromise by saying that the children of Israel could sacrifice their animals and worship God without going away into the desert for three days. Moses said that was unacceptable, so Pharaoh agreed to let them go. Moses warned Pharaoh not to change his mind again. But as usual, "Pharaoh hardened his heart again and refused to let the people go" (Exod. 8:20-32).

Plague five: Every Egyptian horse, sheep, donkey, camel, goat, and cow died. Even after Pharaoh confirmed that not one Israelite livestock animal had died, "his heart remained stubborn." He once again refused to let the people go (Exod. 9:1-7).

Plague six: Skin boils broke out on every Egyptian person and animal. Pharaoh still would not listen to Moses and Aaron. His heart remained callously hard (Exod. 9:8-12). Do you get the feeling that Pharaoh had an attitude problem with arrogance?

Plague seven: A hailstorm (in a Middle Eastern desert!) destroyed everything in the Egyptians' fields—people, animals, crops, and trees; the hail did not touch the place where the people of Israel lived. "Then Pharaoh urgently sent for Moses and Aaron. 'I finally admit my fault,' he confessed. 'The Lord is right, and my people and I are wrong. Please beg the Lord to end this terrifying thunder and hail. I will let you go at once'" (Exod. 9:27-28). Moses agreed to ask the Lord to stop the hail. But he told Pharaoh that if it stopped, it would only prove that God ruled the earth. Then Moses delivered his parting shot: "'But as for you and your officials, I know that you still do not fear the Lord God as you should'" (Exod. 9:30).

Sure enough. When the hail stopped, Pharaoh dug in his heels and refused to let the Israelites go. This time Pharaoh's officials were fed up with him: "How long will you let these disasters go on?" they pleaded. "Please let the Israelites go to serve the Lord their God!" (Exod. 10:7). So Pharaoh summoned Moses and Aaron and negotiated with them. First he said that all of the Israelites could go worship God. Then he reneged and said only the men could go (Exod. 9:13–10:12).

Plague eight: Locusts covered the face of the earth until it was black, and they ate everything that was green. Pharaoh quickly summoned Moses and Aaron and said, "I confess my sin against the Lord your God and against you. . . . Forgive my sin only this once, and plead with the Lord your God to take away this terrible plague" (Exod. 10:16-17).

Notice how quickly Pharaoh got the focus off his sin and onto his real concern—the locusts. He still focused only on his discomfort and not his rebellion. He wanted to keep his hardened heart. He repented only to escape the pain. And once again, God granted Egypt mercy and removed the locusts (Exod. 10:13-20).

Plague nine: Darkness covered the entire nation for three days (except where the Israelites lived). "Then Pharaoh called for Moses. 'Go and worship the Lord. . . . But let your flocks and herds stay here. You can even take your children with you'" (Exod. 10:24). Moses told him no deal, the livestock must go too. Pharaoh's heart got hard again (should we be surprised?), and he was not willing to let them go (Exod. 10:26-27).

Pharaoh was getting tired of all this affliction. He told Moses to get out of his sight and that he never wanted to see his face again. Moses said that was fine with him (Exod. 10:28-29).

Pharaoh had an uncooperative internal posture. He thought that Moses was the problem because every time Moses came around, all these bad things happened. Pharaoh thought that all he had to do was get rid of Moses. Pharaoh just didn't get it. His own heart was the problem, but he refused to see it.

Plague ten: Every Egyptian firstborn son and animal died. This plague did not affect the Israelites. Moses ended his admonition with these stern words: "'Then you will know that the Lord makes a distinction between the Egyptians and the Israelites. All the officials of Egypt will come running to me, bowing low. "Please leave!" they will beg. "Hurry! And take all your followers with you." Only then will I go!' Then, burning with anger, Moses left Pharaoh's presence" (Exod. 11:7-8).

Moses is telling Pharaoh that he will leave on his terms. Pharaoh was in no position to tell him anything anymore. Pharaoh has been chastised. Everyone in the country, including his own officials, will bow down to Moses. That is a huge slap in the face for Pharaoh. In Egypt, the pharaoh was considered a god. Everyone had to worship him, even his officials. Pharaoh refused to be brought to his knees. Moses (speaking for God) gave him every opportunity to cooperate with God's plans.

Pharaoh never took advantage of all those chances to learn his lesson. He definitely took the hard road. He didn't want anyone, even God, telling him what to do. Wouldn't you think that after all this pain and suffering Pharaoh would have admitted his arrogance?

Israel's Attitude Adjustments

Some people would argue that God would never inflict this much suffering on his own children. After all, all this was done to Pharaoh and Egypt, not God's beloved Israel.

Don't forget that God loves all people, even pharaohs and Egyptians. God did not enjoy making the Egyptians suffer. He is trying to send this message to the whole earth: "I alone am God. I am powerful. Worship me and you will be glad you did. Fight me, and you will not only lose, but you will also suffer in the process."

Israel had a ringside seat to witness God's powerful determination. They had an eye-opening demonstration that God doesn't take no for an answer, not even from the great pharaoh of Egypt. They witnessed the intensifying destruction when Pharaoh hardened his heart against God. God may have been hoping that Israel would get the idea to not resist him. Did they benefit from that lesson? Like too many children, they did not remember very long.

The entire book of Judges records examples of Israel's rebellion against God. Each time the people cried out to God for mercy and help. Each time they repented, and God rescued them. But the people soon forgot about God and returned to their stubborn ways. Each time their suffering was greater than the time before.

The book of Hosea illustrates how God pursued the rebellious Israel. God told the prophet Hosea to marry Gomer, a prostitute. Gomer stayed with Hosea long enough to bear him three children. The names of two of their children literally mean "not loved" and "not my people." God used Hosea, Gomer, and their children to send a message to Israel. Gomer represented Israel, and Hosea represented God. Gomer left Hosea and prostituted herself with other men. Hosea and God would confront her with her behavior. God told Hosea to continue to love her, despite her rebelliousness.

This striking passage from the book of Hosea illustrates God's intense love for his stubborn people.

"When Israel was a child, I loved him as a son, and I called my son out of Egypt. But the more I called to him, the more he rebelled. . . . It was I who taught Israel how to walk, leading him along by the hand. But he doesn't know or even care that it was I who took care of him. I led Israel along with my ropes of kindness and love. . . . For my people are determined to desert me. . . . Oh, how can I give you up, Israel? How can I let you go? . . . My heart is torn within me, and my compassion overflows. No, I will not punish you as much as my burning anger tells me to. I will not completely destroy Israel, for I am God and not a mere mortal. I am the Holy One living among you, and I will not come to destroy. For someday the people will follow the Lord. I will roar like a lion, and my people will return trembling from the west. . . . I will bring them home again." (Hosea 11:1-11)

This is the love that kept after his children until they submitted to him.

The book of Isaiah offers another picture of God patiently engaging in the battle of the wills with his children. God confronted his rebellious children and severely disciplined them. But they refused to be broken and repent! God was deeply saddened; Israel's arrogance was unbelievable.

God told his children exactly what he expected from them. He pleaded with them to listen and obey. God hated their meaningless acts of sacrifice. He didn't want just their external obedience; he wanted their submissive hearts. He offered them a way, but they were not interested (Isa. 1:18-26). God warned them how painful his judgment would be. He would melt his people down like liquid metal and skim off their impurities (Isa. 1:25). Talk about painful!

Somehow hard work or an attitude adjustment full of exercises doesn't sound as rough as being smelted by fire. God's attitude-adjustment sessions seem a lot rougher than the tools this book describes. By disciplining his people God shows us how he feels about rebellion.

The New Testament also gives us examples of how God used discipline in people's lives to soften their hearts. Jesus confronted bad attitudes throughout his ministry. The group that received the most steady confrontation was the Pharisees, the religious rulers who thought they had a corner on obedience. But Jesus revealed their obedience for what it was: adherence to a set of rules without submission to God.

Jesus was not afraid to confront the people with whom he spent the most time—his disciples. He was more patient with them because they were more humble than the Pharisees. One time two brothers, James and John, asked Jesus privately if they could have seats of honor next to him in his kingdom. Jesus tried to explain that they would have to endure a great deal of suffering to be given those seats of honor. They said that would be no problem. Jesus kindly told them that his Father would be making that decision. Jesus not only put them in their place, he reminded them that he too was living in submission and obedience to his heavenly Father (Mark 10:35-45).

Many people mistakenly think that Jesus talked only about love and getting along with each other. They think that the God of the Old Testament has somehow changed. Jesus addressed this issue clearly: "Don't misunderstand why I have come. I did not come to abolish the law of Moses or the writings of the prophets. No, I came to fulfill them. I assure you, until heaven and earth disappear, even the smallest detail of God's law will remain until its purpose is achieved" (Matt. 5:17-18).

In fact, Jesus challenges us to keep a law even tougher than the one in the Old Testament! "You have heard that the law of Moses says, 'Do not commit adultery.' But I say, anyone who even looks at a woman with lust in his eye has already committed adultery with her in his heart" (Matt. 5:27-28). Jesus set very high expectations.

The life of the apostle Paul is a powerful example of how a person allowed suffering to change his attitude. Remember how hostile Paul was toward God and the church? God allowed Paul to endure physical hardship to wake him up to the truth. God used hardship to change Paul's internal posture. It changed Paul's life dramatically. Paul realized the value of hardship. "So now I am glad to boast about my weaknesses, so that the power of Christ may work through me. Since I know it is all for Christ's good, I am quite content with my weaknesses and with insults, hardships, persecutions, and calamities. For when I am weak, then I am strong" (2 Cor. 12:9-10).

Through these biblical examples we can see that God takes our attitudes seriously. He engages in the battle for our hearts and is willing to go to great lengths to connect our hearts to his. As parents, we can follow that example as we use discipline to unite our children's hearts with our own and ultimately with God's.

Do not withhold discipline from a child; if you
punish him with the rod, he will not die.
— Proverbs 23:13, NIV

Appendix C: Dealing with Difficult Teenagers

TEENAGERS WHO NEED SERIOUS
ATTITUDE ADJUSTMENTS

This section is for those of you who are at the end of your
rope. Or maybe you know someone who is ready to throw in
the towel with their teenagers. This is for those of you who
may be considering sending your teenagers into a treatment
program.

You have diligently tried all the tools in this book with
your teenagers. They haven't responded to long talks aimed at
trying to understand them better, practicing specific ways to
cooperate, prolonged days of just working around the house,
and long exercise sessions to try to break through their stubbornness.

You may want to consider an even more intense attitude-
adjustment session. Before attempting this kind of interven-
tion, however, consider these things.

1. Get help. If you think your teenagers might respond to a
prolonged, intense physical attitude session and if you aren't

sure you can handle it physically or emotionally on your own, call for some backup. Arrange for a close relative or friend (preferably male) to come over and be on hand in case you need help. Tell your assistant(s) what the game plan is so they are not surprised. Ask them to wait for your direction and follow your lead.

If, when it comes time for the attitude-adjustment session, your teenagers ask why the others are there, simply say something like, "Uncle Mike and Coach Smith are here because they care about you. They are not here to talk to you or to try and settle you down. We've tried that several times already, and frankly, you have not responded. Your attitude is still extremely poor. That is going to stop as of now."

2. Stand your ground. This is where it gets intense. This is when you have to do your best imitation of a Marine drill sergeant in boot-camp training. You have to be in your kids' faces, literally and figuratively. You want to confront them with their bad attitudes and pull out your shopping list of how they have been rude, arrogant, and selfish. This reminder is accompanied by a whole series of physical exercises designed to wear down their resistance to you. They have to feel what it is like to surrender to you. You and your support team have to tear them down until they lose their haughty attitudes. They have to become pliable. You and your friends can work it like a tag-team wrestling match. Take turns wearing down your teenagers. If they refuse to do the exercises, then you have the strength of extra bodies on hand to help them. If they complain of being physically exhausted but still maintain a bad attitude, they must still have enough energy to hold on to that attitude. Your job at that point is to exhaust them so they cannot hang on to their stubborn attitudes.

Don't be dissuaded by any "battlefield conversion." Kids are not stupid. They know when they are overmatched. They may try to talk their way out of the ordeal. Don't settle for a shallow apology. Remind them of the abundant chances you have already given them to change their attitudes only to have the change last for a short time. (Sounds like Pharaoh; see appendix B.) Remind them of all the broken promises they have already made. Don't fall for their I've-finally-seen-the-light conversion. They need to feel the painful consequences of their disgusting attitudes. They need to know how much they affect others with their attitudes. They need to experience how much you and others who love them hate their attitudes.

Some teenagers are smart enough right from the start to see they are outmatched this time. They will promise to do better from now on. That's easy to say. Test their sincerity. Explain that they will have the rest of the day to demonstrate fully their "new attitudes." Assign them the hardest manual-labor job you have around the house. Tell them they have to demonstrate a perfect attitude by working full tilt until you decide it is enough. Tell them you are the sole judge of what is good enough and when they are done with the job. If they have truly decided to change their attitude, they will respond with energy and a "yes, sir" attitude. Test them for a while.

If this sounds like provoking them to rebel, it is. You want to provoke the bad attitude to come to the surface. It is hiding right below the surface because you have your reinforcements with you. It's like lancing a boil. You put pressure in the sensitive spot in order to eradicate the infection. Only this time the infection is a poisoned attitude. Go after it. Don't be tricked by easy submission.

As usual, end up with their giving a verbal account of why

they had to do all this, and listen for any trace of blaming someone else for their plight. Look deeply into their eyes to see inside their souls. Look for any trace of resistance. Absolute surrender to your will is the only standard at this point of the relationship.

3. *Prepare for extreme reactions.* In response to your attitude-adjustment session, your teenagers may threaten to run away. Running away should be treated as a serious threat. If you overhear them making plans to leave, ask them directly. Challenge them with what you heard or what you suspect. Tell them how concerned you are and that you want to talk about it. Ask them to tell you what they find so unpleasant at home. Ask them if they have any solutions or suggestions. Listen to them; acknowledge their feelings. Debate their suggestions. Negotiate the structure to protect your concerns. Don't just give in to their demands. Listen to their reasonable ideas. Don't waste your energy on surface issues such as hairstyle and clothes. But also, remember to use the outer appearance as a possible indication of an inner problem. Keep your eyes and ears wide open, but don't see or hear things that aren't there.

If you are convinced that your teenagers might run away, then you should take some action. Go with your teenagers to a trustworthy counselor whom a pastor or family friend could recommend.

But if the situation is critical, if running away seems imminent, then take immediate action. Do two things. First, take away the teenagers' shoes and pants. Give them bathrobes or jogging shorts to wear around the house. It is more difficult to run away without shoes and pants. Second, pull them from any activities until the immediate danger has passed. They will have to stay home from school, church, work, and activities with friends. No activity is worth the risk of their leaving the protection that home affords. They should not be allowed out of your sight. They will be your shadow until you are convinced (not just hopeful) that they are not considering running away. Their safety and your relationship are top priorities. Just as you make your two-year-old hold your hand when you cross the street, your teenagers have to be next to you until they can prove they can accept your reasonable rules without threatening to leave.

This is not like the story of the Prodigal Son. In that story, the rebellious son was an adult. Although it is conceivable he may have been only in his teen years, in that culture he was old enough to make a decision to live on his own. Teenagers cannot survive alone in today's culture. Do not be lulled into any false hope that your teenagers will learn lessons on their own and return home repentant. Broken repentance at the hands of someone else may be life threatening. Teenagers on their own today are easy targets and will be the prey of many unscrupulous adults. Do not risk that happening by letting your teens leave home until they are at least seventeen or eighteen years old. Even at that age, they should have a realistic plan for how they will live independently.

If you are tempted to surrender to your teenagers' power play, then you may both lose. Use your strength carefully, but don't give up when your teens challenge your authority.

Believe me, I know how controversial this tough stance is, especially in this day and age. Be clear about this. I am *not* saying, "Don't listen to your teenagers." You want them to learn to express their needs, wants, opinions, etc. Verbalizing what they want is a good thing. It helps them figure out who they are. Parental guidance is needed for *what* they want and *how* they express it. Don't forget those two critical issues. The stakes are extremely high at this age. Don't just hope for the best. Be proactive in your relationship.

JAKE'S STORY

Jake was a young man with great promise. He was a leader on every athletic team he joined. He seemed to overcome new challenges effortlessly. Everyone knew he could do anything he wanted. Friends loved to be with him. His parents loved him too. They were very proud of him.

But there was a significant flaw in Jake: He didn't think the normal rules applied to him. He had the idea that he had special privileges because of his physical and mental gifts. His parents tried repeatedly to break through his growing arrogance and rudeness. Jake would listen for a while, but he soon tired of his parents' old-fashioned ideas. When they lightened up, he just got even more rude. When they tried to be more strict, he would loudly argue with them. They even got his uncle and favorite grandfather to have long talks with him. No matter what they tried, nothing seemed to make a difference for very long.

Jake began to be dissatisfied with everything. He seemed to get bored easily, even with the things he used to enjoy. He turned to alcohol. He refused to do any work. He whined when he had the slightest ache or pain. Whenever he had money or time, he would waste it on something insignificant, indulgent, or destructive.

When Jake expressed his ideas to leave home and live on his own, his parents were not supportive. His age wasn't a factor; he was old enough to live on his own. But Jake's parents knew he would go downhill even more. They were worried that he might unintentionally or even, God forbid, intentionally hurt someone else with his insatiable, self-centered appetite for pleasure.

Jake's parents did the only thing they knew to do at this point. One morning, before Jake was fully awake (even though it was almost noon), they took him to meet with the town leaders outside of town. Jake sobered up pretty quickly when he realized what was happening. He had heard stories about what happened when parents took a child to meet with the town leaders, but he never thought it would happen to him. Jake listened as his parents told these men how Jake's attitude had deteriorated. Some of the leaders already knew about Jake's situation. They had personally encountered his stubborn self-centeredness.

Jake knew he could not argue his way out of this situation. All he could do was beg. He admitted he had been out of line, but he promised he would change. The men did not seem impressed. Finally, they all came toward Jake and took him by the clothes. Jake collapsed, sobbing, so they dragged him to the spot and dropped him. Jake just lay in a heap. He knew this was it. The men all picked up rocks and threw them at Jake. They threw the stones until they knew he was dead.

This is a shocking story, isn't it? It feels barbaric to our modern sensibilities. But this is a scene from the Old Testament. "If a man has a stubborn and rebellious son who does not obey his father and mother and will not listen to them when they discipline him, his father and mother shall take hold of him and bring him to the elders at the gate of his town. They shall say to the elders, 'This son of ours is stubborn and rebellious. He will not obey us. He is a profligate and a drunkard.' Then all the men of his town shall stone him to death" (Deut. 21:18-21, NIV).

The passage ends with this pronouncement: "You must purge the evil from among you. All Israel will hear of it and be afraid." No kidding! You can believe that every young boy and girl would know what had happened to Jake. For at least a year or so, all any parent would have to say would be two words to get their children to be respectful and cooperative: "Remember Jake."

Every parent would be changed too. They would feel more challenged not to let their children's attitudes get to the point where they would have to have their children stoned by the town leaders.

While you know that I am in *no* way suggesting that we use this method with our rebellious teenagers today, I am challenging us to think about the implications of this Old Testament practice. The point is that sin is serious. Rebellion is not something to be taken lightly. Our eternal destiny is at stake. If spending an afternoon making my children do some exercises, shed a few angry tears, and break down the walls of rebellion will save them from a lifetime of heartache, then it is worth the investment.

We must remember that we live in a society that idolizes rebellion. Our teenagers may think it is cool to rebel and express rude attitudes. But the truths are these:

1. Courage is laudable; arrogance is laughable.
2. Standing up for what is right is admirable; standing up for what just feels good is abominable.
3. Resisting evil is praiseworthy; resisting guidance is pathetic.

God has his own politically incorrect opinion regarding rebellion. He says that rebellion is as bad as practicing witchcraft and that arrogance is like idolatry (1 Sam. 15:23). The apostle Paul puts it this way: "But God shows his anger from heaven against all sinful, wicked people who push the truth away from themselves. . . . Their lives became full of every kind of wickedness, sin, greed, hate, envy, murder, fighting, deception, malicious behavior, and gossip. They are backstabbers, haters of God, insolent, proud, and boastful. They are forever inventing new ways of sinning and are disobedient to their parents" (Rom. 1:18, 29-30). Paul recognizes that disobeying parents ranks right up there with hating God and committing murder. Rebellion and arrogance are so disgusting to God because these attitudes worship the creature, not the Creator.

We must develop the discipline to discipline our children. We must develop the fortitude to correct our children's negative attitudes before those attitudes solidify into ugly character traits.

Notes

CHAPTER 2—ATTITUDE IS MORE IMPORTANT THAN BEHAVIOR

1. Since we will be talking so much about positive attitudes, I thought it would be helpful to list a few positive attitudes. This is by no means a complete list, but it should give you a good start as you begin to work with your children.

Positive attitudes to help your children develop:

appreciative	gentle
attentive	generous/giving
caring	honest
content	humble
cooperative	loyal
courageous	polite
determined	responsible
discerning	responsive
empathic	thankful
energetic	submissive
flexible	

CHAPTER 3—SUBMISSIVENESS IS THE KEY TO ATTITUDE

1. Erma Bombeck, "'No' Won't Win Parents Any Popularity Contests," *Daily Herald*, 10 November 1994.

CHAPTER 4—CONFLICT ENHANCES OUR RELATIONSHIPS

1. Stephen Bly, *The Surprising Side of Grace: Appreciating God's Loving Anger* (Grand Rapids: Discovery House, 1994), 20.
2. Ibid., 29–35.

CHAPTER 5—EVALUATING INEFFECTIVE METHODS OF DISCIPLINE

1. Carolyn Spencer Brown, "To Spank or Not to Spank," *USA Weekend* 22 April 1994: 4–7.

CHAPTER 6—SETTING EXPECTATIONS

1. William Damon, *Greater Expectations* (New York: The Free Press, 1995), 79.
2. Paul E. White, *What about Their Peer Relationships?* (Wichita, Kans.: Family Resources, 1994), 12.

CHAPTER 8—ASSIGNING WORK

1. C. S. Lewis, *The Screwtape Letters* (New York: Macmillan, 1961), 20.

CHAPTER 11—ASSIGNING EXERCISES

1. Dallas Willard, *The Spirit of the Disciplines* (New York: Harper & Row, 1988), 84.
2. Interview with Dallas Willard, *The Door*, 129 (May/June 1993): 15.

CHAPTER 14—ADDING AN ACCESSORY: SPANKING

1. Murray A. Strauss, "Discipline and Deviance: Physical Punishment of Children and Violence and Other Crime in Adulthood," *Sexual Problems* 38 (1991): 133–152, as quoted in *Family Policy*, ed. William R. Mattox Jr., 9, no. 5 (October 1996): 6.
2. Robert E. Larzelere and J. A. Merenda, "The Effectiveness of Parental Discipline for Toddler Misbehavior at Different Levels of Child Distress," *Family Relations* 43 (1994): 4, as quoted in *Family Policy*, ed. William R. Mattox Jr., 9, no. 5 (October 1996): 6.
3. Ibid.
4. *Statistics Sweden* (May 1995): 1–6, as quoted in *Family Policy*, ed. William R. Mattox Jr., 9, no. 5 (October 1996): 6.
5. *Family Policy*, ed. William R. Mattox Jr., 9, no. 5 (October 1996): 7.
6. Ibid., 4

CHAPTER 15—WORKING AS A TEAM
1. Martha G. Welch, M.D., *Holding Time* (New York: Simon & Schuster, 1989), 86.
2. Ibid., 147.
3. Proverbs 29:15 says, "To discipline and reprimand a child produces wisdom, but a mother is disgraced by an undisciplined child."
4. In Isaiah 41:8 and 2 Chronicles 20:7 Abraham is referred to as God's friend. However, I think it is safe to assume that he was a very special case.

CHAPTER 18—USING THE TOOLS WITH TEENAGERS
1. An angry, pouty Scottie Pippen once refused to play the last 18 seconds of an NBA playoff game because he was not chosen to shoot the final shot.
2. Erma Bombeck, "Measure of Discipline Also Measure of Love," *Daily Herald* 6 June 1996.

APPENDIX A: HANDLING TANTRUMS
1. Dallas Willard, *The Spirit of the Disciplines* (New York: Harper & Row, 1988), 99.

About the Author

Steve Sherbondy has been helping children and families for twenty years, serving as a crisis-intervention counselor for behavior-disordered and learning-disabled children in school settings, as a houseparent for troubled teens in the Dominican Republic, and as a child-care worker. A licensed clinical professional counselor, Steve currently counsels families, couples, and individuals at the Harbor Counseling Center in South Elgin, Illinois. Steve earned an M.A. in Counseling Psychology from Wheaton College Graduate School. Steve and his wife, Sharon, provide home-school instruction to their son, Dugan, and daughter, Breeze. The Sherbondy family worships at the Willow Creek Community Church in South Barrington, Illinois, where Sharon is a leader in the drama ministry.